The Work of France

CRITICAL ISSUES IN HISTORY
World and International History

The Vikings: Wolves of War
  by Martin Arnold
Magic and Superstition in Europe: A Concise History from Antiquity to the Present
  by Michael D. Bailey
War and Genocide: A Concise History of the Holocaust, Second Edition
  by Doris L. Bergen
Peter the Great
  by Paul Bushkovitch
A Concise History of Hong Kong
  by John M. Carroll
Remaking Italy in the Twentieth Century
  by Roy Palmer Domenico
A Concise History of Euthanasia: Life, Death, God, and Medicine
  by Ian Dowbiggin
The Work of France: Labor and Culture in Early Modern Times, 1350–1800
  by James R. Farr
The Idea of Capitalism before the Industrial Revolution
  by Richard Grassby
The New Concise History of the Crusades
  by Thomas F. Madden
The Great Encounter of China and the West, 1500–1800, 2nd Edition
  by D. E. Mungello
A Concise History of the French Revolution
  by Sylvia Neely
The British Imperial Century, 1815–1914: A World History Perspective
  by Timothy H. Parsons
The Norman Conquest: England after William the Conqueror
  by Hugh M. Thomas
Europe's Reformations, 1450–1650: Doctrine, Politics, and Community, 2nd Edition
  by James D. Tracy

American History

The Unfinished Struggle: Turning Points in American Labor History, 1877–Present
  by Steven Babson
Conceived in Liberty: The Struggle to Define the New Republic, 1789–1793
  by Lance Banning
The Evolutionists: American Thinkers Confront Charles Darwin, 1860–1920
  by J. David Hoeveler
America's Great War: World War I and the American Experience
  by Robert H. Zieger

The Work of France

Labor and Culture in Early Modern Times, 1350–1800

James R. Farr

ROWMAN & LITTLEFIELD PUBLISHERS, INC.
Lanham • Boulder • New York • Toronto • Plymouth, UK

ROWMAN & LITTLEFIELD PUBLISHERS, INC.

Published in the United States of America
by Rowman & Littlefield Publishers, Inc.
A wholly owned subsidiary of The Rowman & Littlefield Publishing Group, Inc.
4501 Forbes Boulevard, Suite 200, Lanham, Maryland 20706
www.rowmanlittlefield.com

Estover Road, Plymouth PL6 7PY, United Kingdom

British Library Cataloguing in Publication Information Available

Library of Congress Cataloging-in-Publication Data

Farr, James Richard, 1950–
  The work of France : labor and culture in early modern times, 1350–1800 /
by James R. Farr.
      p. cm. — (Critical issues in world and international history)
  Includes bibliographical references and index.
  ISBN-13: 978-0-7425-3399-8 (cloth : alk. paper)
  ISBN-10: 0-7425-3399-9 (cloth : alk. paper)
  ISBN-13: 978-0-7425-3400-1 (pbk. : alk. paper)
  ISBN-10: 0-7425-3400-6 (pbk. : alk. paper)
  [etc.]
  1. Labor—France—History. I. Title.
  HD8429.E37 2008
  944—dc22
                                                          2008038204

Printed in the United States of America

∞™ The paper used in this publication meets the minimum requirements of American
National Standard for Information Sciences—Permanence of Paper for Printed Library
Materials, ANSI/NISO Z39.48-1992.

To Steven L. Kaplan,
the *maître* of work and culture

~

Contents

~

Illustrations

~

Preface

This book on work and culture in early modern France appears in a series on "Critical Issues in World and International History." The "critical issue" engaged in this book is the relationship between what we might call material life—specifically work activities (of both men and women)—and the culture in which these activities were embedded, a culture that helped shape these activities, invested them with meaning, and fashioned the identities of the people engaged in them. My focus will be early modern France (roughly 1350–1800), but much of what happened then and there was general to Europe as a whole. After a brief overview to set the context within which men and women worked, we will explore the work practices and culture in the countryside, the world of the peasant and rural artisan. Our attention will then shift to the towns and cities, the urban world of common laborers (lumped by the French into a general category of the *menu peuple*, or "lesser folk"), domestic servants, craftsmen and women, and merchants. The book concludes with the emergent professions of the "liberal" occupations of law, medicine, finance, and bureaucratic governance. Each chapter is divided into three parts: the first two are synchronic (largely treating constants and continuities) and explore the nature of various kinds of work activities and their cultural aspects; the third is diachronic and examines and explains the changes in the world of work across the economic, social, and political spectrum.

There is a danger of essentialism in organizing a book this way, for men and women slipped between categories. Peasants often doubled as craftsmen

and craftswomen, artisans as merchants, merchants and public officials as financiers, and so on. Moreover, comprehensiveness would be impossible; many
of the things that people did that we might recognize as work will escape
these pages. My defense of such categorization and selectivity rests on clarity
of exposition and analysis, for even though we will see much slippage between categories in the pages that follow, the categories I have invoked do,
in broad fashion, correspond to actual categories of lived experiences, and
they cover the salient activities and practitioners that comprised the work
world of early modern France. Artisans may have engaged in commerce, for
example, but for reasons I hope to make clear, they did see themselves, and
were seen by others, as distinctly artisans nonetheless. The same can be said
for the other actors in this book.

The reader will notice that each chapter is not an encapsulated description of all aspects of the social category under discussion. The criterion for
what to include and what to leave out is always work, and the connection to
it. Thus the reader will find nothing in these pages about, say, peasant rebel-
lions, and, perhaps surprisingly, little about religion. Though much has been
written about Protestantism and the modern work ethic, especially concerning Calvin's teachings about the sanctity of one's calling, the connection between the modern work ethic and Protestantism, in my view, remains tenu-
ous at best and even illusory (we need not look far, for example, to find a
work ethic among French Catholics). Moreover, Calvinism only partly penetrated the French population (never more than 10 percent, and then only
briefly in the sixteenth century) and dwindled to numerical insignificance by
1700.

One might wonder why France merits singular attention in a book like
this, and why the early modern centuries are the chronological focus. Aside
from the fact that a large body of research on the many and varied aspects of
work by other scholars exists for France (thus making a book like this possible), during these centuries France was the most populous polity in Europe,
and had embarked on a path of increasing internal integration. One cannot
deny the importance of France's history to our understanding of the early
modern era. Above all, however, France experienced most clearly the three
salient developments that I have isolated for analysis in this book (intensification of hierarchy, expansion of the market economy, and growth of the
state); in their interconnectedness, these developments created the conditions that in many ways will be the foundation for the modern age.

I owe a debt of gratitude to the many scholars whose research and writing
has provided me with the material to write this book. Over my career I have
learned immeasurably from friends and scholars like Mack Holt, Len Rosen-

band, and Guido Ruggiero. For this book, however, above all stands the work of Steven Laurence Kaplan, and most importantly, among a robust and trenchant body of scholarship that has contributed immeasurably to the history of work in France, stands the seminal volume he edited with Cynthia Koepp in 1986, *Work in France: Representations, Meaning, Organization and Practice*.[1] Kaplan and the contributors to that volume charted an approach to the subject that I have followed in this book. As a group they sought to analyze the culture of work and to reflect on the historiography of work that led historians to the study of work in the first place. My book shares with that one the commitment, as Kaplan and Koepp wrote then, "to consider human labor as it was actually performed and what it has meant to specific groups at particular historical moments."

I am likewise grateful to Purdue University for providing me the invaluable time to write several chapters of this book by awarding me a fellowship in the Center for Humanistic Studies in 2006. Thanks, too, to my colleagues at Purdue University, John Lauritz Larson and William Glenn Gray, for taking the time to read the manuscript and offer suggestions for its improvement. John Larson, a historian of the early American republic and a colleague of mine for twenty years, has always brought a sharply critical and humorously acerbic eye to my work, and his reading of this manuscript is no exception. The many conversations I had with Will Gray over a pint or two of beer at a favored local pub also contributed greatly to the outcome of this book. Whatever its merits, there would have been far fewer without his selfless input. Finally, I thank my wife, Danielle, and my children, Stacia, Quentin, Mason, Jasmine, and Kiran, for helping me through their varied activities to always realize that my "work," like everyone else's in the present as well as the past, is informed by the cultural relations within which we are all inextricably immersed.

Note

1. Steven Laurence Kaplan and Cynthia Koepp, eds., *Work in France: Representations, Meaning, Organization and Practice* (Ithaca, N.Y.: Cornell University Press, 1986).

~

Introduction

The work worlds of early modern French men and women both shaped and were shaped by momentous changes that would transform France and bring it into the modern age. The world of work was especially affected by three salient, interconnected, and at times conflicted developments that I emphasize throughout this book: the intensification of social hierarchy, the extension and integration of the market economy, and the growth of the state's governing apparatus.

What Is Work?

As we begin to probe the work worlds of early modern French men and women, let's start with the following, seemingly simple, question: what is work? The answer is not as obvious as it at first sounds. Certainly, we all have general notions about what work is, but upon closer analysis and reflection these preconceptions often break down, or at least they mask a complexity not easily analyzed. Take the contemporary academic profession of historian as an example. Assumptions abound among the general public that our "work" is comprised of our teaching, and erroneous assumptions easily follow from learning that we teach two, three, or four classes per term, or about six to twelve hours per week in the classroom. Does that mean academic historians "work" only up to twelve hours a week? Despite common public perception, this is almost never the case. Preparation for the classroom often occupies more time than the class does, and many academic historians also are engaged in research and writing (it took many hundreds of hours, for example, for me to research and write this book). For academic historians all of this comprises our "work," including the time devoted simply to reflection. Thinking is working, from this perspective, but obviously, this kind of work is very different from, say, the effort involved in putting a roof on my house. As we will see, there are historical reasons for these divergences of perspectives on the nature and meanings of work. Indeed, divergences continue to the present day.

Over the last twenty years or so, sociologists, anthropologists, and some historians have come to believe that humankind has entered a historical juncture where the meaning of work is undergoing radical change. In 1988, for example, the sociologist R. E. Pahl edited a collection entitled *On Work: Historical, Comparative and Theoretical Approaches*, and he opened his introduction with this: "Work is becoming the key personal, social and political issue of the remaining years of the twentieth century: confusion and ambiguities about its meaning, nature and purpose in our lives are widespread."[1] His comments were prompted in part by the awareness shared by most of us that divisions of labor are changing, even as you read these words, at the global, national, and local levels, and such changes invariably produce new perceptions of and attitudes to work. Some social critics, such as Jeremy Rifkin in his provocatively titled book *The End of Work* (1993), even assert that the new world of information technology is producing an increasingly "workerless" society.[2] Other critics, such as Antonio Negri and Michael Hardt, are theorizing about "immaterial labor," that is, labor that "produces an immaterial good, such as a service, a cultural product, knowledge, or communication."[3] So, what is work? Can we agree with Robert Dubin, who wrote in 1958 in his classic textbook, *The World of Work*, that work is simply "continuous employment in the production of goods and services, for remuneration"?[4] Clearly not, for most of us would agree that some unpaid activities, like housework, are work nonetheless. But if we toss out remuneration, what is it that analytically distinguishes work from all purposeful activity? What marks an activity as work? Or, indeed, as play or leisure? Is work simply, as one scholar puts it, "the use of things and materials of nature to fashion tools with which to make objects, grow food . . . to satisfy human needs and wants"? For many, including me, that is a too narrow utilitarian and materialistic definition, not so much wrong as incomplete.

I find more fruitful the suggestions coming from scholars who accept the definition of work as any activity performed in the sphere of necessity, but who push beyond that definition to the social and cultural world in which it takes place. Such an approach takes us *away* from conceiving of work as defined by the intrinsic nature of the task or activity and *toward* the social and cultural relations in which the task or activity is embedded and through which the activity gathers its meaning and significance.[5] Moreover, to grasp the meanings that individuals bring with them as they face a given task, it is useful to consider the varieties of coercion or rewards and incentives they anticipate, incentives that may not be simply material, varieties that once again are socially and culturally conditioned. We must try to understand how work was perceived and represented in its historical context.

During the early modern period in France (and elsewhere), work was certainly recognized and valued as a means to earn a living, but I argue throughout this book that its significance to men and women of the early modern period *also* was as a cultural marker, a sign of personal identity and social status, a living symbol of who they were, and who they were seen to be. Men and women felt this way in large part because the taxonomic structure of early modern French society was a hierarchical series of graduated ranks of people, a stratified, structured system of hierarchical differences, and everyone sought to establish and proclaim his or her place within it. One knew one's place or "station" through an apprehension of *difference* from other ranks or stations, an awareness of *distinction* from those above and below, and a resulting knowledge of one's *status* in the overarching system. This, in turn, was inseparably bound up with one's personal identity, or one's sense of self and self-worth. One's sense of self was rooted in a subjective experience of difference, but, importantly, this experience was a shared one. Belonging to a "rank" and one's sense of self (and self-esteem), in other words, were linked. Identity was formed through erecting and maintaining boundaries between an imagined "us" and "them," an "us" and "them" that were ranked in the minds of men and women.

Now, let's place "work" in this system. We can now appreciate that it was more than a means to survival or to material accumulation, but just as importantly, that it was a sign of social place, or status. In the steeply hierarchical world of early modern France, or indeed of Europe, the connection between work activity and status was explicit and visible. It was publicly communicated by means of symbolic representation in a cultural system of appearances. Work, in short, functioned as a means of social classification and social control.[6]

Work and Hierarchy

The overall wealth of early modern France increased dramatically, a trend that accelerated in the sixteenth century and continued to the end of our period. France's wealth was also increasingly polarized, both socially and geographically. Though it is possible to offer precise figures in only isolated cases, historians agree that by the end of the Old Regime about 1 percent of the

French population possessed the vast majority of the wealth. We do know, for instance, that in 1789 the nobility of the southern French city of Toulouse (dominated by high royal officials called *parlementaires*) made up only 1 percent of the population but possessed 63 percent of the total wealth of the city. Other studies confirm the picture of polarized wealth, and show that the upper nobility were by far the kingdom's richest people. In a study of Parisian marriage contracts in 1749, for example, we find that three-quarters of the *noble* brides and grooms brought by dowry and inheritance over 50,000 livres tournois (the French money of account at the time). These are huge sums by contemporary standards. Slightly more than one in three wholesale merchant families brought that much wealth to a marriage, and barely more than one in five families from the liberal professions (mostly lawyers and physicians) did. Only about one in twenty nonnoble rentier families (those who lived off investments) were in this category. Needless to say, no artisans or petty tradesmen, much less common laborers, could even dream of possessing such fortunes. What was true for the eighteenth century was no doubt true for former times.

Wealth, of course, was closely correlated to social rank, for rank was made visible by appearance and comportment. During the early modern centuries we see a growing preoccupation with expensive display, a clear indicator that hierarchy was increasingly important. Indeed, in city and countryside the place of every individual was precisely and formally defined from the top of society to the bottom. Family was the basic indicator of place (and hence the importance of marriage to social status), but rank was determined and made visual by a bewildering array of other markers. What one wore or ate, how one walked, talked, or was educated, all demonstrated rank. But the most important marker of status for this study was one's occupation. What one did in one's work life was crucial to determining one's rank in society. Ironically, among the rich the goal of wealth was to leave work behind, for work was a sign of degraded status. Many a successful merchant would withdraw from commerce when he could and invest in land, finance (especially loaning money to the ever-needful crown), or the purchase of government offices, and hopefully (and eventually for their heirs) claim noble status.

With all this attention to display and hierarchy, society became a ballet of deference, a dance that was performed everywhere, but above all in the royal court and the kingdom's cities. This dance was intended to distinguish ranks, to demonstrate who was where in the social hierarchy, and with this deference came what the historian Gaston Roupnel called "dissociation."[7] Of course, the families that entered the desired house of elevated rank wanted to close the door behind them, to freeze the hierarchy and forestall upward social mobility for others. Social treatises justifying this view appeared, especially in the seventeenth century, proclaiming the positive values of an immutable order of society (both sacred and natural). Indeed, the seventeenth and early eighteenth centuries were the high tide of hierarchy. Behind this mythical screen, however, forces were at work—the growth of cities, the state, and the market economy—that generated the conditions for greater upward and downward mobility than ever before.

As we explore this hierarchy, let's begin with the countryside. Men and women who worked in the countryside in early modern France were often simply referred to as peasants. When learned men (mostly city dwellers) wrote about their society they were invariably dismissive of the peasantry, treating it as an indistinguishable lot, scarcely more sophisticated than animals and often worthy of even less attention. Theorists of social order described the peasant as bound by necessity, directly dependent on manual labor. They were consigned without much reflection to the bottom of the social scale, just above the wandering, homeless poor. Peasants, in short, were disdained by elites. Cardinal Richelieu, Louis XIII's prime minister, called them "the mules of the state"; Mazarin, his successor, called them *la canaille*, or "rabble." The inimitable seventeenth-century letter writer and social observer Madame de Sévigné called them "savages"; her contemporary and essayist La Bruyère, "ferocious animals."

Such colorful and derogatory epithets spring from a learned tradition. A very influential treatise written in the early seventeenth century by the lawyer and man of letters Charles Loyseau, *A Treatise of Orders and Plain Dignities* (1610), addressed the notion of hierarchy directly.[8] In this book (which went through at least nine editions before the end of the seventeenth century) he ranked the social categories of France at the time, and in his explanation of the reasons for the hierarchy, the idea of work was central. Beneath the men of letters, financiers, lawyers, and merchants were the laboring classes, the essential criterion for the rank order being the dichotomy between what he called "art" and "labor." Activities requiring intelligence, skill, training, and rules were artful and thus ranked above mere labor, which he associated with fatigue, lack of rules and skills, and degradation. Lawyers were artful so their work placed them higher in the social scale than, say, the mechanical arts, that is, the activities of the artisans, the degree of manual input determining their difference. At the very bottom of his scale was unskilled labor. The mere laborers, a category into which he lumped peasants, could earn, but because they were without training and, in his estimation, had no intellectual component to their activities, they were without occupation, and thus, tellingly, *sans état*, or without rank. He therefore devoted almost no attention to them in his treatise.

The general term invoked to describe rural folk—*paysan*, or peasant—conceals much more than it reveals, however, for historians know, even if

learned Frenchmen like Loyseau refused to, that the social world of the peasantry was extremely complex. What peasants did, what changes occurred in
their work, and what meanings work carried for them were far from simple.
A rigid, finely graded, and complex system of hierarchies held sway within
the village—large farmers, small farmers, tenant farmers, sharecroppers, day
laborers, migrant workers, and so forth, all had their place and knew it.
Within this stratified society, hierarchy and its privileges were widely internalized to the point of becoming a part of tacitly accepted tradition.

Let's go farther up Loyseau's ladder. In everyday social usage a man called
himself an *honorable homme* (literally, "honorable man") if he had scaled the
first rung of social advancement, had taken the first step up from the peasantry. Like peasants, these men still worked with their hands, but distinction
was based on corporate membership. Peasants had no such membership, but
the "honorable man" did. Within this rank, populated by merchants and
master artisans who belonged to guilds, are further gradations of honorabil-
ity. Wholesale merchants (called *négociants*) ranked above retailers, and
among the artisans goldsmiths, jewelers, painters, and sculptors perched at
the top (due to working with beautiful materials or involving the intellect in
production). More "base" were tanners, butchers, and shoemakers because
they worked with more "bodily"—and thus degraded—materials, like blood,
carcass, or even offal.

A *noble homme* was up another rung but, despite the title, was not a no-
bleman per se (who was called a *gentilhomme*, or "gentleman"). Here the fundamental determinant of dignity was the absence of manual labor, and thus
lawyers and physicians often populated this rank. From the perspective of the
noble homme (and those above him), those who work with their hands are de-
valued, often referred to as avaricious, poor, gross, or vile. Manual labor is disparaged, again, because it is bodily, dirty, and tiring.

Above the *noble homme* perched the *gentilhomme*, styled by himself and
others, according to the sixteenth-century writer Brantôme, as the *élu du
monde*—the elect of the world. He promoted the notion that his elevated status was in accord with nature because it was based on birth. Furthermore,
such rank supposedly conformed to a divine plan where superiors are glori-
fied and inferiors edified by their virtuous example. The *gentilhomme* saw
himself as the living image of the divine order in which moral values weighed
as much as economic ones.

But nobility was a juridical status too, and one entered it frequently by a
judicial inquiry. Before the seventeenth century this entailed taking state-
ments from witnesses who would testify that the applicant "lived nobly." Significantly for our purposes, this meant primarily that the man (and his parents and grandparents) lived off their income *without laboring*.[9] This was only

possible, of course, with a certain level of wealth, which required in turn certain economic involvements that would generate such capital. In the seventeenth century the definition and proof of nobility became much more stringent, requiring genealogical tables and more searching investigations, if anything intensifying the social principle of hierarchy.

Because they did not work, *gentilhommes* have no role in this book, but another breed of noble does. This was the "noble of the robe" (*noblesse de robe* as a term, according to the eminent French historian Fernand Braudel, was first used in 1603), or the nobility of officialdom. These men defined their status, like the *gentilhomme*, by the rejection of trade or manual labor, but, as we will see in a later chapter, they were at the forefront of defining "work," their work, in a different, more cerebral, way. Their wealth was drawn primarily from land and office, their fortunes usually inherited, expanded, and consolidated, not made. In other words, their lineage had invariably been launched generations earlier, and a successful merchant often lurks silently in their ancestry.

Men's Work, Women's Work

Hierarchy, of course, did not simply have a social face, but a gendered one as well. In the early modern period we call it patriarchy, and it put an indelible stamp on work and labor. Society was theoretically structured on the microcosm of the family, and a well-ordered society, as theorists wrote constantly, rested on the well-ordered family. Families, in turn, were supposedly regulated and disciplined by the father, the male head of household. Of course, women in this model were construed to be, in the nature of things, inferior to men. We can hardly be surprised, then, to find women's work considered by males as inferior to men's work. Once again, the meaning of work was mediated by ideology, and so was less about the nature of the activity itself than about relationships between men and women. Not long ago historians often assumed that the female sphere in early modern France (and Europe) was within the household, and that women were more concerned with reproduction than production. There followed from this an assumption that women's "work" was confined to the family economy, and, significantly, was unpaid. This was distinctly separate, so the argument goes, from the male-dominated sphere of the market economy where men were remunerated for their labor, their goods, or their services. This is what the ideological definitions of work pointed to, and what historians have often accepted as reality.

Certainly there is some truth to this normative picture, but recent research has forced us to question the rigidity of the boundaries between these spheres, the female family economy and the male market economy. Men,

especially in the countryside, can often be found doing household, supposedly female, tasks, and women can be found engaged in remunerative activities in the market economy (in both *labor* markets and *commodity* markets).
But if the boundaries between household and market were more porous than
we used to imagine, especially in towns and cities, how can we account for
the *increasingly rigid* ideological distinction between men's and women's work
in the sixteenth and seventeenth centuries, the latter inferior by definition
to the former? In a recent book, Mary Hartman suggests that this seeming
paradox has something to do with rising anxiety among men over their identity.[10] Men at the time, like historians recently, were well aware that women
were entering the public sphere of the market in increasing numbers, and in
many cases the demands of family business (in the workshop, in the merchant's counting house, even on the noble's landed estate) required men to
accept their wives as "deputy husbands," to quote Hartman. But just as much
as these men needed these women, they also felt threatened by their intrusion into male activity. It challenged, in other words, the men's notions of
masculinity. Among artisans, for example, guilds became increasingly closed
*brother*hoods, institutions that now excluded women from their ranks. Moreover, all across society (in towns and cities, at any rate—it is much more difficult to discern what male peasants were thinking, although rank hierarchy
structured peasant society no less than anywhere else), men, as I mentioned
earlier, intensified and extended the definitions of work that distinguished
the value of an activity by the degree of its intellectual component. Thus female work was naturally consigned to an inferior status (women, of course,
were deemed by men as less intelligent than men), and male work came to
be an increasingly important marker of status and a measure of worth. Patriarchy and hierarchy marched arm in arm.

A clear example of this process at work is in the defining of "skill." As we
will see in this book, women were working in many early modern manufactories and workshops, and their tasks, like spinning or above all lacemaking,
required a certain motor dexterity and know-how that had to be acquired.
Still, even though female work was needed in the economy, men looked on
this activity as inferior to their own, and arrogated the quality of "skill" only
to themselves. Indeed, skill became a cultural marker of masculinity, yet another attempt to shore up the fragile boundaries between males and females
in the world of work that, as we will see, economic forces were breaking
down. Lacemaking is a good example of these tensions. Seventeenth-century
French fashion meant that lace was in high demand, and so, too, were lacemakers. Oddly, though, in lacemaking regions of France there was high unemployment among men. Or perhaps not so oddly, for lacemaking was femi-
nized work par excellence, and was avoided by men, despite demand in that

labor sector and male unemployment, because making lace would rob a man of his sense of masculinity. Some things, evidently, were more important than earning a living!

Corporatism

The great German sociologist Max Weber pointed out long ago that the first task of the state was to secure obedience, to gain for itself the monopoly of the use of force and convert it into legitimate violence. But state power was expressed in a nonviolent, if no less coercive way, by the invocation of law. And a fundamental function of both force and law was securing social hierarchy. Moreover, according to Braudel, "No state could have existed without the collaboration of the dominant class, and thus when the state intervened against someone it was inevitably the masses who had to be contained and returned to the path of duty—that is to work."[11] The legal framework through which the early modern state exercised its authority over society and work was corporatism.

When men theorize about the meaning and value of work, assumptions about the proper order of society, the economy, or the polity are always present. These assumptions in early modern France were cast in the framework of corporatism, what I have called elsewhere "a rhetorical system for ordering the world and making sense of it."[12] Corporatism as a system of order emerged everywhere in Europe in the twelfth century. By our period it was deeply embedded in the economy, it was inextricably linked to social hierarchy, and it was fundamental to political, legal, and gender relations. France was formally organized into collective bodies of people (usually, but not exclusively, males, corporatism being informed by the theory of patriarchy), each body, or *corps*, possessing privileges that had been granted by the king in exchange for responsibilities owed to him and the public he embodied. Each body was assumed to possess a common interest, and, just as the human body possessed an order-giving soul, so these social bodies had their *esprit de corps* that would be expressed in solidarity. These collective bodies, or corporations, were thus legal entities and were considered legal persons, entitled to own property, plead in courts, and so on. *Corps* were empowered to make their own rules governing their internal affairs and submitting their members to a collective discipline. Corporatism, in short, was the legal armature of the early modern French state and would remain so until the French Revolution.

Chief among the legal privileges of corps, as far as our exploration of work is concerned, was a monopoly over the practices and services the particular corporation performed, and the primary responsibility of the corps was to guarantee order, through subordination and discipline, within its ranks. The emphasis on monopoly, of course, had economic implications, and the emphasis on subordination and discipline had social ramifications. Artisan guilds (called *corps de métiers*, or "craft bodies") come immediately to mind when the word "monopoly" is spoken, and I will have a great deal to say about these institutions in a later chapter, but I emphasize here that corporations included far more than the craft guilds and were institutions with much more than economic functions. Indeed, they were the fundamental cells of social hierarchy, explicitly arranged in descending order and thus visible representations of the society of ranks. Membership in a corps, therefore, placed the individual in his *état* and thereby announced his social status to the rest of society.

Only in the eighteenth century will corporatism come under attack, but its replacement by another comprehensive ideological system, what historians call "liberalism," will be complete only in the nineteenth century and thus lies beyond the scope of this book. Suffice it to say that the Enlightenment opened cracks in the corporate system, the French Revolution widened them, and new political regimes in the nineteenth century finished the job. Where corporatism embraced the principles of collectivism, patriarchy, hierarchy, discipline, and economic regulation, liberalism championed the individual (which could include the troublesome notion of equality), and the principles of "utility" and an unregulated, or "free," economy.

The Market and the City

Understanding work in early modern France requires grasping the importance of hierarchy in all its forms. It also demands consideration of economic forces at work, for it was during the early modern period that France witnessed a dramatic expansion of its market economy and, some historians now argue, sustained economic growth. Both, as we will see, altered the face of work and even its meaning. The expanding market economy had urban nodes and no doubt disproportionately advantaged certain urbanites, but economic growth was not just an urban phenomenon. Economic growth is notoriously difficult to measure, especially during the early modern centuries when sources are lacking for systematic and quantifiable analysis. Still, recent research has shown a quickening of local and regional trade (not to mention burgeoning overseas trade) between and among markets that were stocked with surplus products, both manufactured goods in cities and towns and agricultural products brought in from the countryside. This expanding market economy was demand driven, and though it certainly had its bottlenecks, and its attendant gluts and shortages, over the course of the sixteenth to eighteenth centuries there seems little question that the forces of the market were altering the economy of France (and elsewhere) in profound ways.[13]

At the heart of this economic transformation was the city, and the process of urbanization exerted pressures on markets that had dramatic effects. Indeed, as we will see, cities were the motors of economic growth. Cities in early modern France were fundamentally different from villages in the countryside. Until the seventeenth century, cities of more than two thousand inhabitants were invariably surrounded by walls. In fact, dictionaries of the later seventeenth century defined a city (a *ville*) by its primary characteristics of being enclosed by walls and surrounded by moats and fortifications. Ironically, as the authors were writing these words these characteristics were fast disappearing, but the fact that cities were and would remain physically set off from the countryside was inescapable. The villager who walked through the town gates was struck by a radically different world. Here houses were packed tightly together, and a bewildering variety of people of differing occupations and social status mingled in a bustling spectacle of street and marketplace.

The villager could not miss the construction projects that were going on across the city, as new homes for enriched townsfolk sprang up on sites of demolished medieval dwellings, or additional stories were added to existing ones, making the four-story building a common sight. For a hundred years after 1550 the boom continued. One mid-seventeenth-century commentator was so struck by the height of houses that he mused that it seemed as if two or three cities had been piled atop one another. Many cities, especially Paris, were transformed in another way, as the primary medieval building material of wood, plaster, and thatch gave way to clay tile and stone. Such changes in materials shifted the kind of labor involved in building. Fully half of the building costs of a new townhouse in 1673, for example, were spent on masonry and masons, while a quarter went to carpentry and the remaining quarter toward roofing and the increasingly important interior finishing.

Some neighborhoods experienced more building than others, and these increasingly corresponded to the nodes of wealth and power within the city. Chief commercial streets more and more concentrated the dwellings of wealthy merchants and traders, while some neighborhoods reflected the social concentration of political power. St. Médard Parish in the provincial capital of Dijon is a typical case in point. The highest royal judicial and financial courts for Burgundy were in this parish in the heart of the town, and wealthy royal officials built their ostentatious mansions nearby. Many of the new seventeenth-century homes of urban notables were built as freestanding edifices, set apart from neighboring dwellings (in contrast to their medieval counterparts, which tended to be connected), and set back from the street with wings surrounding an interior courtyard entered from the street through a grand arch. Such an architectural style emphasizing particularity and distinction reflected and reinforced the move toward social "dissociation" that marked all of French society. Not surprisingly, a greater density of lawyers, doctors, notaries, and craftsmen of luxury products clustered in these neighborhoods as well.

The French town of the sixteenth and seventeenth centuries was transformed, in the physical spaces where people lived and in terms of social exchange. Behind all of these factors of urbanization rests, of course, demography, and we should hardly be surprised that the populations of French cities surged, especially between 1500 and 1700 when they more than doubled, appreciably more rapidly than the overall population of the realm that climbed from fifteen million to over twenty-one million. Between 1700 and 1789 growth continued, the total population of France on the eve of the Revolution in 1789 reaching twenty-eight million. Sixty-three provincial cities grew by 32 percent and Paris by 29 percent in that century alone. In 1500 about 10 percent of the population of France lived in towns of two thousand or more inhabitants. By 1725 that percentage had climbed to sixteen (of a total population of well over twenty-three million), and by 1789 to about twenty. These growth rates are all the more striking when we note that death rates in cities (especially among infants who were often put out to wet nurses in the nearby countryside) surpassed birthrates, for urban living conditions were prime breeding ground for disease, and virulent outbreaks of plague and later typhoid repeatedly beset city folk and thinned their ranks. This meant that massive immigration from countryside to city fueled the growth. Demographers have shown that about one-third to one-half of the residents of any given city after 1500 and through the eighteenth century who married there had been born outside the town.

Behind this general picture we can perceive some differences in patterns of urbanization. Certain kinds of cities grew. Port cities burgeoned— Marseille, Nantes, and Saint-Malo all more than doubled between 1550 and 1700. Many migrants came from the countryside, but many also came from other, small towns. Paris was the most powerful magnet, but industrial and commercial cities like Lyon also mushroomed during that century. Lyon surged past one hundred thousand souls by 1700 (it counted only thirty-five thousand in 1515), buoyed by mercantile operations and the fabulous expansion of the silk industry. Most provincial capitals grew substantially as well: Rennes, Aix-en-Provence, Dijon, Montpelier, and Grenoble are classic examples. The latter, for instance, surged from two thousand in 1473 to twenty thousand in 1710.

The Growth of the State

Joining the intensification of hierarchy and the expansion and integration of the market economy was a third salient development that affected the history of work: the growth of the state. Broadly conceived, the primary business of kings was twofold: making war, and attempting to maintain order among their subjects. Thus the warfare state and what historians call the "judicial monarchy" marched arm in arm throughout the early modern centuries. Kings built their power on the administration and distribution of law (to maintain order) and the collection of taxes (to pay for war).

As population grew and the costs of war escalated, kings needed ever-increasing numbers of specialists in justice and finance to accomplish these objectives. Indeed, the sums of money required to wage war were vast, and because taxes proved inadequate to the need, kings beginning in the fifteenth century struck on the useful expediency of venality of office—the selling of government posts. The result was a swelling class of government officials of dizzying variety, but also a group of men who had a private, proprietary stake in public power. As we will see, moving farther from the center decreased the effectiveness of royal control of this mass of officials, who comprised a burgeoning social entity that gathered an ever-growing share of the kingdom's wealth into its hands. In economic terms, they deeply affected the demand structure and contributed greatly to the transformation of France's market economy.

Not surprisingly, these officials perched at the top of the social hierarchy and were keenly concerned with demonstrating their superiority and wealth in terms of status. In the seventeenth and especially eighteenth centuries we can easily detect a growing concentration of the nobility in cities, especially Paris. The social ideal of the *honnête homme*, or civilized man, assumed the city and the social exchange that occurred there as part of his definition, a definition that rested on social distinction expressed through rank-specific appearance, consumption, and comportment. By the 1780s in most towns, despite the growth of merchant wealth, the richest inhabitants were nobles.

Cities became the sites of administrative and legal authority, the apparatus of the state, and home to hordes of officials, all going about the "work" of government. Demographic figures confirm this. The number of officials exploded, especially between 1500 and 1700, and most of these men and their families lived in cities. The number of royal venal judicial and financial officials quadrupled between 1515 and 1665, reaching an estimated forty-six thousand. By 1778 the number of royal officials had grown only slightly, to fifty-one thousand, but cities continued to draw wealthy people to them.

Obviously, the administrative structure also mushroomed. By 1700, for example, there were twelve Parlements in France (the highest judicial courts in the kingdom), several quite venerable. The courts in Dijon, Bordeaux, Toulouse, Grenoble, and Paris all date from before 1500, while the court in Aix-en-Provence was established in 1501, in Rouen in 1515, in Rennes in

1554, in Pau in 1620, in Metz in 1633, in Besançon in 1676, and in Douai in 1686. The ballooning of the number of royal judicial institutions and officials to staff them did not stop there. In 1552 Henri II established thirty-two Présidial courts (primarily in smaller towns and largely hearing criminal cases), but their numbers more than doubled by 1600, and had swelled to one hundred by 1764. Justice was also dispensed in bailiwick and seneschalsy courts (*bailliages* and *sénéchausées*, respectively), and even *greniers à sel* (the last hearing cases pertaining to the salt tax). Over four hundred towns had one or more of these various courts.

In several of these towns these judicial courts were flanked by financial ones. By 1715 we can count eleven *Chambres des Comptes* (royal courts charged with auditing royal accounts), and twelve *Cours des Aides* (charged with tax matters). Francis I established sixteen financial districts called *généralités* (which became intendancies in the seventeenth century), a number that grew to twenty-two under the reign of Louis XIII. Louis XIV added eight more; thus thirty towns had intendancies by 1700.

The three salient developments that shaped the nature and meaning of work examined in this book—the intensification of hierarchy, the expansion and integration of a market economy, and the growth of the state—did not occur in isolation. Rather, they affected one another in profound ways, creating tensions in the lives of men and women at all levels of society. Hierarchy rested on ideological assumptions of static, immutable order, while the market economy and the growth of the state brought dynamism and social mobility. As the forces of growth gathered steam, they could not help but confront the dominant ideology with troubling implications. Indeed, as we will see in the chapters that follow, the ideological intensification of hierarchy (and patriarchy) and the corresponding emphasis on the importance of status in the seventeenth century was in part a response to unsettling market and governmental forces and the social changes that accompanied them.

The renowned French historian Roland Mousnier described French society as a "hierarchy of degrees . . . distinguished from one another and arranged . . . according to the esteem, honor and dignity attached by society to social functions."[14] Another distinguished French historian, William Doyle, adds that "no hierarchy can exist without reference to power differentials, and power differentials unrelated to wealth are quite inconceivable. . . . Thus, orders [or hierarchical social ranks or "estates"] were intended to divert attention from something dangerously important—the economic structure of society."[15] In other words, the ideology of hierarchy, voiced clearly by such influential theorists as Charles Loyseau, was an attempt to shore up a certain vision of proper social order, and an ideological masking of forces (economic and governmental) that, as more and more recent research is demonstrating, were threatening the social structure at its foundations.

The implications of these tensions for a cultural history of work like this one are profound. When one views these tensions as the context within which the heightened preoccupation with status took place, one can better understand the ideological masking (rank hierarchy and patriarchy) that was so essential to the definitions of work's meaning. One can certainly see this in the Loyseaus of this world, but also among peasants, artisans, merchants, and emerging professional men and government officials. Social identity was rooted in more than just employment, or work activity, and every bit as much in a maintenance of place asserted by other demonstrations of status.

In the pages that follow I hope to demonstrate how three salient developments I have been discussing in this introduction—the intensification of hierarchy, the expansion and integration of the market economy, and the growth of the state—shaped the history of work. Work and labor are basic to the creation of the human environment, and so we will explore the varied ways that French men and women worked, and how and why these activities changed over the early modern years. But work is more than just an economic activity, as important as that is, for it is also a cultural one that carries meaning. Work activities—making things and performing services that are of value to oneself and to others—are how men and women make contact with material reality, *and* how they achieve status and self-esteem and thereby, in part, invest their lives with meaning.

Notes

1. R. E. Pahl, ed., *On Work: Historical, Comparative and Theoretical Approaches* (Oxford: Blackwell, 1988), 1.

2. Jeremy Rifkin, *The End of Work: The Decline of the Global Labor Force and the Dawn of the Post-Market Era* (New York: Putnam, 1994).

3. Quoted in Kellie Robertson and Michael Uebel, eds., *The Middle Ages at Work: Practicing Labor in Late Medieval England* (New York: Palgrave, 2004), 2.

4. Robert Dubin, *The World of Work* (New York: Prentice Hall, 1958).

5. See Richard L. Simpson and Ida Harper Simpson, eds., *Research in the Sociology of Work*, vol. 5, *The Meaning of Work* (Greenwich, Conn.: JAI Press, 1995).

6. See the fundamentally important article by Steven L. Kaplan, "Social Classification and Representation in the Corporate World of Eighteenth-Century France: Turgot's Carnival," in *Work in France: Representations, Meaning, Organization, and Practice*, ed. Steven L. Kaplan and Cynthia Koepp (Ithaca, N.Y.: Cornell University Press, 1986), 176–228.

7. Gaston Roupnel, *La Ville et la campagne au XVIIe siècle: Etude sur les populations dijonnaises* (Paris: SEVPEN, 1955).

8. Charles Loyseau, *A Treatise of Orders and Plain Dignities*, ed. and trans. Howell A. Lloyd (Cambridge: Cambridge University Press, 1994).

9. Fernand Braudel, *Wheels of Commerce*, trans. Siân Reynolds (London: Harper Collins, 1986), 484.

10. Mary S. Hartman, *The Household and the Making of History* (Cambridge: Cambridge University Press, 2004).

11. Braudel, *Wheels of Commerce*, 516.

12. James R. Farr, *Artisans in Europe, 1300–1914* (Cambridge: Cambridge University Press, 2000), 277.

13. See Jan De Vries, "The Industrial Revolution and the Industrious Revolution," *Journal of Economic History* 54, no. 2 (1994): 249–70; and De Vries, *European Urbanization, 1500–1800* (Cambridge, Mass.: Harvard University Press, 1984).

14. Quoted in William Doyle, "Myths of Order and Ordering Myths," in *Social Orders and Social Classes in Europe since 1500: Studies in Social Classification*, ed. M. L. Bush (London: Longman, 1992), 218.

15. Doyle, "Myths," 221.

CHAPTER ONE

~

Peasants

What Peasants Did

In everyone's estimation in early modern France, peasants were closely associated with the land. Their labor turned mere earth into valuable crop-producing fields. Peasants occupied and worked the *terroir*, a term that did not mean simply "the land," but generally included buildings, courtyards, gardens, vineyards, fields, meadows, pastures, wasteland, woods, forests, and the network of paths and cartways that connected it. Technically, few peasants owned the land they worked. By the mid-seventeenth century 90 percent of the property of France was owned by lords (called *seigneurs*, who were not necessarily nobles), but by custom many peasants acted as if they were the proprietors—they sold land, bought land, exchanged land, and handed land down to their heirs. For this freedom to dispose of property they needed the consent of the seigneur, however, and gained it by paying the lord a variety of fees. For instance, there were annual dues called *cens*, which acknowledged the lord as owner; there were *lods et ventes*, fees paid the lord when land was sold; and there were *champarts*, or fees paid the lord with every harvest. By the seventeenth century, for reasons we will see, many landholdings of the French peasantry had become quite small (many as small as about two hectares, or five acres), while others had grown large.

On these lands—depending on whether we look at the northern half or southern half of the kingdom—many peasants were engaged in sharecropping and tenant farming. Sharecropping became more prevalent among the peasantry in the seventeenth century (for reasons we will discuss shortly), and was the dominant arrangement in most parts of France outside of the great wheat plains of the northern and eastern provinces and the Paris basin where tenant farming was common. In sharecropping arrangements the lessor and lessee shared the profits the land produced, the lessor providing the land and half the livestock and seed. The lessee provided labor, the other half of the livestock and seed, equipment, tools, and smaller animals (chickens, pigs, goats, etc.). Significantly, the lessee also had to pay all taxes, tithes (the annual fee owed to the church), and seigneurial dues and fees.

Tenant farmers, on the other hand, held land in lease and worked it as they saw fit. They paid rent to the owner, but provided the livestock, tools, equipment, seed, and hired labor. All profit (or loss) was theirs. This kind of farming required considerable capital investment. In the sixteenth century leases varied from twenty-seven years, or fifty-four, or even ninety-nine, but in the seventeenth century they became more standardized at six or three years. Terms then commonly lengthened in the eighteenth century to nine years. In these arrangements the tenant generally paid the rent in money, kind, or a combination before 1700, although after that cash payments predominated.

Behind this general picture lies bewildering diversity. Peasant landholding was very unequally distributed across the kingdom, thus providing the material base for a steeply hierarchical social world in the countryside. Moreover, there were sharp geographical and even linguistic differences. It is useful for analytical purposes to divide the kingdom of France into four zones, each with its own distinguishing characteristics.

The first zone, which held about one-third of the population of the kingdom, spans northern France from the Loire River in the south to Flanders in the north, and from upper Normandy in the west to Champagne and Burgundy in the east. The terrain was relatively flat and open, and was dominated by cereal grain production—oats, barley, wheat, and rye—and small herds of livestock, mostly sheep and cattle. About one-third of the land in any given year would lie fallow, allowing that land to restore nutrients necessary for cultivation over the next two years. This zone was marked by large villages surrounded by open fields laid out in long strips (ten times as long as wide, adapted to the heavy wheel and mold-board plow), and it is here we find most of France's large tenant farmers. Fields and villages were linked by foot- and cartpaths, and as one's eye swept across the landscape surrounding the village he would see a vista that was interrupted by a windmill or two. The great city of Paris sat in its center.

Figure 1.1. Map of France

The second zone comprises western France (lower Normandy, Brittany, Anjou, Maine, and Poitou), and held about a quarter of France's peasant population. Rolling hills with soils less fertile and less suited to grain production distinguish this zone from the first one. Dotting the countryside were small fields enclosed by hedges laid out in concentric rings or ellipses. These fields were often flanked by waste, marshland, woods, and open pasture. Villages, more like hamlets, were smaller and more widely dispersed than in northern France.

As we move south we enter our third zone, Mediterranean France (which included the provinces of Languedoc, Provence, and Guyenne). As in the west, here we find stretches of waste, heath, grasslands, and marshland, but the climate is quite different. Hot and dry summers here were good for growing olive and fruit trees, and for cultivating silkworms in mulberry trees, but poor for growing cereals. The soil was lighter and less fertile than in the north, which made for easier and cheaper plowing but lower yields. A good yield ratio of wheat in the north would have been 6:1 (grains produced on a plant per seed sown), but in the south the ratio would have been much lower. Consequently, peasants in the south grew a wider variety of agricultural products. Such diversification, despite the small property holdings that defined the landscape, supported a relatively dense population, nearly as dense as the fertile Paris basin. Irrigated gardens and terraced fields were common, and extracted exhausting toil from the peasants who worked them.

Our last zone comprises large stretches of terrain ill suited to permanent cultivation—the mountainous regions of the Pyrenees and the Alps, and the barren stretches of the Massif Central in central France. These regions were thinly populated, holding about 15 percent of the peasant population.

In 1500 France held about fifteen million souls, and by 1800 about twenty-eight million. Of these men, women, and children, well over 80 percent were peasants, clustered in about forty thousand communities. France's peasantry was very diverse, so in certain respects it would be more appropriate to speak of peasantries, with divergent experiences and outlooks on life.

Figure 1.2. Louis Le Nain, *Repas de paysans,* 1642, Musée du Louvre

Still, there are certain common characteristics that peasants shared. First and foremost, the centerpiece of the peasant's value system was the family rooted in its independent household.

The requisite strategies to establish and maintain the household put relentless pressure on all family members to work. Peasants everywhere were engaged in seasonal work, their labor following the rhythm of the agricultural calendar. During spring planting and fall harvesting everyone—men, women, and children—was engaged in these all-important tasks. For the rest of the year peasants performed a dizzying variety of jobs, often with little specialization of tasks. Villagers could not afford to confine women's proper role to the home, although household tasks like cooking were reserved for them. Only the miller, smith, and inn- or tavernkeeper fit the mold of a clear division of labor. The construction and maintenance of a mill were expensive (thus few peasants owned them) and grinding grain with wind or water power was a full-time job. Cutting or gathering wood for cooking and heating was a constant chore, and many men and women, as we will see, were employed in household tasks like spinning, weaving, and knitting. Every male peasant was something of an artisan, and men and women might double as petty merchants, but, unlike today, there were no retail shops to speak of in France's early modern villages (at least before the second half of the eighteenth century). Many tasks were interchangeable between men and women, but women more than men milked the cows and goats, and, with children, fed the small animals in the farmyard.

In general, women's work related to the family economy as a series of gradations. They could work as partners or assistants to men in various activities, or they could work in the household at an altogether different task from men, or they could work outside the household to generate additional income to help support the family. Importantly, women as much as men participated in the local market (the household economy was decidedly *not* sealed off from the market economy, contrary to what historians used to assume), buying and selling farm products on a regular basis, and hiring themselves out if necessary as milkmaids, weeders (especially in the spring), or farm servants. Among the more prosperous families, women were often involved in the business management of the farm. Usually, paying wages and buying and selling land were a male prerogative, but in some parts of France like Comtat, Brittany, Angoumois, and the Ile de France, women could be found signing legal documents and selling and buying land jointly with their husbands.

Some tasks were monopolized by men, of course, like plowing and wielding the heavy cutting implement, the scythe. Male peasants, like women, hired themselves out as day laborers or part-time servants, sometimes with their horse and cart if they owned one. Or they would offer their services as plowmen. Poaching small game in the nearby woods and forests (which were owned by lords, but often were not well policed), like weaving, spinning, and knitting, could bring an important supplementary income to the household.

In the peasant family everyone worked. By the age of five children were washing dishes, moving rubbish, pulling up weeds, and tending chickens. By seven girls were helping to cook, watching over younger siblings, tending small livestock, raking the garden, and helping with spinning and sewing. Boys at seven were moving and guarding livestock, and wielding pitchforks and hoes. They helped spin and weave cloth, or fix threads under the loom, and at ten boys might be shepherds, cowherds, or servants in other households.

Amid this welter of activity, a distinct social hierarchy held sway. At the top of the pyramid of the laboring peasant's world was the *laboureur*, or farmer. He owned a plow and animals to pull it, and enough land to support himself and his family. Indeed, the ownership of land was an important marker of social status. This type of farmer was most common in the northern and eastern parts of France and in the Paris basin. Some especially large farmers might hire out their horses, plows, and carts to smaller farmers, or they might lend seed, wood, and even money. The debtors of these large farmers often were peasants who worked smaller parcels of land in the village, and frequently would repay their debt in labor.

These men who hired out as farm laborers owned very little land, and so were considered inferior to the *laboureur* and ranked below him in the social hierarchy. Depending on the geographic region, they were variously called *manouvriers* (derived from the French words *main*, meaning hand, and *ouvrier*, meaning worker), *journaliers* (derived from the French word *journée*, meaning day, thus day laborer), or *brassiers* (from the French word for arm, *bras*). Whatever the term, these peasants were hired laborers who worked with their hands and used simple tools, usually made of wood. Metal-bladed sickles were a prized and less common implement, and the larger scythe was scarcer still because of its expense. This group of farm workers was a notoriously difficult bunch to discipline. On a farm with only one boss it would be hard to keep an eye on everyone. In the early seventeenth century in his influential treatise *Le Théâtre de l'agriculture*, Olivier de Serres complained about the "malign nature of most hired hands, which is the very reason why they merely feign any effort when their master is away."[1]

Many a *manouvrier* owned his own tiny plot of land (usually less than two hectares—about five acres—considered the minimum to support a family),

and clung tenaciously to it because of the status it conferred, but the laboring world of the peasantry comprised many individuals who were not even
that fortunate. At the bottom of the social scale were the homeless or
transient men, women, and children who struggled to survive by all kinds
of manual work, from making simple baskets to picking fruit. These folk
shuffled from village to village with no permanent abode, and, along with
other itinerants like peddlers or folk healers, were regarded with deep suspi-
cion and fear.

Historians have long known that peddlers and vagabonds were mobile
populations, but recently we have come to realize that there was more mobility among even domiciled peasants than historians once thought. Dimin-
ishing landholdings contributed to this. The propertyless laborer (both male
and female) was constantly on the move looking for work, frequenting *louées*,
or hiring fairs, that were held at certain times of the year. Here men and
women looking for work would gather to be hired as servants, or as hands by
larger tenant farmers. Familial marriage strategies at times also could contribute to this mobility. Throughout our period peasants steadfastly clung to
a value system that placed the family and land it owned at the center of the
independent household. Indeed, marriages were arranged only when the future husband and wife were ready to set up their own hearth. This strategy
pushed some individuals into a wider world often beyond the native village
where, as we will see, landholdings were shrinking in size and sometimes disappearing. The wealthier peasants sometimes had to search beyond the locality for leaseholds for their sons or appropriate husbands for their daughters, while the poorer peasants had to seek labor opportunities wherever they
could. In short, the desire to establish independent households contributed
to geographical mobility.

All these itinerant French men and women tramped along roads that were
rough thoroughfares—often dust-choked ruts in the summer and muddy
sloughs in the winter. The network of roads was very complex and very
dense, usually comprising single cartways, tracks, or even footpaths. These
roads were full of people, carts, and wagons, men and women walking with
hoe or spade to work in a field or vineyard. They were joined by women
heading to the local market, fair, river port, or nearby town or city with baskets of eggs, chickens, or a bolt of cloth. They shambled along with itinerant
potters and peddlers with fish, earthenware bowls, or cooking pots, dodging
oxcarts and wagons carrying stones, barrels of wine, sheaves of grain, hay,
dung, or wood.

When we think of peasants, we tend to think of agriculture and land, and
certainly throughout the early modern period peasants were engaged prima-

rily in agricultural work and closely identified with the land. However, peasant work was more complex than this. Consider what the intendant Bal-
ainvilliers in Gévaudan reported in the eighteenth century: "Every man is a
fabricant. There is not a single *journalier*, artisan, or *laboureur* who does not
work on his own account out of his home, in which he is occupied when agricultural work is lacking; his wife, his children spin and prepare wool, and, especially in winter, a feeble lamp illuminates these different tasks well into the
night."[2] Indeed, throughout the early modern era, rural industry was both important to the economic well-being of peasants and, in some places, very extensively developed. Who would guess that in 1600 in Picardy, a province in
the northern cereal-producing plains, looms far outnumbered ploughs? Supplying looms with thread and yarn required a host of other activities, most
importantly, spinning, and rural spinning and weaving were not confined to
a few regions of France. In some places linen production from flax dominated, in other areas woolens were the primary textile, and in parts of the
south of France it was silks. The countryside was a vast reservoir of cheap
and, at certain times of the year, underemployed labor.

Flax spinning and linen weaving were important supplementary occupations for peasant women and men in some parts of France, notably in the
north near Flanders. Women did most but not all of the flax spinning, pulling
threads with a handwheel (these threads were too fragile to adapt to the new
cotton-spinning machines that appeared in the eighteenth century), and
then transposing the thread onto bobbins that they gave to weavers (mostly
but not exclusively male) for warping on the looms. It could take a weaver
up to three weeks to manufacture a bolt of fine linen because linen weaving
was a difficult skill acquired through informal but demanding apprenticeship.
Woolen production followed similar paths, with men and women spinning
the yarn and men weaving it into cloth. The finishing of linens or woolens
(fulling, bleaching, and so on) was usually done in towns and cities, the cloth
sometimes transported there by the peasant family itself, or by contracting
merchants who, by the way, were not just from the city. Especially in the
eighteenth century we find a swelling population of village merchants whose
enterprises could be quite large and sophisticated, men who still owned and
farmed land but whose energies were spent mostly on the cloth business.

Silk had long been imported from the Middle East and Asia, but beginning in the late fifteenth century we find in France the cultivation of mulberry trees necessary for silkworms to produce their fibrous cocoons. From
meager beginnings mulberry trees and silkworm production expanded significantly in the seventeenth century in the countryside of Provence and the
Comtat and then spreading to Languedoc and Dauphiné. Silk weaving re-

mained an urban occupation (first in Lyon, although in the eighteenth century Tours and Nîmes became important silk-weaving centers), but cultivating the trees and raising the worms became an important source of supplementary income for peasants. French silk was considered of mediocre quality, and so great was the demand for silk that upward of 80 percent of the raw material was still imported, even in the eighteenth century.

Work and Culture

The work world of the peasantry was embedded in cultural relationships that gave it meaning and form. First and foremost was the peasant's connection to the land. Even if a peasant engaged in rural manufacturing, and increasingly over the early modern centuries more and more did, all peasants still sought to "own" and work land, even if it was but a small parcel. And this connection to the land immersed the peasant in three fundamental and shifting relationships that will go a long way toward providing us with an understanding of peasant work. First, there was the economic relationship to the market, or markets—those of land, commodity, and labor. Second, there was the social relationship to family, gender, kin, and fellow villager. And third there was the political relationship to the seigneur, the state, and the village *communauté*. Let's explore each of those in turn.

Market Relationships

Given the present state of research we cannot fully subscribe to the view that peasants were locked in a Malthusian prison that conditioned a conservative, tradition-bound mentality. Demographics did, however, have much to do with the economic, political, and social conditions of peasant life, and population levels cannot be ignored when we try to understand these conditions. There were times when overpopulation (relative to resources available) did seem to contribute to famine or cyclical economic downturns, and relative underpopulation encouraged economic expansion and growth. Moreover, *urban* population growth was a motor of primary importance that drove the rural economy throughout the early modern period, even at times when the total population of France was stagnant. Demand from cities had far-reaching effects in the French countryside.

But demographics are only part of the story. Perhaps the most important agent of change was the market, and over the early modern centuries we can see its increasing if uneven penetration into peasant lives. As urban demand accelerated, market forces were exerted on the countryside, and peasants responded in a variety of ways, none of which suggest that they were hidebound traditionalists averse to change. Indeed, one fundamental characteristic of the peasant was his adaptation to shifting demand through specialization—from growing grapes to weaving cloth to engaging in commerce. Peasants do not seem to have seen an antithesis between a world of tradition and one governed by profitmaking and competition.

These findings seem to lend support to Jan De Vries's theory about an "industrious revolution" taking hold in the seventeenth and eighteenth centuries. De Vries argues that European men and women worked harder (cutting back on leisure time, extending the workday) in order to generate surplus products that would in turn increase the household income. More income meant increased discretionary spending, an activity that was increasingly deemed necessary to provision the family with desired items available only in the marketplace. This helps explain why French peasant households were increasingly stocked with consumer items made elsewhere. These consumption patterns—in other words, demand—stimulated both a new attitude toward work (industriousness as a positive value) and an accelerated integration of the market economy. Combined they were requisite preconditions for the "consumer revolution" that historians agree took off in the late seventeenth century.

Social Relationships

Market relations changed the peasant world in other ways, notably in escalating tensions between the collective life of the village and the villager's pursuit of individual self-interest. Networks of interdependence coexisted, often awkwardly, with keen calculation of economic interests. Pressures from economic conditions constantly forced peasants to weigh the benefits of the pursuit of individual advantage with those of the collective life. But against this unstable backdrop, and perhaps as a way to shore up social relations, was an increasingly finely graded hierarchy in the peasantry. A common legal phrase in marriage contracts or guardianship arrangements was "as he belongs to his rank and status" ("comme il appartit à son état et condition")—stressing a strong and pervasive sentiment that everyone belongs to a social group that is situated at a certain level of the social hierarchy. The increasingly fine gradation of this scale everywhere, not just in the countryside, was a primary characteristic of the early modern era (only to be partially dismantled by the radical idea of social equality that made some headway in the eighteenth century). The scale was characterized—and visualized—by a range of criteria that were continually expressed by clothing worn, food consumed, place occupied in the church or village assembly, and marks of respect given and received. For peasants, an especially significant marker of status was the connection to land—how much was owned and how it was worked. Even the families that were drawn to rural industry tenaciously held on to land, even tiny parcels of it. Such possession, aside from being useful collateral for loans, was a symbol of still belonging to the rural community and holding a recognized place within it, and distinguished the owner from the inferior landless day laborers and migrants.

The kind of work one did, in other words, labeled and placed. This was especially true for men, less so for women (who were identified not by the work they did or the land they owned, but by familial status—daughter, wife, widow). The routines of life were profoundly marked by the conditions of work, and work deeply stamped social relations. This was a society of inequality, and one that was accepted by everyone from the king to the lowest peasant as natural and sacred. Distinction was the key. A rigid and complex system of hierarchies existed within the village (small farmer, sharecropper, day laborer, migrant worker, and so on). The farmers with a plow belonged to a higher rank from those without one. Similar material indicators of status (and reflections of the gap between rich and poor peasant) were the quality and quantity of farm implements and the number of horses one possessed. A chronic problem for the small farmer was the high cost of animal traction.

Family was the base of social organization, the source of solidarity, and around this node daily life and work were structured. Social status and rank were reinforced through family and kin groupings as well. Endogamous marriages within rank were very common, at least since 1600 and probably earlier. Research shows that day laborers married daughters of the same, as did small farmers, large farmers, and so on, in rates upward of three-quarters. Marriages consolidated alliances and merged properties within the village or, as among big farmers, established bonds with other wealthy families in other parishes. The advancing polarization of wealth in the countryside, a development we will return to shortly, encouraged these developments. In the Norman village of Neuville, for example, *laboureurs* comprised only 5 percent of the population, but by the mid-eighteenth century they controlled the village's principal resources. Their marriage contracts show increasing liquid wealth, and as their wealth grew they became a more tightly knit group by intermarriage.[3]

A finely graded legal and economic hierarchy structured social relations in the countryside, and hierarchy and its privileges, though no doubt resented by many, were widely internalized among the peasantry. Submission to rank had become traditional, and a prime characteristic of rural culture. Distinct social ranks, however, did not preclude close interrelationships up and down the peasantry. A small farmer might borrow a plow from a large farmer, and in exchange provide a certain number of days' labor. This is the reciprocity of inequality, and it ensured the preeminence of a small section of the peasantry. Such dependency was further reflected in complex systems of clientage that ran through the village, a cultural dominance that was often reinforced by the ability to read or write. Indeed, the ability to read became a great distinguisher, as the illiterate became dependent on the literate as mediators with the church, the state, and the law. In the seventeenth century literacy increased, largely due to little schools established by the reforming church to teach the faith, and by the eighteenth century we find some peasants even acquiring books.

Political Relationships

The political culture of the peasant was local in nature, and centered on the village community, the *communauté*. The lord and the state (or, more commonly by the eighteenth century, the proliferating legal professionals and urban royal officials to whom the lords and the crown had either sold or delegated privileges), of course, exercised authority over him and theoretically could expect deference and subordination from him. Fundamentally, such authority was felt in similar ways, for the seigneurie and the state were both mechanisms for surplus extraction from the land in the form of dues, fees, sharecropping and rental arrangements, and taxation.

In terms of work, the village community was a more important political body than either the seigneurie or the state. It was a *corps*, and so held an important and legal place in the corporate world. It was recognized by customary law and by the monarchical state beginning in the mid-fifteenth century. Like all such bodies, it had a juridical personality, and it was the fundamental fiscal unit for tax purposes. There were about forty thousand village communities in France, although their vitality varied greatly from place to place. In Flanders, Hainault, and Artois, for instance, they were feeble, but in Burgundy and Provence powerful.

The political nucleus of the community was the assembly, and it typically would meet five or six times a year, sometimes more, sometimes less. All heads of household were members, and in some places this included women. This body would set the date of the harvest, determine the use and management of communal lands, elect officials, debate expenses, and in some locales, distribute the tax burden among its members. The amount to be levied on the community as a whole was, depending on the region, determined by royal officials called *élus*, or by representatives of provincial estates, but in some places the community then nominated tax assessors and collectors who would then determine the allocation within the community and organize collection.

Clearly considerable power was vested in the communal officials, but despite appearances, these were not democratic bodies. The poorest members of the community had no political voice. Big farmers and, increasingly, notaries and lawyers dominated, the ability to read and write making them natural mediators with the world beyond the village, especially the seigneur and the state. These people interpreted the legal documents under which peasants were increasingly obliged to lead their lives, and not surprisingly, they manipulated the system to their advantage. Indeed, the divisions within the communities increased in the early modern centuries. Escalating taxes ignited rancor within the community about distributing assessments, and not surprisingly, accusations of corruption and favoritism flew. The vibrant land market exacerbated the problem, and peasants knew it. As common (and taxable) lands more and more came on the market (as we will see), they were often purchased by city-dwelling men of privilege, and when such privilege carried tax exemption for the property as it often did (especially in the northern half of the kingdom), the tax burden fell even more heavily on the remaining common lands—and the peasants who worked them. Such relations of political authority, then, had much to do with the nature and history of the work world of the French peasantry.

What Changed in the Work World of the Peasantry?

The extension of commerce in and among France's cities during the sixteenth and seventeenth centuries is undeniable. Equally obvious is the fact that this commerce enriched city dwellers much more than rural folk. The results could be spectacular, as in Lyon, a city that emerged in the sixteenth century as a major European banking, commercial, and manufacturing center. Other cities (and their merchant classes) profited enormously from burgeoning long-distance trade. Atlantic port cities like Saint-Malo and Dieppe, for example, were entrepôts for trade in fish brought from the Grand Banks off the coast of Newfoundland, while Nantes became a bustling center prospering from the Atlantic sugar and slave trade with the West Indies and Africa in the seventeenth and eighteenth centuries. Bordeaux's big merchants profited handsomely from the booming export trade in quality wines and brandy. In 1550 about 210,000 hectoliters of wine were shipped out of this port city, but over the next ninety years that volume would more than double to 510,000 and would be joined by brandy exports of over 7,000 hectoliters. By 1700 wine exports lurched to 750,000 hectoliters, and brandy to 140,000.

Urban merchants, as we will see in more detail in a later chapter, also benefited from the restructuring of manufacturing. It is well known that beginning in the late fifteenth century and accelerating in the seventeenth and eighteenth, woolen and linen manufacturing moved to the countryside. Merchants (who continued to base their operations in cities) seeking cheaper labor employed rural workers to spin yarn and weave cloth, and then sold the products in distant markets. Thus the labor may have moved to the countryside, but the profits generated from the industry were sucked into the city. The woolen and linen industry may have relocated to the countryside, but silk production remained in towns like Lyon, Tours, and Nîmes (the last tripled in size in the eighteenth century due to the growth of its silk stocking industry catering to South American markets).

Of course, as the example of rural manufacturing illustrates, cities did not live in economic isolation from the countryside. Population growth in cities had a huge impact on the countryside. Escalating demand increased pressure on rural productivity, and forged new and more extensive networks of transportation to reach urban markets. As the market economy increasingly became dominant, the city became something of a pumping station, drawing in money, raw material, people, and food, and spewing out goods. Most cereal, wood, stone, meat, and cheap wine that provisioned towns came from the nearby countryside, and cities had voracious appetites. Parisians in 1637, for example, consumed an average of 155 liters of wine per person, and a total of 368,000 sheep and lambs, 40,000 cattle, and 68,000 calves. A city of 100,000 inhabitants would require anywhere from11,000 to 26,000 square kilometers to provision it.

This points to a very important development that will be fundamental to our understanding of the peasant's world of work: the extension of the town dweller's control over the countryside. Between 1500 and 1789, the dominance exercised by cities over France's economic and political life increased substantially. Theorists of the city, like Alexandre Le Maître in 1682 in the *Metropolitée*, assumed a hierarchy of city over countryside. According to him, by right and law the city commanded the countryside; like the head in the human body, it directs and controls. During the early modern centuries we see a massive extension of the city dweller's control over land, especially the land in closest proximity to the city. The profits of agriculture, including land rent, were drawn into cities and into the coffers of its richest citizens. Add to that urban-based fiscal extraction (land rent, seigneurial dues, tithe, royal taxes) that increased sharply over the sixteenth and seventeenth centuries, and we see that cities took much more from the countryside than they returned to it. And of course, the revenue pulled from the countryside was very unevenly distributed in the urban population. It favored the wealthy, and further reinforced the hierarchical contrasts between the summit and the base of the social pyramid.

Until recently historians assumed rural France from the late Middle Ages to the mid-eighteenth century was an immobile, unchanging society. Some of the greatest French historians of the twentieth century subscribed to this view—Marc Bloch, Emmanuel Le Roy Ladurie, Pierre Goubert.[4] Supposedly this was a time of economic stagnation, of repeated subsistence crises, of paltry agricultural output. In explanation, historians tended to point to the prevalence of peasant-owned farms that were so small that subsistence farming was the only option. This meant that the inhabitants of these farms were perennially poised on the brink of starvation. With this material situation, it was argued, came a mentality that was risk averse and opposed to innovation. Peasants were thus mired in a world of little trade and outmoded technology.

Historians had constructed this grim picture based largely on demographic evidence (the ebbing and flowing of population) and on tithe returns (each year the church demanded a percentage of the agricultural product, and measuring these exactions could, so it was argued, provide an indicator of total production). It seemed to them that the French peasantry was locked in a Malthusian cage, prisoners of the ineluctable relationship between resources the land could produce and the number of mouths it could feed. Growth could be only cyclical in such a system, and occasional famine an inevitable and predictable, if tragic, occurrence. French peasants, accordingly, developed a conservative mentality, fearing that any departure from traditional practices would hasten the arrival of dearth. They clung to the ways of their forefathers, and so the forces of change could only come from the outside and be imposed on them.

But what if total population bears only a remote relationship to agricultural productivity? This has been demonstrated in other times and places, so why not early modern France? Perhaps the percentage of people living in cities would be a better indicator of growth? What if we shift our focus to other kinds of sources than demographic? Might a different image appear, one that may force us to reconsider the role and extent of economic growth in early modern French agriculture? Such is the argument of historians like Philip Hoffman, Jonathan Dewald, and Liana Vardi.[5] In the past twenty years or so historians like these have shifted their analysis to labor, commodity, credit, and land rental markets, and by scrutinizing wages, prices, and leases, which Hoffman has done, they fundamentally revise the traditional picture of early modern French agriculture.

It is true that French peasants experienced repeated subsistence crises, but these crises were often not related to the failings of agriculture or an innovation-resistant mentality of French farmers. Rather, the culprits, as we will see, were epidemics, war, and taxation schemes that were periodically imposed by government. Moreover, even though few French peasants had enough land to be self-sufficient (recall that that required at least five and more likely ten hectares of farmable land to support a family, feed livestock, and pay tithes, seigneurial fees, rents, and taxes), it would be erroneous to conclude that this made them averse to innovative alternatives or that they were isolated from a market economy. Indeed, we now know that even "subsistence" peasants were involved in a fair amount of trade. How was this possible?

In a word, specialization. Historians are now aware that this was much more widespread across the early modern era than was once thought. As we have seen, peasants worked in cottage industry (usually textiles), and did so long before the eighteenth century. They also tuned production to suit the soil, climate, the local costs of transport, and above all, the demand in nearby urban markets. A central argument of this book emphasizes the importance of the growth of cities and the trade networks that increasingly connected them in creating markets that were a primary motor of economic growth. Attuning production to these conditions, which we now recognize peasants did, testifies to an innovative peasant mentality eager for profit. It might mean giving up cereal production for a more intense cultivation of orchards or grapes (and vineyards spread relentlessly throughout the kingdom during the early modern period, especially near towns and cities). Or it might entail more assiduous attention to clearing away weeds and brush from fields, or creating better and more extensive drainage. It might entail a novel use of an implement, like a scythe. This heavy tool had long been used to cut grass, but with demand from urban markets on the rise it was increasingly used to harvest grain. Or it might mean grazing a small flock of sheep on one's land, and on the village commons, and then driving them to market or selling them to a merchant. None of these activities were revolutionary, but were incremental and specialized adaptation to geographic, climatic, and, above all, market conditions. These adaptations had an aggregate effect and resulted in growth, discontinuous, sporadic, and regional though it may have been. There was no sudden conversion to efficiency with the advent of capitalism introduced from the outside, but in fundamental ways agricultural productivity *was* determined by outside forces, by urbanization, prices, epidemics, warfare, and taxes. The conditions for growth also turned on the city and access to urban markets. It thus depended on effective transportation and lower transport costs, and if roads were better in certain areas (like the Paris basin) then trade was facilitated and specialization encouraged.

Just as it makes sense analytically to divide the kingdom of France into geographical zones, so too can we analyze the changes in French agriculture by time periods. Between the mid-fourteenth century and the end of the eighteenth French agriculture passed through six distinct phases, each with its own dominant characteristics. Phase 1 of our analytical model stretched from about 1330 to 1450, phase 2 from 1450 to1560, phase 3 from 1560 to 1660, phase 4 from 1660 to 1720, phase 5 from 1720 to1780, and phase 6, the revolutionary period, from 1780 to 1800.

Phase 1, 1330–1450

The years from 1330 to 1450 were times of misfortune for many French peasants, and the two chief scourges were disease and war. In many parts of rural France, the 1330s and 1340s were marked by dearth as the population had multiplied to the furthest extent of resources available to feed it. In 1340 France was relatively densely populated with eighteen to twenty million inhabitants, a figure that would not be reached again until 1560. What happened in between was catastrophic mortality. By 1420 the kingdom's population had been cut in half, victim of waves of plague that swept France in fearful and frequent intensity. The first visitation is well known—the Black Death. In 1347 infected rats carrying the deadly pathogen *pasteurella pestis* (named in the nineteenth century after being identified by Louis Pasteur) disembarked from Italian trading vessels in Messina, Sicily, and spread terror and death in their wake. Within four years one in three Europeans had died, infected in their turn from fleabites (fleas living off the blood of infected rats literally transfused the pathogen into human bodies). The contagion hit France by 1348. It abated in 1351, but returned with equal deadliness in 1360–1361, and then again from 1373 to 1375. When plague struck areas already weakened from famine, the mortality was truly astronomical. It returned in regular, deadly epidemics several more times: from 1380 to 1383, 1399 to 1401, 1420 to 1421, 1438 to 1441, and 1450 to 1453. For hundreds of years thereafter plague would continue to visit European populations, with deadly effect, but not in the epidemic proportions characteristic of its first one hundred years in Europe. The last plague epidemic in France occurred in Marseille in 1721.

With such mortality, obviously plague disorganized the rural economy. However, it was not the only culprit. War was also frequent and intense. The Hundred Years' War erupted in 1338 when an English king, Edward III, laid claim to the French throne by what he construed to be rightful inheritance. It lasted until 1453. Actual battles were waged only in certain parts of France, but the havoc wreaked by this war was more far reaching. During times of "peace," roving bands of unemployed soldiers became organized bands of brigands and proliferated. Many of these soldiers were younger sons of nobles who could no longer survive on the family estate because of the disruptions of war and plague. These estates, naturally, lost tenants and workers, and so could not be run in the traditional manner.

Moreover, war was expensive, and was paid for by ever more frequent royal fiscal exactions (taxes) and outright extortion and confiscation by the armies. The burden fell on the peasantry. Royal fiscal exactions had actually begun before this war, with King Philip the Fair in the early fourteenth century. Exceptional at the outset, they soon became regular and permanent. In 1341 the *gabelle* (a tax on salt) was introduced, followed by *maltôtes*, or *aides* (levies on consumables), and the *fouage* (later called the *taille*, a hearth, or household, tax).

Disease, war, and fiscal depredation took their toll on the rural economy. Families, the fundamental economic units, were decimated, and the relationship between the great estates and the peasant was fundamentally altered. Marginal lands were abandoned first, and over time entire villages were deserted as peasants died or headed for towns or other estates, where they could exact more favorable farming arrangements from lords in need of men and women to work their land. Over the course of this phase, the number of *feux*, or hearths (peasant households), diminished by half.

The disaster was also felt by lords. Estate revenues plummeted. With the threat of peasant flight and competition with other lords for a workforce, not only did real wages for farm workers rise and land rent decline, but lords lost the ability to levy feudal dues and charges, and in many places were forced to abolish serfdom altogether. Most notably in the northern and eastern grain belt of France, there arose a rural aristocracy of *laboureurs*, those fortunate few peasants who were able to capitalize on the conditions that spelled misery for so many.

Overall growth, of course, declined in the century after the Black Death first appeared. But important changes took place in the French countryside. Most notably, the relationship between the seigneur and peasant was altered, and a sharper hierarchy within the peasantry emerged, with the independent landowning or tenant farmer, the *laboureur*, at the top.

Phase 2, 1450–1560

The years from 1450 to 1560, phase 2 of our analytical model, were generally a time of demographic and economic restoration, especially up to the 1520s.

Population grew, the seigneurie was reconstituted, and agricultural production increased. Just as disease, war, and fiscal exactions had been the culprits causing the woes of the previous century, so now they influenced the return to prosperity. The plague became less virulent. Historians and epidemiologists are unsure of the reasons for this, but it is likely that the microbe itself mutated into a less lethal form. Whatever the reason, epidemics were less frequent and the mortality rates from contagion declined. War on French soil also disappeared after peace with the English came in 1453. French kings and nobles still waged war, of course, but the battlefields shifted to northern Italy and the foe became the Habsburg dynasty. With the relocation of war, French peasants were now spared the scourge of roving armed bands of soldiers, and so the French countryside experienced over a century of relative peace. And finally, though royal fiscal exactions did not disappear, they noticeably lightened, at least until the 1540s.

A new climate of security prevailed, and historians point to the halcyon years of 1460 to 1520 as a "golden age" of French agriculture. The French countryside was repopulated; indeed, due primarily to a declining death rate, by 1560 the population of France had reached its preplague level. In other words, between 1450 and 1560, the population of France doubled. Moreover, land was plentiful and relatively cheap to buy or rent. Landlords eager to gain tenants were accommodating in their rents, and with the population rising, food prices rose as well, thus pushing up agricultural profits.

Economists and historians agree that economic growth is notoriously difficult to measure, and during a time when records for such measurement were sparse and incomplete, we can only infer growth from a variety of indicators. First, there is no evidence of famines during this golden age, suggesting that, despite the growing population, the fruits of agricultural growth were spreading, albeit certainly not equally, across rural society. Moreover and even more importantly, peasants were increasingly oriented toward the market, further suggesting surplus production. And cities and towns, like the countryside, saw their populations swell. City dwellers, of course, do not grow their own food, and so rely on production in the countryside. As urban demand grew, peasants geared their production to meet it, and so increasingly specialized what they grew. It is during this period that we see an acceleration of regional specialization, in grapevines, for example, or olive trees. The great wine-producing centers of France—Burgundy, Alsace, the south Atlantic coast—all saw vast stretches of land converted to vineyards during these years, and the substantial growth in production resulted in expanded shipping of large quantities of wine to urban consumers. The same can be said of olive trees in the south—already prevalent, they became ubiquitous.

Urban demand pressed not only the production of food and drink, but also of cloth. The textile industry had been largely urban based before this time, but growing demand drew country folk into it, and the putting-out system, or cottage industry, began to take hold in certain regions. As a result we see the beginnings of an important shift in the division of labor in this important industry, as certain tasks left the city and shifted to the countryside. For example, in 1464 in Dijon, nearly a quarter of all artisans in this town of about eleven thousand people were involved in the textile industry, but by 1556 barely one in ten were, despite the fact that the population of the city had grown by nearly 40 percent. The number of spinners, weavers, and above all, carders in Dijon declined absolutely during this period, yet the number of cloth merchants increased (indeed, the number of household heads engaged in commerce *generally* increased by nearly 200 percent). Textile production, or at least certain stages of it, was moving to the countryside. City merchants would provide the raw materials to peasants, pay by the piece produced, and move the finished items along the various stages of production. Peasant men, women, and even children would card or comb the raw wool, and women and sometimes men would spin it into yarn that the men would then weave into cloth on looms provided by the merchant (or financed by him). We cannot miss the important fact that more and more peasants during this time were drawn into this manufacturing network.

Growth and the penetration of the market in peasant lives had other, important effects. Market forces generally do not distribute the products of growth equally, and during this phase they most certainly did not. An increased polarization of wealth is starkly apparent during these years, and a sharper social hierarchy emerges as a result. Prime beneficiaries of the favorable conditions were the landowning and tenant farmers who had survived and even prospered during the previous phase of widespread misfortune. They had the means to solidify their preponderant economic and social position, becoming the *coqs de village*, as they were often called. They formed lasting local dynasties, and dominated the village community, monopolizing its posts. At the other end of the social scale were more and more men and women dependent on these wealthy families for their livelihood—as hired workers, or debtors. As long as economic conditions were good, everyone could benefit (or at least avoid famine), but if conditions deteriorated, the ranks of the lower orders could only swell.

Agricultural growth, then, spelled significant change in the world of the peasant. We can perceive an evolution toward greater contacts with towns and cities, and with some of the inhabitants of them—notably merchants, notaries, and government officials. This is a trend that will accelerate, in fits and starts to be sure, for the rest of the early modern era. As early as the 1520s, however, darkening clouds begin to gather on the horizon. More and more lands are showing signs of overexploitation (signaled by lower crop yields). This is accompanied by a continued rise in prices and a decline in real wages (first and most notably in the north, then slowly in the south). By 1560, in fact, the purchasing power of wageworkers was half what it had been in 1490. As a result, we see in the historical record in the 1520s, for the first time in a generation, a return of famines, and by 1560 a clear increase in pauperization. To make matters worse, in the 1540s royal fiscal exactions increase, and in the 1560s, war resumes on French soil.

Phase 3, 1560–1660

As we enter the third phase of our analytical model, 1560–1660, we cannot help but be struck by the impact of war, governmental fiscal exactions (largely to pay for war), disease, and even climate on the work world of the French peasantry. With the eruption of the murderous civil wars that involved such deep religious hatred that historians call them the Wars of Religion, France was torn apart. From 1562 to 1595 Protestant and Catholic forces struggled for control of the monarchy and their armies visited devastation on many parts of the kingdom. Crops were destroyed and farmsteads pillaged by the combatants, obviously disrupting not only production but also the avenues of exchange. The years from 1589 to 1595 were especially bad, but for nearly a half century the economic and social life of the countryside was severely disorganized. The kingdom experienced a brief respite until the 1620s, but in the 1630s as France became engaged in the Thirty Years' War (1618–1648), the impact of war was felt yet again. The eastern provinces suffered the misery of invading and destructive imperial armies, but perhaps most painful for peasants everywhere in France were the taxes levied to fund the war.

Indeed, the misfortunes caused by war had been compounded by a sharp increase in the tax burden for decades before the Thirty Years' War. Consider these increases in the *taille*, the direct royal tax on property and personal wealth (a tax that fell most heavily on the peasantry). In 1559 the crown levied 6.7 million livres on the kingdom, a figure that lurched to 18 million by 1588. In 1610 it held at 17 million, but by 1635 had shot up to 39 million, and by 1642 had reached 44 million. Worse still for the peasantry, indirect taxes proliferated. Total imposts collected by the crown in 1620 stood at 31 million livres, soared to 85 million by 1639, and hit 118 million two years later. For reasons we will explain shortly, while taxation was escalating, more and more wealthy elite French families were escaping it through legal privileges that exempted them from the levies. Thus peasants, even poor ones, were paying an ever-greater percentage of a sharply growing tax burden. By the 1660s France's two million rural day laborers (of a total population of eighteen million) were paying taxes that amounted to about a fifth of royal revenues. Louis XIV's minister Vauban in 1700 summarized that a *manouvrier* earned about ninety livres a year, from which he paid fifteen in *taille* and *gabelle*. Peasants who farmed five or six hectares of good wheat land and owned a cow, a pig, a half dozen sheep, and a few hens, would pay forty livres in royal taxes, or the equivalent of a couple of good cows, or ten sheep. Of course, peasants also had to pay the church its tithe, and the landlord his dues and rents (or, if sharecropping, half the crop). Indeed, with the reconstitution of the seigneurie that was occurring during the previous century, seigneurial dues were reimposed, and varied from light to crushing (the *lod et ventes* and the *champarts* in the north and east, for example, were especially heavy). We can estimate that the church, crown, and lord took about two-thirds of what the land produced.

This escalation of exactions on the land and the peasant coincided with a renewed offensive of the plague in the 1630s. With war and a cooling of temperatures (often referred to as the "Little Ice Age" that appears to have commenced in the 1580s) that slightly shortened the growing season, we see a return of famines, poor harvests, and rising prices that will last through the 1650s. Better times will wait until 1660, and as a result the population of France dipped from twenty-two million in 1640 to eighteen million in 1660.

The population of France had begun an upward climb in the second half of the fifteenth century, growth that lasted until the 1630s. Given that French laws in most places stipulated that patrimonies be divided equally among surviving children, population growth led to a gradual but inexorable shrinking of peasant holdings from one generation to the next. By 1550, 80 percent of the peasants of France may own a house, a garden, and a few hectares of arable or vines, but not enough to be self-sufficient.

In such a fragile position, peasants were extremely vulnerable to poor harvests, and when such harvests inevitably struck, to get through the season peasants had but one option: debt. Beginning in the second half of the sixteenth century, peasant indebtedness soars, and when debts cannot be repaid (sadly, too often the case for, recall, war resumes and the tax burden increases in the 1560s), two options present themselves: foreclosure or sale. In either case, so begins a massive expropriation of peasant land that will last for the rest of the Old Regime, but its high-water mark will be 1560 to 1650. Predictably, pauperization and sharecropping grow, as do the ranks of rural wageworkers who scrape a living from physical labor, doing odd jobs wherever needed.

At first glance, this seems a contradictory picture—peasant immiseration amid economic growth. We can begin to resolve this paradox by answering the questions: To whom were peasants indebted? And who foreclosed or, more frequently, purchased land from a desperate peasantry? As we have seen, the late fifteenth and early sixteenth centuries witnessed the growth of a market economy that put capital in the hands of *laboureurs*, and these successful farmers became creditors for their fellow though less-fortunate peasants, and were active buyers in the land market. One result, then, is the growth of a small but influential class of big farmers, especially in the cereal plains of the east and north of France, and the decline and even disappearance of middling farmers.

But *laboureurs* were not the only beneficiaries of the situation. Royal notaries also became very powerful and influential among rural inhabitants, and many amassed wealth by loaning money and purchasing land. But by far the greatest profiteers of the distressed peasantry were royal officials. The numbers and wealth of this new, urban class burgeoned in the early modern period. Take Dijon as an example. In ducal Burgundy in 1464 Dijon could count only a handful of high officials, but by 1556 their ranks had swelled by over 1,000 percent, and by 1643 by another 140 percent. By the mid-seventeenth century they numbered almost 5 percent of the total population of this important regional capital. The same story can be told in many other cities across the same period—Rouen, Montpelier, and above all, Paris. And these increasingly numerous men were the most prominent land buyers. They bought land for status, to be sure, but they also expected to draw wealth from it, and so often they were keen on imposing the dues and fees that by law seigneurs had the right to extract. The same reasons that pushed peasants into the land market rendered them vulnerable to the reconstitution of the seigneurie that these new lords effected. Many an urban noble family (called the *noblesse de robe* because of the long black gowns the men wore as uniforms of their high office) could trace its affluent roots to the acquisition of properties in the late sixteenth and early seventeenth centuries. And the much-prized possession of a seigneurie, especially a titled one, granted these upwardly mobile (even upstart) families the enhanced social status they so craved.

Under such circumstances, how could peasants survive? For many, perhaps 10 percent, a life of severe poverty beckoned. These landless folk lived a wandering life in search of short-term work and charity. Most peasants were better off than this, however, and survived by combining a complicated range of resources. Many still owned or rented small plots, and with whatever capital they could scrape together, rented and worked additional plots. On these small holdings, as we have seen, they often specialized, gearing production for market demand rather than growing food for direct consumption. Thus, even in grim times—or perhaps even because of them—the forces of market integration were exerted on the factors of production—labor, commodity, and land.

Viticulture well illustrates this adaptation to market forces. In 1600 vines were grown throughout the kingdom, most on small plots of land of one to two hectares. Most of these were peasant owned (85 percent of the vineyards in the Ile de France were). The market for wine grew as local and long-distance demand grew. Thirsty city dwellers regularly haunted the numerous small taverns that dotted the suburbs and prompted peasants to grow vines nearby, even all the way up to the city walls. Wine was also produced for export. Burgundian vine growers and winemakers (called *vignerons*), for example, sold wine to merchants for shipment down the Saône and Rhône rivers to Lyon, or up the Seine to Paris, while Gascon peasants in the southwest had a longstanding and growing wine market in England.

Such demand meant that vineyards produced two to three times the value as would the same quantity of land put to the plow. True, vine tending, harvesting, pressing, and vatting were much more labor intensive than grain farming (two to three hectares of vines kept a peasant family fully occupied), but grapes could be grown on land unsuited to grains, and so were a useful source of money to be spent in the market, to pay taxes, or to buy or rent more vineyards.

Phase 4, 1660–1740

This phase was a mixed bag. For some cereal-producing peasants good times returned in 1660, and for twenty years the specter of famine disappeared. Bumper crops provided plenty of food, but they also put downward pressure on prices, thus hurting the *laboureur* more than the wage laborer. Still, in many areas the second half of the seventeenth century was a time of growth—gradual and incremental, but growth nonetheless. Historians have discovered that peasants were now using a wider array of farm implements, and more horses than ever before. Fields were thus clearer of weeds and, with more fertilizer from more draft animals (in the area around Paris it has been estimated that fertilizer use increased by 50 percent between 1650 and 1700), crops produced greater yields. Facilities for storing grain and transporting it improved as well. The first canals were being dug in the seventeenth century, first linking the Loire and the Seine, then later in the south the Canal des Deux Mers connected the Garonne River with the Mediterranean Sea.

By 1675 the population of France had risen to twenty million, but crisis once again loomed on the horizon. In the 1690s misfortune returned to many a peasant's world and lasted for twenty years, and truly good times would not return before 1740. The famine of 1709, for example, was among the worst France had ever experienced. By 1717 the population had dipped to nineteen million. Nonetheless, everywhere exactions from the state, the church, and the landlord continued apace.

Phase 5, 1740–1780

Only in the 1740s does the situation improve, evidenced first by a rising population. By 1770 France's population had reached twenty-five million and by 1789 about twenty-eight million. Burgundy seems typical of this dramatic demographic surge; its rural population grew by almost 40 percent between 1715 and 1789. There were other indicators of economic growth besides population increase. Improved and cheaper transport was one (private tolls were gradually being eliminated by the crown), and the cultivation of new crops like maize (especially in the region around Toulouse) was another. Accelerating agricultural specialization (the flexibility of peasant polyculture in response to demand continued to be one of the peasantry's most prominent characteristics) fueled commercialization and market expansion as more specialized products went to markets. All of this was accompanied by an increasing monetarization of the countryside. Village shops popped up, complementing the existing markets and fairs, and a wider array of consumer goods were purveyed in them.

No major technological changes took hold in the French countryside at this time (no historian will call this time of growth an "agricultural revolution"), but more lands were brought under cultivation, more diverse crops were sown, and, in some areas, more fertilizer from draft animals was used. In Burgundy, for instance, crop production expanded as lords and commoner farmers, both large and small, cleared wasteland for cultivation and brought more common lands (meadows and pastures) under the plow. In some places yield ratios inched upward. The incentive was an upward spiraling of grain prices. These prices began slowly at first in the 1730s, then moved up briskly in the 1760s. And landowners of all descriptions tried to cash in. Rents rose sharply (after having stagnated for a hundred years), and seigneurial obligations were exacted with increasing efficiency, especially harvest dues (*champarts*) and woodland rights (wood prices shot upward as well). These windfall profits were then reinvested in land acquisition, usually at the expense of the smaller peasantry. In Neuville in Normandy, for example, by 1776 the wealthiest 5 percent of landowners owned over half of the land.

Demand in the land market was further buoyed by buyers who were making money from commerce and rural industry (farmers and rural merchants), notably trade in spun cotton in Normandy, or in the linen industry in the Cambrésis. In the latter region between 1680 and 1789, real land value, spurred by demand, increased two and a half times. This "seigneurial reaction" of the eighteenth century was not an appeal to a feudal tradition, but a response to contemporary economic conditions. Landowners had an increasing trust in land as a source of profit. Books like Desponniers' *L'Art de s'enrichir promptement par agriculture* (*The Art of Enriching Oneself Promptly by Agriculture*), a best seller in 1762, and in 1784 another by Arnould called *L'Art d'augmenter et de conserver son bien, ou règles générales pour l'administration d'une terre* (*The Art of Increasing and Preserving One's Goods, or General Rules for the Management of Land*), are written testimony to this mentality. So are the increasing costs of leases, the reviving of ancient claims to a property, the assault on common lands, and a lively real estate market.

A strong stimulus to economic growth in the countryside came, ironically, from nonagricultural activities related in some fashion to rural industry. In some areas of Normandy cotton spinning was taken up in the eighteenth century, and became a principal economic resource for many a peasant household. The Norman cotton industry built on a woolen industry that was well established earlier. In the 1620s Rouennais cloth merchants sought out cheaper and more docile labor in the countryside to spin and weave cloth that they would then sell in distant markets. By the eighteenth century *laboureurs* were cashing in as well, using their draft animals and carts to transport spun cotton to merchants who had commissioned the work, or employing their capital to serve as middlemen, buying raw cotton from merchants, putting it out to peasant spinners, and then selling the thread back to the merchant.

Farther to the north in Cambrésis a dynamic linen industry combined with prosperous agriculture.[6] As elsewhere, peasant holdings had become smaller over the years, but even though the plots were increasingly tiny, again, as elsewhere, peasants diversified in response to demand. As middling and small farmers disappeared, peasants turned to spinning flax and weaving linen, and wages from the industry allowed many to live independently. By 1750 two out of every three village households in this region were occupied with linen manufacture. The spread of rural industry in this area in the eighteenth century was dramatic, with looms especially proliferating in peasant cottages after 1750.

During the first half of the eighteenth century rural weavers sold their linen cloth directly to urban merchants, but by midcentury they relied increasingly on rural intermediaries. Indeed, the biggest difference in rural industry here between the eighteenth century and previous centuries was the surge in the numbers of rural merchants who came to dominate. The first group of rural merchants to rise to prominence were sons of *laboureurs* or weavers who had sufficient landed assets to raise loans through mortgages, or family connections to back their borrowing in *rentes* (interest-bearing annuities, effectively personal loans). After 1750 there was an enormous extension of credit, however, and land was increasingly its basis. Again rural merchants insinuated themselves in the business. Bills of exchange secured by landholdings proliferated, negotiated by the rural merchants through banking establishments and urban wholesalers, as did simple promissory notes that were easy to arrange and, again, were negotiated with rural merchants. These rural merchants, like the peasants themselves, adapted to circumstances, often attaching the linen trade to the agricultural marketing networks that were expanding at the time.

All of this was driven by seemingly insatiable demand. Fine linen from this area was prized as a luxury product by urban notables who wanted their undergarments, cuffs, collars, and handkerchiefs made from it. About a quarter of the production was sold in France, but more moved north into Brabant, the Low Countries, Germany, and the Baltic states, from whence it was re-exported to Italy, Spain, Portugal, and the French Caribbean colonies.

Cloth production was beset by periodic recessions, but over the eighteenth century rural industry increased in profitability as demand grew and production soared. Between the 1730s and the 1780s real income had increased 20 percent. This was a freewheeling business, essentially unregulated, and in the 1780s competition, especially from English fine cottons, caused a sag in demand. These cottons were cheaper and after a free-trade treaty was signed between Britain and France in 1786, the linen industry in the Cambrésis was beset by overproduction, falling prices, predictably rising defaults on credit, and, ultimately, bankruptcies. Many weavers were thus driven out of the industry and returned to farming.

Phase 6, 1780–1800

Growth in the French countryside marked the four decades after 1730, but during the 1770s it began to flatten out. These may have been good years for the wealthier sectors of the peasantry, but when rural wages did not keep pace with rising prices it could only hurt the vast population of *manouvriers* (recall that most peasant households survived by supplementary income from wageworking family members). Indeed, their purchasing power was cut by a quarter over these years. After 1776 tenant farmers began to be pinched as well, as rents now rose faster than prices.

The 1780s to 1800, what we might call the revolutionary period, comprise the final phase in our analytical model.[7] France in the 1780s experienced not only a prolonged recession in the textile industry, but also periodic collapses in the market for wine and sharp fluctuations in grain prices. The years 1788–1789 were especially severe, and economic crisis beset the entire kingdom. In 1788 storms and high rainfall hit the northern cereal plains, while in 1788–1789 the south suffered a brutal winter so intense that many olive trees froze. Spring shortages followed and prices shot up.

The ensuing food crisis coincided with a political crisis, one that had been brewing for some time. A monarchy strapped for revenue and annually facing bankruptcy escalated the fiscal pressure on French subjects, especially in indirect taxes, and the lion's share, as usual, fell on the peasantry. Moreover, the taxation system was grotesquely unfair, with various taxes disproportionately levied from region to region, and even parish to parish. No one could miss the irrationalism or the seeming injustice. Whether the peasants were in fact being taxed more heavily than ever before is an open question that historians still debate, but it does seem clear that peasants *felt* that to be the case. And to compound the resentment they felt, the tax system exempted many of the kingdom's wealthiest inhabitants from paying anywhere near their proportional share, and this "privilege" threw an even heavier burden on peasant shoulders. The resentment was not directed at the king, however, but rather toward his ministers and, more specifically and pervasively, against the privileged seigneurs.

Recall that a seigneurie was a system of land tenure dating from the Middle Ages. In earlier times it was also a jurisdiction of rights and a unit of judicial administration, but for the peasants of the eighteenth century what it meant more than anything was a mechanism for rent collection, a central cog in the system of surplus extraction. As we have seen, seigneurs, or lords, possessed certain legal "rights" to collect this money, and the most lucrative (and the most resented by the peasantry) continued to be the fees on property transactions (the *lods et ventes*) and harvest dues (the *champarts*). These "rights" were often put out to lease by absentee landlords, and the weight of exaction was uneven geographically. Even so, they were pervasive, touching every peasant somehow everywhere in the kingdom. In 1788, when the king prepared for elections to the Estates General, he asked for his subjects to list their complaints in *Cahiers de doléances*. One constant complaint by peasants was against the feudal regime, specifically against seigneurial impositions. Opposition to seigneurialism, then, had the potential to be a transcendent rallying cry for the peasantry when an opportunity presented itself.

The revolution that erupted in 1789 presented just such an opportunity. In March peasant unrest broke out, and its wrath was directed at symbolic instruments of seigneurial oppression—weather vanes and grain measures were broken, and property registers and tax documents were destroyed. The rioting intensified in the summer, and in some places seigneurial châteaus were pillaged. As harvest began, many peasants simply refused to pay seigneurial dues. In a politically expedient response to such unrest, the National Assembly, which had convened itself in June and declared itself the true representative of the nation, on the night of August 4 abolished feudalism and ended the church tithe. Expediency of another sort set in the next week, however, for from the fifth to the eleventh there was passed more legislation that restricted the extent of the abolition of the fourth; this was done in hopes of deterring a generalized assault on property. Forced labor and serfdom were gone, but dues relating to ownership and the use of land—and this included the detested harvest fees—were not abolished. As an indemnity for the loss of revenue by the landowner, these dues could only be removed through purchase at twenty to twenty-five times the annual value, an amount few peasants could afford. When word of this reached the countryside, many peasants felt betrayed.

Peasant insurrection continued in some areas into 1792. Revolutionary regimes responded to the agrarian situation, but historians search in vain for a consistent agrarian policy by the governments. In August 1792, with the new nation at war and peasants resisting conscription, the National Assembly offered a palliative, abolishing all seigneurial dues unless there was clear documented evidence of the nature of such rights (and with destruction of records in the summer of 1789, many such records had been destroyed). Then, when the National Convention was controlled by Maximilien Robespierre and his colleagues on the Committee of Public Safety in 1793, all feudal dues were abolished, but ground rents were specifically exempted from their definition. The closest revolutionary regimes came to formulating a policy was the Rural Code enacted in September 1791, and this will stand as one of the most durable items of revolutionary legislation. It was a compromise. On the one hand it embraced the absolute right to property that had been enshrined in the Declaration of the Rights of Man and Citizen in 1789 as an inalienable natural right, and so appealed to rural property owners, including the wealthier peasants. On the other hand, it also protected collective rights such as common pasturing, which was so important to poorer peasants.

The Revolution certainly brought changes to the French agrarian regime. The seigneurial system ultimately was abolished. Moreover, the property market continued to open up. Revolutionaries remained true to the principle of the natural right to private property so explicitly evoked in the Declaration of the Rights of Man and Citizen, and so any remaining fetters to real estate transactions were removed. Moreover, the sale of national lands contributed to the opening up of the real estate market. Revolutionaries confiscated lands from the church and from *émigrés* (people who feared the revolution and left France) and sold them to provide money for the state (and its creditors, many of whom were the revolutionaries themselves), to support the clergy in the absence of a tithe, and to provide backing for the new currency, the *assignat*. More than ever, ownership of land was the pivot of social and economic differentiation in the countryside.

But how did these changes affect the peasantry? The sale of national lands benefited mostly nonpeasants, but of the peasants who did purchase land, nearly all were those who already held land rather than those who sought to acquire property for the first time. Thus, one condition remained much as before: the peasantry was divided between a small minority of wealthy peasants with larger farms, and a large majority of poorer peasants with meager holdings.

Notes

1. Quoted in Philip T. Hoffman, *Growth in a Traditional Society: The French Countryside, 1450–1815* (Princeton, N.J.: Princeton University Press, 1996), 44.

2. Quoted in Denis Woronoff, *Histoire de l'industrie en France* (Paris: Seuil, 1998), 80 (my translation).

3. Jonathan Dewald, *Pont-St.-Pierre, 1398–1789: Lordship, Community and Capitalism in Early Modern France* (Berkeley: University of California Press, 1987).

4. Marc Bloch, *Les Caractères originaux de l'histoire rurale française* (Cambridge, Mass.: Harvard University Press, 1931); Emmanuel Le Roy Ladurie, *The Peasants of Languedoc*, trans. John Day (Urbana: University of Illinois Press, 1974; orig. ed. 1966); Ladurie, *The French Peasantry, 1460–1660*, trans. Alan Sheridan (Berkeley: University of California Press, 1987; orig. ed. 1977); and Pierre Goubert, *The Ancien Regime*, trans. Steve Cox (New York: Harper and Row, 1973; orig. ed. 1969).

5. Hoffman, *Growth*; Jonathan Dewald and Liana Vardi, "The Peasantries of France, 1400–1800," in *The Peasantries of Europe from the Fourteenth to the Eighteenth Centuries*, ed. Tom Scott (London: Longman, 1998).

6. See Liana Vardi, *The Land and the Loom: Peasants and Profit in Northern France, 1680–1800* (Durham, N.C.: Duke University Press, 1993).

7. P. M. Jones, *The Peasantry in the French Revolution* (Cambridge: Cambridge University Press, 1988).

CHAPTER TWO

~

The *Menu Peuple* (the "Lesser Folk")

What the *Menu Peuple* Did

The social and educated elites of early modern France called the underclass of French society the *menu peuple*, or "lesser folk," and when they bothered to acknowledge their existence at all, the collective portrait the underclass offered was unflattering in the extreme. Consider how an anonymous author of a police report in 1709 described Parisian society. At the top was the nobility of the robe and sword, followed in descending order by the established and rich financial and commercial classes, members of the liberal professions (primarily physicians and lawyers), the great merchant guilds of the Six Corps, retail merchants, and master artisans.

> Finally, there are port workers, industrial workers, the journeymen joiners, carpenters, plasterers, masons, locksmiths, tanners, bookbinders, parchment makers, tailors, tinsmiths; in a word, of all the . . . laborers, to whom must be added the Auvergnats, the Savoyards, the water carriers, coal heavers. . . . There are, moreover, lackeys, grooms, pages, domestics, runners, servants, huntsmen, guards, kennelmen, stablemen, ostlers, apprentices, bakers' boys. . . . The slime of Paris, despite its blackness and infection, contains nothing as infamous as the race of men called crooks, cheats, Greeks, Egyptians, astrologers, fortune tellers, English. All this pack of rabble gets up in the morning not knowing where or what they will eat, where they will warm themselves or sleep. They live only on swindles, thefts, rapine, and wrong-doing; they kill, burn, rape or poison for their own account or for others; happy with an *écu* or asking their weight in gold to commit a crime, in accordance with the state of their purse,

whether it be empty or full, and their appetite more or less strong. Such are
. . . the different classes of which Parisian society is composed. One must add
the whores, public or hidden, all devoured by evil and vice; they live with
thieves who they support most of the time with the fruit of their debauchery,
and who blackmail them, a slang term, that is, who force them to give them
money, when these creatures refuse to do so.[1]

This anonymous author lumped all manner of folk in the lowest category
of society, and made little distinction between the working poor and beggars
and criminals. Other authors, like the eighteenth-century Parisian physician
and moralist Philippe Hecquet, attempted to make distinctions within the
poor, and his central criterion was work. For Hecquet, in a well-ordered society the poor should be industrious and obliged to work to make a living.
Society, he adds, should not allow the poor to become indigents without any
means of support and unintegrated into the social organism.[2] In 1790 the
Comité de Mendicité (Committee on Begging) for the revolutionary government echoed this model in a systematic inquiry into the problem of
poverty. In very traditional fashion that goes back hundreds of years, the
committee distinguished between the worthy poor and the unworthy: "The
true poor, that is, those without property and without resources, seek to acquire their subsistence by their labor. . . . The unworthy poor, that is, those
known as professional beggars and vagabonds, refuse all labor, upset public
order, [and thus] are a scourge in society and call for its just severity."[3] These
descriptions of the poor are polar opposites; either no distinction is made between the laboring poor and the criminal indigent—all are worthless—or
clear distinctions are made between those who work and those who do not.

A parish priest named d'Athis comes closer to reality. In writing to his
bishop in 1774, he recognized the imprecision of a distinction between laboring poor and indigents, reporting that "the day laborers, . . . journeymen
craftsmen and all those of whom an occupation does provide for a living . . .
are [also] those who [may] become beggars. Being boys, they work and when
by their work they can acquire a suit of clothes and pay the expenses of a
wedding, they marry. They feed a first child, [but] they have great difficulty
feeding two, and if a third follows their labor is no longer sufficient to meet
the expenses."[4]

This priest's pitiable observation reflects how precarious the family economy in the 1770s was. Nowhere could a day laborer support a family on his
own. Indeed, when the revolutionaries were drafting a new constitution in
1790, they decided to separate the citizenry into two groups, active and passive, and intended to grant suffrage only to active citizens. Those who earned

less than seventeen to twenty sols per day were classified passive, and fully 40 percent of the male population of France fell into this category. The Comité de Mendicité estimated that it cost thirty-five sols a day to feed a family of five, so clearly entire households were required to work to survive, a fact that forced most French men, women, and children into what Olwen Hufton calls a "makeshift economy."[5]

What we have said thus far describes the eighteenth century, but had it always been thus? Yes and no. Poverty became a pressing social issue in the sixteenth century as population growth pressed against available resources, and starvation and annihilation by disease sporadically struck villages during the seventeenth century. But if the eighteenth century was no longer haunted by the specters of famine and plague, with population growth resuming we actually have more impoverished workers and indigents than ever before, thus ever broadening the base of the social pyramid.

An Economy of Makeshifts

Hufton described an economy of makeshifts as one where men, women, and children worked at whatever tasks they could find to piece together a subsistence living for the family. Thus the laboring poor of France were a highly disparate group, and a shifting one where people often specialized in not specializing in anything. Behind the generic names in town or countryside for day laborers—*gagne-deniers* (penny earners), *journaliers, manouvriers, gens de bras, hommes de peine,* and so on—was a complex and diversified reality. The countryside was full of unemployed occasional and seasonal workers, a sort of reserve of cheap manpower and heavy labor. Most of these laborers were agricultural, finding work during spring planting and fall harvesting (women and children were often employed during the growing season as weeders), but men often could periodically be found digging ditches or building roads. The countryside also was populated by petty tradesmen who flourished along the borders of forests as woodcutters, charcoal burners, or operators of forges and makers of small hardware. Itinerant knife sharpeners and menders of pots and pans were ubiquitous as well. Everywhere we find men, women, and children improvising in work and adapting to a variety of casual occupations just to survive.

In some areas of France, men, women, and children were irresistibly pulled toward smuggling, an illegal but widespread activity that could be profitable. Indeed, by the eighteenth century perhaps as many as a million people were involved in it. The most common smuggler dealt in a basic commodity, salt, but by the eighteenth century other contraband like tobacco became increasingly prominent. Throughout the early modern period the monarchy had levied a tax on salt (the *gabelle*), but the assessment varied by province. Some areas like Brittany had a low tax rate, while others like nearby Anjou, Maine, Normandy, and Picardy had a high one. As a result, contraband salt poured into the high tax provinces from the low ones (for example, Normans and Angevins, obviously, would rather buy smuggled salt than pay for the legal but highly taxed, and thus the higher-priced, alternative). The government "farmed" the tax (receiving a prepaid lump sum from a contractor in exchange for the lessee's monopoly right to collect the tax and pocket whatever difference he could manage). These contractors were viewed as shameless profiteers (they were), and smuggling was so widespread that it was virtually beyond regulation and control—despite the constant complaints lodged by the legal contractors with the government. Smuggling was so hard to police not simply because it was ubiquitous, but also because much of the salt was transported in very small amounts. Chunks of salt could be hidden under the crust of a loaf of bread, or granulated and mixed into a tub of butter. Children could carry a couple of pounds under their clothing and, in the eighteenth century, earn up to fourteen sols in clear profit from the load. This proved an irresistible practice because such a payoff was equal to a daily wage of an agricultural laborer. An adult male carrying a load from Brittany to Maine could clear twenty livres for the trip, equivalent to a month's wages as a laborer. Not surprisingly, whole villages were supported by smuggling.

Mirroring the organization of work in towns, some smugglers formed hierarchical bands of *chefs*, *valets*, and *journaliers*. The *chefs* headed the bands and were the entrepreneurs who had enough capital to purchase the contraband in bulk, the horses to carry it, the weapons to defend it, and the cash to hire the *valets* and *journaliers*. The *valets* were the *chefs*' permanent employees, and *journaliers* their spot market hires as the jobs required. We will encounter this core-periphery structure in the workforce again when we shift our attention to urban artisans in the next chapter. The *chefs* were much like merchants, for they had to know their markets, and depending on demand and supply would move their contraband over wide areas.

The economy of makeshifts was not just a rural phenomenon. Many urban dwellers lived lives of marginal expedience as well. Indeed, it was not unusual to find men alternating work in fields and unskilled labor in towns, flowing back and forth as demand required. In fact, we know much more about casual and opportunistic work and workers in cities and towns than in the countryside. Unskilled labor was an essential element of the preindustrial city and its economic life. As Haim Burstin cautions us, if we confine our analysis of the working world only to guilds, we only partially grasp the role of unskilled workers and, thus, form a distorted and inaccurate picture of the world of work and the urban economy.[6] It is true that guild masters absorbed throngs of unskilled workers through a spot labor market, but countless more day laborers toiled beyond the purview of the guildsman. It is difficult to ascertain how many people comprised this urban world of unskilled labor, but historians have estimated that wageworkers made up *at least half* of the urban population, and when we add the hordes of street merchants, hawkers, and servants, the proportion of the *menu peuple* among all city dwellers approaches two-thirds or even three-fourths.

Eighteenth-century municipal guides and picturesque literature describe the activities of the unincorporated (that is, nonguild) worker as they present the spectacle of the city streets. We read and, in our mind's eye, then see the streets teeming with unloaders, dockworkers, porters, errand runners, road sweepers, and water carriers, as well as innumerable petty trades engaged daily in countless acts of service or fabrication, of sale and resale of anything that anyone might possibly buy. A bourgeois of Reims wrote in his journal in 1663 that "the people . . . find markets for their work, but at very poor prices so only the shrewdest can subsist."[7]

Authors like Louis-Sébastien Mercier, keen if opinionated observers of the world around them, including these poorest workers, provide in words invaluable images of this makeshift economy. Mercier describes "brushers-down" thus: "the brusher-down lies in wait at the street corner" for a passer-by with mud-spattered stockings and shoes. For "two liards only, a halfpenny," he cleans your stocking and shines your shoes. "There is no monopoly among these wandering Savoyards," and their work is not regulated by the authorities. Mercier's description of the ragpicker is even more poignant. "See the man himself, with his forked stick; watch how he lifts God knows what from the muck on it, and stows the trophy away in his basket. . . . These vile rags, his gleanings, are primal matter, which later and under another form will adorn our bookshelves . . . for this is the raw material of all paper, this rubbish that the rag-and-bone man gathers."[8]

Modern readers are struck by the bewildering and chaotic spectacle of the city streets of early modern France, and in this we share the opinions of contemporaries. Mercier presents a vivid image of Les Halles, that central marketplace in the heart of Paris. "At one in the morning six thousand peasants arrive, bringing the town's provision of vegetables and fruits and flowers, and make straight for the Halles. . . . As for the market itself, it never sleeps. . . . Perpetual noise, perpetual motion. . . . First come the fishmongers, and after these the egg-dealers, and after these the retail buyers; for the Halles keep all the other markets of Paris going. . . . The food of the whole city is shifted and sorted in high piled baskets . . . everyone bawls his loudest; and you must know their jargon . . . in this bedlam of sound—street criers who . . . make day hideous with their performances, and against whose voices neither shut windows nor thick walls avail." Indeed, more than once does Mercier bewail the cacophony of the street vendors' cries. "Cries make a babel of our mean streets, cries raucous, or toneless, or shrill. 'Mackerel, live mackerel, new caught!' 'Fresh herrings, all a-shiver!' . . . 'Sea-fresh, sea-fresh' means oysters. Portugal, Portugal!' (These are oranges). Add to all these the voices of . . . the umbrella-sellers, old-iron vendors, and water-sellers, men screaming like women, women shouting like men. The din never ceases, no words can give any idea of the abomination of this piteous vocal torment when all the cries meet and mingle."[9]

A chaotic world of constant motion.

No wonder early modern French vocabulary distinguished poorly between *manouvriers, journaliers, gagne-deniers, dechargeurs*, or *portefaix*. These workers did similar tasks, and could be paid by the job or by the day. A similar vagueness characterizes terms like *regrattiers, revendeurs*, or *fripiers* (generally hawk-

Figure 2.1.   Etienne Jeaurat, *La place Maubert*, Bibliothèque nationale de France

ers of both genders of innumerable types of secondhand goods). Elite men ever since the sixteenth century published engravings called *Les Cris de Paris*, visual descriptions of activities whereby each kind of seller was recognized by a particular call. Historian Daniel Roche suggests that these were futile attempts by "cultivated opinion" to reduce this gigantic and disparate world to coherence and comprehension by investing "the world of labor with a normative coherence, a homogeneity of role and function."[10]

Historians note that attempts to bring an analytical order to this world are frustrated by shifting economic conditions that pushed and pulled workers into countless varieties of activities. Still, there are two primary distinctions in the world of work that help us to make sense of it. The first is whether an occupation or activity was incorporated or not. We will leave the incorporated world of guilds to a later chapter and confine our attention here to the "unskilled" workers. Tellingly, the term in French for "unskilled" used by the public authorities and cultivated society at the time was *sans qualité* ("without quality" or "without position") or *non-qualifié* (unqualified), which speaks to the lack of social status of the worker (signaled by membership in a guild) as much as his or her technical ability.

But if society's elites lumped all unskilled workers in a socially indistinguishable mass (recall the anonymous author of a police report in 1709 that opened this chapter), workers themselves were less inclined to do so. In times of good employment, a stratified hierarchy tended to emerge among many of the unskilled workers, mirroring the rest of society. Economic crises conspired to frustrate these ordering aspirations, however, rendering unskilled work more homogeneous, the crisis acting, in Burstin's words, as a "social leveler, diluting occupational distinctions."[11] Despite the desire to establish a sense of rank hierarchy by and among the unskilled, in fact the distance between even skilled artisans and unskilled penny earners (*gagne-deniers*) was not always great and, especially in hard times, could disappear altogether. To cite a telling example, the term *tonnelier* in eighteenth-century Paris could mean barrel cooper (a skilled artisan), or longshoreman, an unskilled worker who unloaded casks of wine at the city's wharves. Both occupations probably drew from the same men, the barrel cooper resorting to unloading casks during slack times in the barrel-making business.

And then there were the ubiquitous street merchants, men and women who sold everything from old hardware to lemonade, anything for which there was a market. These denizens of the makeshift economy ranged from the fruit sellers, fishwives, and ragpickers to the shadowy characters found in every city—the fortune-tellers, quacks, and charlatans who peddled balms

and unguents. All purveyed their goods in the secondhand markets that dotted France's cities. Mercier describes those of eighteenth-century Paris thus:

> The markets rise on a strange foundation; nothing less than the house in which
> our glorious Molière was born, and which still exists in part. There along the
> arches are ranged the used clothing stalls, ill-lit on purpose, that stains may be
> less noticeable, and colors deceive the eye; thus the suit of solemn black,
> bought and paid for, is transformed before your eyes, by the mere light of day,
> to purple or green, and spotted at that. These stalls all have their touts, who
> call your attention, none too civilly, to their wares; yield to the wiles of one,
> and you will have all the rest of them at your heels. The stallholder's wife,
> child, assistant, and dog, all bellow in your ear at once; and the din continues
> till you are well out of their clutches, and out of the gloomy precincts of their
> chosen trade.[12]

Equally striking is his description of the Fair of the Holy Ghost.

> On Mondays. The wives, sisters, aunts and cousins of these hucksters hold a
> kind of sale of their own, called Fair of the Holy Ghost, in the Place de Grève.
> . . . They sell only women's and children's clothes, and all who must make their
> money go a long way, shopkeeper's wives and such, get their bonnets, linen,
> cloaks and even shoes there, ready-made. . . . The fair itself is an amazing sight;
> a whole province might have been unfrocked to clothe its stalls. . . . The buyer
> neither knows nor cares whence comes the corsets she sells (stolen and fenced
> not uncommon)—both buyers and sellers are women. . . . By nightfall the
> whole mass of clothing is gone, magicked away, not one poor scrap left; but the
> fair itself is inexhaustible, and reappears without fail the following Monday
> morning.[13]

A Mobile Population

We might usefully define mobility in early modern France as the uprooting
of oneself from one's native community and moving elsewhere, perhaps only
temporarily, in search of a livelihood. Such a condition was a common phenomenon. Consider the following typical example from the eighteenth
century:

> At Saint-Jean d'Ollières there were 270 households, making a population of
> 1,190 adults and 810 children under the age of 14. On 1 October of every year
> 200 adult males left to cut wood; they returned nine months later for two
> weeks' work on their own harvest before heading south for three weeks' work
> on the olive harvest of Provence. Two hundred other men and 100 children
> under 14 left on 1 November, intending to return at Easter to comb hemp in

the Berry; if they could not find work they made for Paris as odd-job workers and beggars because at all costs they must not return until Easter, for there were no resources at home to feed them. After Easter (and a short period sowing their own fields) . . . this group moved off to Provence to pick mulberry leaves for the silkworms, and this kept them occupied, albeit spasmodically, until the early autumn. Three hundred children left the village annually as sweeps, and the number of pedlars [*sic*] . . . who left defies enumeration. . . . Only women and young children spent any time at home (even the aged were expected to go on the roads to beg).[14]

This example reveals one common kind of mobility experienced by millions of French men, women, and even sometimes children: that of seasonal migration where the migrant returned home annually after following work opportunities elsewhere. The immense contrast in employment conditions in different parts of France pushed and pulled migrant populations here and there. Vast numbers of people would follow harvests—above all, grain, grape, and olive. A massive exodus of inhabitants of hilly and mountainous terrain (mostly beneath the Alps) flowed onto the plains in the autumn seeking temporary work anywhere it could be found and often ending up as water carriers, mason-assistants, or hod carriers on construction sites in towns. Indeed, the seasonal migrant was a man of limited skills, and thus could work only at such occupations as harvester, woodcutter, charcoal burner, or peddler (selling anything that possibly could be sold—pins, needles, combs, skins, medicines, poisons, what have you—or mending anything that needed mending—pots, pans, chairs, and the like). Some children, too, joined the population of migrants, for bands of child chimney sweeps from mountainous areas moved into the plains during the "dead" agricultural season. They were hired out by their parents to "chiefs" (often also a peddler) who paid the parents a fixed sum in advance, and who then kept the earnings of the band. When spring came, like the men from Saint-Jean d'Ollières, all of these migrants would trudge back home to work on their small plots of land.

Above all it was the uplands of the inhospitable Massif Central, that vast rocky plateau that spanned much of the south-central part of the kingdom, and the mountainous Savoy that disgorged the most migrants. Indeed, "Auvergnat" or "Savoyard" often was invoked by urban dwellers as a generic name for the poor immigrant, a loose characterization that concealed a curious division of labor among some migrants, for we know that a disproportionate number of men from the Auvergne were water carriers; from the Limousin, masons; from the Lyonnais, porters or sedan-chair carriers; from Normandy, stonecutters, pavers, or thread sellers; and from Savoy, peddlers, chimney sweeps, and shoe shiners.

Many of these migrants were seasonal, returning home periodically, but tens of thousands more represented a second type of migration, that of permanent displacement and relocation. This type of migration was usually that of the country dweller relocating to a town or city. This is hardly surprising, given that throughout the early modern period in France cities and large towns experienced sustained growth, which translated into employment opportunities. In fact, the population growth of France's larger towns and cities is explained largely by immigration from the countryside (and from small towns), for poor hygienic conditions in cities precluded their populations from reproducing themselves (that is, the death rate of native urban dwellers exceeded their birthrate).

Consider Lyon in the eighteenth century. In the first half of the century about a thousand immigrants per year relocated there, a figure that nearly doubles in the second half of the century. This means that between 1700 and the Revolution in 1789 about 120,000 immigrants settled in Lyon. Lyon's total population in 1700 was about 97,000, and in 1789 just over 145,000. Thus, the town was full of dwellings like the following: one five-story apartment house in the early 1790s had thirty-six tiny rooms, and only ten of the inhabitants were native Lyonnais. There was a hairdresser from Nevers, a cabinetmaker from Vesoul, a hatmaker from Dauphiné. Of course, Lyon was above all the center of silk manufacture in France, and so it drew and absorbed thousands of unskilled workers. Boys could be assimilated as apprentices and taught a skill in the industry (70 percent of the apprentices during this century were born in the countryside), but the many girls and young women who flowed toward Lyon and were absorbed by the industry were put to work as unskilled assistants. Lyon was also a port city (at the confluence of the Saône and Rhône rivers), and many men found work as dockworkers, loaders and unloaders, transporters, deliverymen, and the like.

Perhaps the urban occupation that absorbed most immigrants (and certainly most girls and young women) was domestic service. Nearly every town or city from the sixteenth century onward could count servants as 10 to 15 percent of its inhabitants, and nearly all of these folk hailed from the countryside. In fact, many migrants left their villages and hamlets for the express purpose of coming to a particular city to work as a servant. They followed paths of family members or neighbors who had gone before them and who had sent word back home of employment prospects and contacts. Indeed, it was not unusual for a servant to find work in an urban household of an aristocrat who owned land near his or her village.

Predominantly Male Activities: Construction, Loading, and Transporting
Analyzing the *menu peuple* is challenging and frustrating for historians because its composition can shift in an instant. A highly mobile population, it
floats in an out of work, found one moment in an established artisanal workshop employed at nonskilled tasks, but at another moment unemployed and
begging in the streets. Or these folk might congregate in the suburbs of cities
(called *faubourgs*), and there hire themselves out as gardeners, vine tenders,
or, if they could obtain a small cart, transporters, hauling anything and everything that an artisan or a merchant wished to move. The ranks of the *gagne-
deniers* were filled by rural immigrants, but they could be joined by skilled
workers thrust into their midst as a result of economic crisis.

The imperatives of the makeshift economy pushed and pulled men and
women in myriad directions, thus making analysis of what they did all the
more difficult. Still, we can make out at least four kinds of *gagne-deniers* that
were monopolized by males. First, there were the simple unspecialized day laborers, the *hommes de bras*, who had nothing to sell but their muscle and were
employed on the spot to accomplish a countless number of tasks involving
heavy labor. Huge armies of manual laborers were hired in construction.
Consider that it took about seven thousand tons of stone to build one large
urban dwelling in the seventeenth century, and we can appreciate how many
laborers would be drawn into this type of work. Moreover, construction was
not just a private matter, for significant public building projects were constantly under way, be they fortifications, wharves, roads, public squares, or
theaters. These hopefuls would appear at dawn in a specified place in town—
in Paris it was the place de Grève; in Dijon, the place Saint-Michel—and be
hired for the day as a digger, a hod carrier, a stonecutter, or what have you.
These were the most miserable of all the *gagne-deniers*. Unlike journeyman
artisans (as we will see), these male laborers had no collective organization
in their work, and so were totally unprotected from competition (which
drove their wages to the lowest possible level).

Then there were the longshoremen in the ports of harbors and rivers.
These loaders and unloaders of barges also lived by their brawn, but unlike
the *hommes de bras*, could be well organized in bands (as we will see) and so
protect themselves (and their wages) from competition. Likewise often organized and so able to eke out a better living than the simple *hommes de bras*
were the various deliverymen (often called *portefaix* or *crocheteurs*) who
hauled (often on their backs) specialized loads of certain types of goods—
there were men who only carried charcoal, or wood, or hay, or salt, or plaster, or grain— to customers in town. The most fortunate workers within this

group were the unloaders of goods at customs points. They invariably restricted their own numbers and were protected from competition by the public authorities. Due to their privileged monopolistic position they earned a
reputation of extorting high fees from merchants and walking off the job to
drink in taverns if their rate demands were not met.

Mixed-Gender Activities: Textiles, Street Vending, and Domestic Service

As we have seen, rural industry came to dominate textile manufacturing during the early modern centuries, and vast numbers of men, women, and children were employed in it. In Languedoc in 1680, for example, fully 450,000
weavers can be counted. But if textile manufacturing was primarily a rural activity, it was not exclusively so. Indeed, some cities, like Tours, Nîmes, and
Lyon, housed droves of textile workers. In eighteenth-century Nîmes, 43 percent of the population was linked in some way to the production of silks, and
in Lyon silkworkers (*ouvriers en soie*) were the most numerous category of urban workers. Women workers comprise a surprising percentage of the workforce in eighteenth-century Lyon, albeit in the lowest-skilled and poorest-re-
munerated ranks. Many women specialized within the silk industry. The silk
thread winders (*dévideuses*) were the most numerous and poorest, but they
were joined by stitchers (*ourdisseuses*) and embroiderers.

Indeed, in every city women's work was concentrated in four areas: that
related to clothing (including washing it), petty retail, domestic service, and
prostitution. Every city throughout the early modern centuries counted legions of seamstresses and embroiderers. In some towns, like Grenoble,
women dominated the workforce in certain industries. By 1787 Grenoble
was producing 160,000 pairs of gloves a year and exported them as far away
as England and Russia. Of the 6,000 workers employed in the business, 4,000
were women who spent their days stitching and embroidering. Women not
only dominated the sewing of clothes, they also monopolized the washing of
it. The banks of rivers that coursed through towns were dotted with laundry
boats full of washerwomen (*lavandières*) washing the clothing of mostly well-
to-do city folk.

Countless women also were petty retailers, perhaps outnumbering men in
this trade by three to one. Many were widows, while others were married to
journeymen, unskilled workers, or servants and engaged in this activity to
supplement the family income. Women who hawked used clothing were
called *fripières*, while women who sold anything that someone might possibly
buy bore the more general label of *revendeuses* (resellers, or street vendors).

There was great diversity and enormous variation in what servants did, in
their working conditions, and in their relationships with their employers.

Most were jacks (or jills) of all trades, doing whatever the employer required, although some, especially in the largest households, did specialize in certain tasks. Most servants did not remain long with an employer, for changing jobs frequently, especially after 1750, was often the only way to get paid, to force the master to settle up. The average term of employment of a servant between 1600 and 1750 was four years, and between 1750 and 1820 it was only eighteen months.[15]

Given the lack of specialization of tasks in domestic service, contemporaries gave servants a broad definition. Dictionaries defined them not by the work they did, but by the fact that they lived in a household not their own in a state of dependency on a master, and thus were akin to children. In his dictionary Furetière defined the servant in 1701 as "a member of a household, under a household head," and the *Encyclopédie* in the mid-eighteenth century characterized the domestic as "someone who lives in another's household and shares his house." For many servants, the rhythm of work was very erratic, marked by short bursts of activity followed by extended periods of idleness. There was a hierarchy among them, and considerable differences of wealth and even lifestyle. And there were legions of them. Historians have estimated that servants comprised the single largest category of workers in early modern French towns, perhaps as much as one-fifth of the unincorporated workforce. In 1789 100,000 servants lived in Paris, or about 15 percent of the total population. About the same percentage inhabited Avignon in the same year, Nancy in 1766, and Aix-en-Provence in 1695. Earlier figures are hard to come by, but one historian estimates that between one-fifth and one-fourth of the population of Lyon in the mid-sixteenth century was employed in domestic service.

Families of even modest means employed maids or manservants. In Toulouse in 1750, for instance, half of the city's households had at least one servant. Not surprisingly, however, the greatest employers of servants were the middle class and nobility. The middle class comprised about 28 percent of the total households of Toulouse in 1750 and employed over one-third of the servants, although lawyers and doctors employed more servants than merchants did. The nobility comprised 9 percent of the city's households, and employed 43 percent of the servants.

Most urban servants were immigrants (it has been suggested that 90 percent of the servants in towns were immigrants from the countryside), the sons and daughters of poor peasants, and above all rural day laborers. Most hailed from especially poverty-stricken areas. The majority was drawn to cities from nearby, but it was not unusual for males to migrate across long distances (women seldom did). Wherever the migrants came from, however, cities were flooded with young migrants looking for work, many of whom ended up in domestic service.

A Female Trade: Prostitution

Prostitution, the exchange of sex for payment, may justly be considered a form of work in early modern France. Such a lifestyle, of course, was exploitative, degrading, nasty, brutish, and violent. The threat of physical harm, venereal disease, and pregnancy were ever present. In many ways, however, it was not so different from the experience of other women of the *menu peuple*, and the "choice" of entering this trade must be considered against the work and lifestyle opportunities otherwise available to poor, vulnerable, immigrant, and often homeless females. These women had few options, and the promise of a modicum of material security—food, clothing, a roof over their head—may have seemed a worthwhile exchange for engaging in a dangerous trade that respectable society judged dishonorable.

Prostitution and procuring were almost entirely female occupations. Prostitutes ranged from women selling sex on an occasional basis to women housed in a brothel and provided food and clothing by their madam in exchange for the proceeds garnered from commercial sex. Some rented rooms and after contracting for sex in the street, brought their customers to them. Streetwalkers did just that, working the streets, public squares, passageways, and markets in all of France's cities. Often they gathered near holy places. In Grenoble many could be found in the lower court of the Recollets church, just outside the Augustinian monastery, and in the garden of the Jesuits. In Dijon, many gathered under the portico of the parish church of Saint-Philibert and in the shadow of the monastery of Saint-Bénigne, while in Paris a favored haunt was just outside the church of Saint-Merry. Not surprisingly, taverns too were favored sites to do business. In fact, any woman seen in a tavern was immediately assumed to be a prostitute.

Historians find it very difficult to determine how many prostitutes there actually were in early modern French cities. Moralistic writers invariably overstated their numbers. The godly brothers of the Company of the Holy Sacrament in seventeenth-century Grenoble, for example, thundered that the city swarmed with harlots. Louis-Sébastien Mercier wrote that during the reign of Louis XV Paris had at least 30,000 prostitutes, a sizable number for a city with a total population, by his reckoning, of 575,000 souls. Mercier's contemporary Rétif de la Bretonne put the number at 20,000, but historians today consider both gross overestimates. Even though it is impossible to say precisely given the sources available and the current state of research, a more acceptable number would be 10,000 to 15,000.[16]

Since 1561 prostitution had been illegal in France, but authorities were ill prepared to suppress the trade. This was true in the sixteenth, seventeenth, and eighteenth centuries. Mercier writes that occasional arrests were made in Paris (he refers to monthly roundups), however, and the unfortunate women were summarily convicted and hauled in crowded open wagons to the Salpetrière, the hospital-prison for, among other miscreants and indigent folk, these *débauchées*.

The populace hooted at the women as they passed through the streets, Mercier tells us; some of the convicted covered their faces in shame while others were more brazen, "more inured to infamy, [and] receive and retort the insults of an unruly populace in the most indecent language."[17]

Actually, arrests of prostitutes are the best sources we have for a sociological profile of them. In Paris, according to a sample of arrests by the police in 1765, 1766, and 1770 and studied by the historian Erica-Maria Benabou, half of the more than two thousand women arrested were aged between nineteen and twenty-six, and three-quarters between eighteen and thirty. Nearly one in seven were over thirty-five (four were even over sixty-five), but only one in two hundred was under fifteen. The most common age was twenty-two,

Figure 2.2. Etienne Jeaurat, *Le transport des filles de joie à l'hôpital*, Bibliothèque nationale de France

and the arithmetic average of the entire sample was twenty-six. Benabou finds that 87 percent were single, only 5 percent were widows, and the small remainder were married. Not surprisingly, two-thirds of the women were immigrants.[18]

Nearly all of the arrested women declared a trade other than prostitution, and this was not simply a cover for dishonorable activities. Rather, it reflects once again the makeshift economy within which all of the *menu peuple* worked. These women worked at different jobs to make ends meet, prostitution being one of them. The majority (54 percent), like many women of the underclass, worked in textiles in some fashion, commonly as seamstresses. A *couturière* could refer to a female seamstress of women's clothing, an unincorporated trade until 1675, or a simple nonspecialized sewer; most of the prostitutes worked as the latter. Hairdressers were also common among prostitutes, as were shopgirls, food and fruit sellers, and domestic servants.

Procuring was nearly monopolized by women, and many of the bawds were widows. And though they were usually retired prostitutes, they rarely came from the lowest ranks of society. More often their fathers or husbands had been artisans, petty officials, or small-scale merchants.

These madams and prostitutes were commercial women working in an economic sector that was highly competitive and, though we have no reliable figures, certainly a sizable one. Mercier estimated that Parisian men spent fifty million livres a year on prostitution. More reliable sources tell us that in the seventeenth century sex could be purchased for an écu (three livres) or a gold louis, but it must have been cheaper than that for sex with desperate unfortunates who filled the ranks of common prostitutes. Whatever the rates, the recruitment of "fresh flesh," in historian Kathryn Norberg's poignant words, was the lifeblood of the business.[19] In provincial cities like Grenoble, much recruiting was done in the countryside. Some procuresses made regular trips there, and often arranged with parents, usually mothers, for the prostitution of their daughters. Shockingly to modern sensibilities, these girls were not kidnapped, but rather "sold" by mothers whose desperate straits left them little choice.

So great was the attraction of Paris to migrants, male and female, that many Parisian madams could remain in the city to recruit. The bawds would frequent fairs and festivals on the lookout for vulnerable young women. Another favored and promising site of recruitment was at the doors of the Salpetrière, awaiting the discharged. Anne Bonnard, a madam in Dijon in 1689, recruited young women recently released from the Maison du Bon Pasteur, a convent in Dijon for former prostitutes.[20] A deal offering food, clothing, and shelter in exchange for commercial sex, even if the madam took all the earnings, may have been too attractive to pass up for many women in these circumstances.

Living Conditions, Economic Conditions

For the relentless social observer Mercier, "the people of Paris is, of all the people of the world, the one that works the most, is the worst fed. . . . The poor Parisian, bent under the eternal weight of toil and work, erecting, building, forging, plunged into quarries, perched on the rooftops, transporting enormous burdens, abandoned to the mercy of all the men of power, and crushed like an insect as soon as he wishes to raise his voice, makes a meager living—and then only with difficulty and in the sweat of his brow. It is sufficient only to keep him alive, but incapable of assuring him a serene life in old age."[21] His depiction of the living conditions of the working poor was no rosier. Consider what he wrote about the poor of the faubourg Saint-Marcel just outside Paris: "An entire family occupies a single room . . . where the windows have no curtains, where the kitchen utensils roll with the chamber pots. The furnishings altogether are not worth 20 écus. . . . The children are naked and sleep pell-mell."[22]

A contemporary of Mercier estimated that on the Ile de la Cité in the heart of Paris, ten families, or forty to fifty people, were jammed into each building. Mercier adds that because landlords never granted credit, every three months "three or four thousand families were on the move; these are the people who cannot find the money for their rent. They shift their few pieces of furniture from garret to garret."[23] This was a mobile population even after migrating from countryside to town. Wageworkers were a populace of renters, contributing heavily to a key distinguishing trait in the world of work (and its hierarchy) besides incorporation: whether the worker maintains a fixed domicile or not. The transient and unincorporated worker, according to eighteenth-century dictionaries, was simply one of "the crowd of little people . . . the rabble."[24]

Of course, workers lived in these conditions because they could afford no better. What we know about income of this working underclass is scanty, especially before the eighteenth century, but regardless of their poverty they were still taxed, and because some taxes were assessed according to wealth, they give the historian some sense of the *relative* distribution of wealth in society. One such tax, the capitation of 1788, for instance, reveals that for Lyon the average assessment of unskilled nonspecialized workers was 2 livres 5 sols, and that of silk workers 2 livres 11 sols (there were 20 sols in a livre). Compare those assessments to the artisans' at 9 livres, that of the liberal professions of medicine and law at 30, and that of wholesale merchants (*négociants*) at 40.[25]

An assessment of two livres or so may not sound like much, but one historian has estimated that a Parisian male day laborer annually earned 230 livres for 250 working days (which lasted fourteen to sixteen hours per day) at the beginning of the eighteenth century. This comes to less than a livre a day—when he worked. Unskilled workers were not always employed, however, and living expenses pressed the worker's purse every day. Rent alone cost thirty livres a year, a figure that escalated across the century to seventy livres at the time of the Revolution. It is true that wages increased as well across the century, but the general increase in prices (and not just rents), especially the brutal explosion in 1788–1789, wiped out most gains. The economic importance of women's work thus comes more sharply into focus. It was essential for a working family to survive.

The living and working conditions of servants were diverse, ranging from miserable to relatively comfortable (given the alternatives to men and women choosing this occupation), depending on the master. Conditions for females were uniformly worse than for males—with fewer prospects for social advancement and more vulnerability to unwanted sexual advances from masters or their sons. Wages were paid annually or when the servant left employment, and though the rates were quite low (especially for women who received about half the wage paid men), the master provided food, clothing, and usually housing. Domestic service was an attractive employment option, however, not because of the living conditions but because of the opportunities, slim though they were, to better oneself. Being a day laborer was a dead end with no chance of upward mobility, but domestic service, despite its degraded status and lack of independence, attracted the better-educated and more resourceful immigrants.

Money could be made in service, more than in agricultural day labor or urban wage labor. Indeed, some servants made more money than some artisans. For female servants, this meant the opportunity to save wages for a dowry, and thus escape service for the more respectable ranks of marriage. Many male servants were called on to handle the household finances of their masters, and in the process learned the rudimentary mechanisms of finance. And, given the provision of food, clothing, and shelter by their master, servants had the opportunity to save money and to invest it. Some of the better-off male servants used their capital to enter petty commerce, while others loaned money at interest in personal *rentes*. Many of the fortunate servants in fact became small-time rentiers, moneylenders to the *menu peuple*, and sometimes even moneylenders to their own masters.

Work and Culture

Among Day Laborers

For the working poor, labor meant endless toil. These men and women were trapped in an iron cage of poverty and were cut off from "respectable" society. Most of the *menu peuple* possessed little but their labor—no property, no tools, no equipment—and they did not define themselves according to their role in the process of production (there was no sense of a working class, in other words). For the countless men and women who worked at whatever tasks they could find in a makeshift economy, identifying with a particular task as we often do today was, obviously, not an option. For them, labor was a synonym for the absence of goods. For some, as we will see, the new ethic of industriousness and work discipline seems to have taken hold, and through this they entered the world of consumption and the possession of cheap populux items, but most of the working poor throughout our period exhibited what economists call "leisure preference," a mentality of present gratification whereby they would cut back on hours and effort when work was plentiful, wages high, and grain prices low.

Is this all there is to say about the meaning of work among these folk? From the perspective of those *outside* this unfortunate mass of people, one would say yes. In early modern France, work was seen as a means to place one in society and to identify one with a group. Participation in social life was conditioned by submission to certain bonds of the group—family, corporation, neighborhood, religious confraternity. Respectable folk looked on the day-laboring poor as dangerous precisely because they seemed not to have ties to communities, these or any other. They were *gens sans aveu*, masterless men and women who had no bonds to the social framework. They were not linked by a common membership in a guild or corporation, and they had no formal relationship with a master. They were also seen as "unskilled," a descriptor that meant not simply a lack of dexterous motor ability, but also and more importantly, a status lacking in dignity. Skill was recognized through corporate status, and the working poor were outside of this world. They were, quite simply, "without status" (*sans état*).

But perhaps we can say a bit more about work and community *among* the *menu peuple*. Even if respectable society refused to grant them a place and a rank in society, we know that ties among them could be very strong, especially among males. The *crocheteurs* of Lyon simulated corporate status and clearly organized themselves into disciplined bands, defending their "turf" against interlopers. Other groups organized themselves by their work and place of origin and colonized distinct areas of different cities. Sedan-chair carriers from Lyon, for instance, settled in the suburbs of Saint-Germain and Saint-Jacques in Paris, while the Savoyards clustered in the quarter of the Ville Neuve near the Porte Saint-Denis, and in the suburbs of Saint-Jacques and Saint-Marcel. All possessed a keen exclusivity and sought to protect a hold on a given trade.

Many of these workers lived together in what were effectively surrogate families, sometimes as many as fifty jamming into a single dwelling. There were probably 100,000 such folk in Paris in the late eighteenth century. Among the Savoyards, newcomers were received into *chambrées*, living quarters and associations of about ten males that were part family, part informal guild. They lived according to rigid rules that guaranteed reciprocal aid within the group and that laid out an explicit hierarchy with the eldest as leaders and a chief at the top who was the group's treasurer and tutor of the young boys. Each member had an assigned place in Paris where he went in the morning. When he returned in the evening he deposited what little money he had earned in a community box called the *tirelire*. These funds were sacrosanct, according to Mercier, for what was not spent on the group's maintenance was sent back home to the boys' poor parents. Indeed, Mercier reports that he heard that one boy was found stealing from the group, was put on trial by his fellows, and was hanged.

We know next to nothing about women in this world, but we catch glimpses of some women at work in their own space (without male oversight) acting in concert to protect certain work "rights." One such feminine work environment was the laundry boats moored in the Saône River in Lyon. We know from visual images that these women did not hesitate to use their washing paddles as weapons to ward off interlopers. These washerwomen likely did not share the assumptions of respectable society that, cued by the image of the "unruly woman" that always carried with it implications of social and therefore sexual disorder, condemned them for their "bawdiness," and associated them, just like the female ferryboat pilots and women street vendors, with prostitution.

The best-studied work world of "unskilled" labor is that of madams and prostitutes. Increasingly over our period, procuresses brought their prostitutes into their dwellings and provided food and clothing in addition to shelter. We can imagine a kind of surrogate family here as well. Occasionally we hear prostitutes and bawds themselves describing their work. Jeanne Gavinet, a woman arrested for prostitution in Dijon in 1660, boldly admitted to the crime. When reproached by neighbors for her scandalous behavior, she retorted that "she was mistress of her body" and that she would do with her body "what seemed good to her." She also displayed an awareness of hierarchy within her trade, for she told another neighbor that she was not a "public whore," but rather had sex "only with honorable men."[26]

Prostitutes like Gavinet and madams in every city seemed to have viewed their work as a business selling a commodity. Nicknames like La Joyeuse (the Joyous One), Dame Bonnefeste (Lady Good Times), or Laurence La Chatte (the Pussy) were advertising monikers. Such a lifestyle was both exploitative and independent. It was degrading, nasty, and brutish, with the constant risk of physical harm, venereal disease, and pregnancy. But it must be considered against the miserable living conditions and work otherwise available to poor, vulnerable, immigrant, and homeless women.

Among Domestic Servants

As in so many other aspects of the work life of the *menu peuple*, when discussing the meaning of work domestic servants require special attention. Economists and philosophes in the eighteenth century had little good to say about servants, especially lackeys who publicly displayed idleness and were the very embodiment of unproductivity. Physiocrats tended to argue that service often was simply employment for sumptuary purposes, and thereby robbed workers from productive sectors of society. Messance wrote that servants were "hands made useless to agriculture, manufactures, and commerce."[27] The great encyclopedist and philosophe Denis Diderot agreed and added a moral pejorative to service. For him, service "is the most abject of occupations, and it is always sloth or some other vice of character that causes one to hesitate between the livery and hard labor. If a man with broad shoulders and strong legs chooses to empty chamber pots rather than to carry loads, he necessarily has a vile disposition."[28] Condemning domestic service for similar reasons was Turmeau de la Morandière. He wrote in 1753 that "all of these superfluous people have no merit but the insolence and wickedness that proceeds from idleness, and no talent but that of consuming considerable goods to the detriment of the whole body of civil society."[29] A late-eighteenth-century police handbook succinctly stated that servants were "the scum of the countryside."

It was not just society's elites, however, who looked down on servants. Servants had a mixed reputation among the lower classes as well. On the one hand they were envied for what seemed an easy or even idle life, and they were resented for their arrogance and posturing of superiority (they were expected to be physical representatives of their masters, even going so far as to violently defend the honor of their masters). Artisans especially looked on servants as inferior beings because they had willingly surrendered their independence, a value closely linked to honor that, as we will see, ran to the very core of artisanal identity.

Like the rest of the *menu peuple*, servants were outside the corporate regime, and so had no legal basis for social recognition. But there was a gap between servants and other urban workers that was not simply behavioral, but spatial and sartorial as well. Those servants who lived with their masters were cut off from neighborhoods and the bonds of sociability that wove through them. As creatures of display, pages, lackeys, and coachmen dressed in livery, and so further marked themselves off from other poor workers. It is nearly impossible to say what work meant to them, but historians like Sarah Maza and Cissie Fairchilds conclude that the servant's psychology was one that may have lacked a sense of identity. Treated almost as a thing by the masters, these men and women lived a depersonalized existence.

With such pejorative characteristics attached to domestic service, why did so many men and women choose it as their occupation? In terms of work, living conditions, and potential financial rewards, it was one of the more desirable employment opportunities available to the working poor. From the outside and from above service may have had no status, but within the ranks of the servants themselves, a clear status hierarchy existed, and one that suggests, at least for some, a sense of pride in the work they did. The cook specifically carried a prestige within the household because of the acknowledged skill that was required. Along with secretaries and personal body servants, in large noble households cooks formed the aristocracy of the servant world.

What Changed in the Work World of the *Menu Peuple*?

Among Day Laborers: Hardship, Consumerism, Organization, and Regulation

Throughout the early modern era, the working poor were continually poised on the brink of indigence. With an economic downturn large numbers were either thrown out of work or underemployed for what work there was. And the economic cycles of the era guaranteed hardship and misery for France's day-laboring masses. The sixteenth century was such a time. Historians have few sources at their disposal to offer precise figures, but the general picture is clear enough. Following the "golden years" of 1460 to 1520 when urban employment was relatively high and the countryside prosperous, population growth put pressure on available jobs. Population growth also spurred a rise in prices (joined by the influx of bullion from the mines of America and eastern Europe), and because wages did not rise proportionately, the result for many was penury and often unemployment. Take Lyon as an example. In

1529 the lower orders rose in a great food riot called the Grand Rebeyne, forcing the city's authorities to provide public assistance to quell the revolt. The city fathers determined that the minimum requirement in bread for an adult male was a pound and a half per day, and for the average family seven and a half pounds. To purchase this much on the open market would have cost a journeyman artisan half his daily wages. Another 10 percent had to be spent on drink (in Lyon, the poor man's drink was water mixed with "marc," the dregs of a barrel after the better wine has been drawn off), and another 10 percent on other foodstuffs (cheap cuts of meat, vegetables, cheese, etc.). Thus 70 percent of one's income went for sustenance. Conditions even worsened as the century progressed. The historian Richard Gascon has calculated that real wages in the building trades in Lyon between the 1550s and 1590s were cut nearly in half by inflation. If 1550 is taken as an index of 100, real wages fell to 83 by the 1570s, 71 in the next decade, and 60 in the desperate 1590s.[30]

In the seventeenth century real wages for day laborers appear to have leveled off, as did prices, but urban populations continued to swell and so the problem of underemployment in towns and cities continued, affecting a quarter to a half of all urban male household heads. Obviously, this contributed to beggary and vagrancy, an increasing and pressing social issue throughout France. As we have seen in the previous chapter, the specter of famine haunted the seventeenth-century countryside, and many day laborers, finding no work in the cities and trudging back to their native villages, no doubt fell victim to it.

In the eighteenth century death came not from hunger, as famine all but disappeared from the kingdom, but from epidemic diseases like typhoid and dysentery. And the poor hygienic conditions of cities contributed mightily to this mortality. Wages did improve in eighteenth-century cities, but the great majority of the laboring poor still earned only about one and a half livres a day or less. To make matters worse, a renewed rise in prices ate into the buying power of an already meager sum. According to Ernest Labrousse, the price of food, heat, and light shot up 62 percent between 1726 and 1789; another historian estimates that between 1700 and 1780 rent doubled. For the average urban day laborer, half or more of the daily wage was spent on bread alone, and in seasons witnessing a spike in bread prices, it could consume it all.

This is a grim picture indeed, and one that was even bleaker for many single women, certainly in Grenoble where Kathryn Norberg has studied their fates. She finds that single women there suffered a progressive deterioration of their fortunes, especially as they aged. By the 1770s a woman without dependents, notably a washerwoman or a street vendor, could not support herself on the income that her work now brought. This meant that she had to rely on charity from the hospital for her daily bread. Younger women might find work as stitchers in the booming glove trade, but this task (where the worker was paid by the piece) required speed and dexterity, skills older women lost to age. Few options remained but drifting to washing and street vending.

The bleak picture presented thus far is based on certain kinds of sources, notably those that indicate wages and prices, and so speak in averages. There is no denying that hardship and penury were the fates of millions of urban workers, but historians have found evidence of another development that at first glance seems to challenge this image of indigence. After-death inventories, for example, list household possessions at the time of death, and historians have been surprised by what day laborers owned. It is not uncommon to find cheap, "populux" items—snuffboxes, pipes, umbrellas, and the like— knockoff imitations of the luxury items owned by the upper classes. Evidently, the common workers of the eighteenth century were drawn into the consumer orbit. This evident penetration of what historians call the "consumer revolution" into the ranks of common workers raises awkward questions. If real wages still lagged at this time, how could workers afford to purchase these populux items? There are two possible explanations. First, averages hide the more successful workers, the figures being dragged to lower levels by the underemployed or the indigent. Closely textured research into the conditions of the day-laboring classes, although still few in number, does suggest great variety in their income abilities (wages of construction workers, for example, are found to have risen in the eighteenth century while those of unskilled loaders remained flat). Second, and probably related to the first, is the taking hold in the households of some of the common workers of what historian Jan De Vries calls an "industrious revolution." We have seen evidence for this in the countryside, but it appears to have been an urban phenomenon, too. Some workers (husbands, wives, and children) were working harder and longer at their jobs, exchanging leisure time for work. The generation of a surplus, modest though it may be, thus made it possible for some families to enter the market as consumers, and they spent some of their money on cheap imitations of luxury goods.

Let's take a closer look at the conditions that could provide income differentials among the working poor and that, in turn, may be behind the industrious and consumer revolution taking hold among some day laborers. Some unskilled—and unincorporated—workers appear to have been successful in cornering a specific task at a specific site in various cities, a monopoly made legitimate not by law or statute but by habit of practice. And monopoly, of course, allowed them to charge more for their work without being undercut by competition. We find this most commonly among longshoremen who established and defended the "right" to unload certain articles in certain places. As early as 1588 in Lyon we find evidence of such practices among the charcoal haulers. In that year Pierre Labay, police commissioner on the docks in Lyon, wrote that "some *gagne-deniers*, combining to form monopolies, do not allow other *gagne-deniers* to work, and threaten and assault any *gagne-deniers* who do not belong to their group, not allowing them to load any charcoal without the permission of the band."[31] Despite Labay's concerns, these loaders (also called *crocheteurs*) continued to organize into bands with clear leadership structures and monopolized the work at certain ports to the exclusion of other bands. Sometimes these crocheteurs would subcontract labor, hiring *journaliers* for fifteen to twenty sols per day for work that earned the bands three to four times that amount.

These bands looked much like guilds. Indeed, by the late seventeenth century we find evidence of dues and entry fees in the bands as well as rules for dividing band earnings among its members. Technically illegal, the Consulate of Lyon (the highest municipal authority) recognized them informally simply by not dispersing or suppressing them. It thereby granted them a certain approximation of a corporate identity. We even find them mentioned in consular ordinances in the late seventeenth and early eighteenth centuries.[32]

The crocheteurs of Lyon were not the only unskilled workers behaving as shadow guilds. Water carriers in Paris fought incursions onto their turf, and clearly thought of their monopoly rights, like any guildsman would, as a form of property. Water carriers were even known to sell their business (and its rights) upon retirement.[33] Displaying a similar corporate ethos but without formal legal recognition were the *gagne-deniers* of Paris. A 1786 uprising by them reflected a collective sense of the value of their labor and how to secure and protect their work through monopoly. In that year a new, rival company arose seeking to monopolize package delivery in the city, and so hundreds of *gagne-deniers* who specialized in this task mobilized in the place Maubert, unsuccessfully as it turned out, to claim and defend their rights.

The dockworkers in Marseille were organizing themselves along similar lines, claiming corporate rights against interlopers into their territory and tasks, even though they were not incorporated themselves. Indeed, in the *cahiers de doléances* drafted just before the Revolution in which French subjects were given the opportunity to vent complaints of any kind, these dockworkers demanded that cut-rate competitors called *robeirols* be formally proscribed from working in the port.

The women working in the washing boats moored in the Saône in Lyon jealously guarded their turf, too (wielding their washing paddles as weapons to brain interlopers if necessary), as did the female boat pilots ferrying passengers across the rivers in the same city. In many cities we thus find what we might call "shadow corporations," unskilled men and sometimes women united—without legal sanction—to defend and maintain exclusive labor rights against interlopers.

The response of the authorities to these activities was, at least until the eighteenth century, ambivalent. The *crocheteurs* of Lyon organized themselves into a veritable community, even calling themselves a "corps," but though the Consulate treated them like a corporation, they were never officially recognized as one of the seventy-two *communautés d'arts et métiers* of the city. Pierre Labay, on the other hand, signaled the fear that the authorities had of organization among the unskilled and the threat to order that it might pose, and gradually in the seventeenth and especially the eighteenth centuries the authorities established greater control over these bands. This is part of a much broader history, the increasing emphasis on the discipline of labor, which we will discuss at length in the next chapter on artisans. For the authorities (and for the incorporated artisans) the fundamental question became this: how to control the unskilled workers who are outside the corporate framework? The Parisian lieutenant general of police Lenoir reflected the growing sentiment in his *Mémoires* in the 1770s and 1780s: "The mass of 200,000 men . . . from the first to the last individual, [must be] well classified, registered, and controlled by rules of discipline and subordination."[34]

We know precious little about how this regulation of the world of the unskilled worker was effected. Arlette Farge finds the *lettre de cachet* (a royal order of imprisonment that bypassed the normal legal procedures) was used surprisingly frequently on *gens sans état* for petty offenses, like fencing stolen objects in the marketplace. We also know that during the eighteenth century the royal mounted constabulary (the *maréchaussées*) were ordered to hunt down workers who had fled their contracts. Thanks to the research by Dean Ferguson on Lyon, however, we now have a better picture of the nature of the emerging regulatory system in an important French city.[35] He finds that formal discipline of the unskilled worker accelerated in the second half of the eighteenth century. A civic ordinance of 1741 signaled the change, for in that year the Consulate suppressed the traditional privileges of the various bands of unskilled workers (*crocheteurs* and the like) and moved toward a more rational scheme for regulating unincorporated work. The new policing system came in two forms. First, prescribed rate schedules were drawn up by the Consulate and imposed on groups of workers, and second, the policing of space came more precisely into prominence. For example, a rate schedule was established by the city and imposed on the *crocheteurs* for the loading, unloading, and delivery of different goods, taking into consideration the distance of deliveries and the weight of the products (charcoal had a different rate than grain, for example). No longer, moreover, were the *crocheteurs* free to carve out their turf at the wharves and maintain it by intimidation or violence, for now they were assigned places there by the city. Ferryboat pilots, too, had their fares standardized. They were also assigned prescribed mooring sites for their boats and each boat was registered with a number painted on its side. Sedan-chair carriers were likewise regulated. An ordinance of 1779 assigned a place to queue up, much like a taxi stand today, and the Consulate set eighteen different rates depending on the time of day and distance of the trip. Street vendors suffered similar fates. These men and women were required to register with the police, providing name, age, and residence. They were then issued a copper medallion that served as a kind of license verifying their registration and that had to be worn while doing business. The Consulate then assigned them to specific locations on the streets or in markets.

Prostitution underwent significant changes in both organization and policing as well. Prostitution was legal in France in the late Middle Ages, when many municipalities actually owned and operated brothels. The logic of legality was that the sexual appetite of the city's young males would be satisfied and the sexual honor of its respectable females protected. Prostitution beyond the confines of the public bordello was technically forbidden, but commercial sex was tolerated as long as public disorder did not result from it.

During the sixteenth century things changed. Public whorehouses were closed in many cities between 1500 and 1560, a result of a shift in moral attitudes (influenced by the Reformations, both Protestant and Catholic) and a dramatic increase in the incidence of venereal disease, especially syphilis. The growth of professional armies (and disorderly and often violent soldiers frequenting brothels) further contributed to the demise of legal prostitution. During the seventeenth century as the morality of the Catholic Reformation took hold in the hearts of many an elite man and woman, prostitutes were arrested and imprisoned in convents, like the Maison du Bon Pasteur in Dijon, La Charité in Lyon, or Saint-Pélagie in Paris. The express purpose of these institutions was, hopefully, to reform penitent prostitutes.

Prostitution may have been criminalized and increasingly stigmatized, but suppression by the authorities was only sporadically attempted and was never entirely successful. Indeed, throughout the early modern period prostitution flourished. Even after Louis XIV appointed the first Parisian police chief in

1667 and gave him broad powers, including those to arrest and prosecute prostitutes, prostitution remained widespread. As many as eight hundred women might be arrested in a year and hauled off to the Salpetrière, but the policing essentially remained episodic and unsystematic. It was not until 1803 that regulation of prostitution took hold as it had among other unskilled trades. In that year a dispensary was established, run by the Parisian police, where prostitutes had to register and undergo pelvic examinations (the authorities were concerned about public health and equated prostitution with disease).

As social distinctions became more pronounced within society in the seventeenth century, a sharper hierarchy emerged within the trade of prostitution. At the upper reaches of society appeared courtesans, women of manners whom elite men sought, but even among the more common prostitutes a hierarchy took hold. The evidence from Dijon suggests that streetwalking dominated the practice between the closure of the municipal brothel in the mid-sixteenth century and the late seventeenth century. Streetwalking would of course continue, but in the late seventeenth century and throughout the eighteenth we see a growing incidence of houses of prostitution run by madams offering clients a range of services, from simple venal sex in brief encounters to evenings of food, drink, and of course sex, in private quarters.

By Mercier's time this hierarchy was clearly in place. As he writes, the best bordellos with clients of noble rank were furnished with "sumptuous beds" in "vast rooms." "At the top of the ladder you see the ambitious and haughty women, who aim always at the highest [client]; nothing less than a financier will serve their turn. . . . Below these come the opera-girls, dancers, actresses. . . . The eye traveling down this structure of disorder rests uncomfortable upon the great mass of common prostitutes, leaning in doorways, leering from windows. . . . These may be hired like hackney carriages at so much an hour." Attending these women were the *marcheuses*, "creatures old and penniless, creeping out into the world from some hospital with the scars of their past life upon their faces." Too old for prostitution, their former trade, they instead work the streets finding clients for "poorer-class prostitutes, those in furnished rooms, whose only equipment is a pair of shoes and one white petticoat." The very bottom of Mercier's hierarchy, "horrors . . . buried too vilely deep for the casual eye to discover; [are] the hideous women of the Pont-au-bled." The hierarchy, moreover, was a fluid one. Mercier remarks that "the changes to be observed in the hierarchy are amazing. Up or down the women go, and take precedence or lose it, according to whether chance accords them protectors with more money or less. It is all pure luck . . . that some little person is lifted to the skies overnight . . . [while] another, having outlived her moment, falls back into poverty."[36]

In Domestic Service: "Bourgeoisification" and Feminization

As with most of the people who comprised the working poor, we know very little about domestic servants before the eighteenth century, other than that they were very numerous and comprised many men as well as women. Over the course of the eighteenth century, a period much more studied by historians, we can see dramatic changes in service and thereby infer what the experience of the servant likely had been before that.[37]

The first notable and noticeable change in domestic service concerned pay. Prior to the eighteenth century, typically servants had been hired *à récompense*, meaning that for their work they received food and shelter and some monetary gift at the end of their employment. Masters preferred to pay lump sums for loyalty or for continuing for a long time in their service. These sums were then used by servants as a dowry, or to purchase tools to practice an artisanal trade. In the eighteenth century we see a shift to more regular wage payments (although the previous practices do not disappear), and over the course of that century wages rose steadily. Indeed, in the 1770s and 1780s servants' wages shot up "spectacularly," according to historian Cissie Fairchilds.

Wages increased substantially for servants of both genders, but men tended to fare better than women. From the 1720s to the Revolution women's wages were up perhaps 40 percent, according to historian Sarah Maza, but men's wages rose 67 percent.[38] Moreover, wage increases varied among different categories of servants. In Aix-en-Provence, for instance, "skilled" males (valets, tutors, and cooks, for example) did best, with nominal wages averaging 90 livres per year in the 1730s, and 250 by the1780s. By the 1780s wages paid unskilled males (lackeys, chair carriers, and the like) rose as well, but, not surprisingly, more modestly (from about 87 livres in the 1740s to about 120 in the 1780s, for an increase of about 38 percent). The wages of "skilled" females (chambermaids, governesses) began to increase in the 1760s, lurching from an annual average of 62 livres to 85 in the 1780s, and those of "unskilled" female servants (kitchen maids and the like) climbed from 26 livres in the 1730s to 56 in the 1780s.

These rising figures may seem impressive, but recall that prices everywhere in France rose from the 1720s to the 1780s by about 60 percent, wiping out the gains, and then some, of everyone but the skilled males. These servants stand alone as the fortunate ones, especially those long in the employ of the same master. They fared well, moreover, not only because of rising wages but also because, more than any other kind of servant, these men tended to live with their masters and so were protected from the worst effects of soaring prices for food and rent (these being absorbed by the employer). It is not unusual to find these fortunate male servants acting as bourgeois, saving and investing in real estate, annuities, and loans. Indeed, these privileged male servants were increasingly distinguished from the lower sort. According to the *Dictionnaire des Trévoux* in 1762, the term "*serviteur* signifies only those who serve for wages, like valets, lackeys, porters, etc.," while "*domestique* includes all those who act under a man . . . who live in his house . . . like intendants, secretaries, clerks, men of affairs."[39]

The sharp erosion of real wages for unskilled male servants may account for another dramatic change in domestic service—its feminization. To take one example among many, in Toulouse in 1695, of the 70 cooks listed in the capitation tax rolls, all but two were men, but in 1789, of the 225 listed, 173 were women. Everywhere we see a relative decline in the numbers of male lackeys and porters and an increase in the numbers of female servants whose tasks are primarily confined to the house (serving meals, cleaning). This feminization of domestic service is related to an important cultural change that accelerated in the second half of the eighteenth century: a more clear distinction between the public and private spheres, and the association of males with the former and females with the latter.

Prior to this cultural shift (and even up to the Revolution in high aristocratic and noble households), lackeys had been hired for the purpose of display. Lackeys did little or no visible work—indeed, they were *expected* to be idle in the public eye because, as status symbols of their aristocratic masters, they demonstrated to all that their masters were men who did *not* work. Indeed, all servants were employed, at least in part, for reasons of status. They not only saved the aristocrat from doing ignoble or undignified tasks, but also provided a public proclamation of his social rank. For nobles, servants displayed obedience and deference, and so were a public demonstration of the master's right to rule.

To be sure, aristocratic households continued to employ large staffs of servants, and display continued to be significant to their identity, but gradually over the course of the eighteenth century these staffs were reduced in size (except in very large aristocratic households) and, at the same time, the employment of servants (usually a single female or two) spread more broadly among the population. The feminization of domestic service in the latter half of the eighteenth century, then, was an unprecedented development. It coincides with the separation of the domestic and the public spheres. Increasingly, service comes to be associated with the domestic sphere, and thus acquires feminine characteristics, especially the devaluation of women's work.

Notes

1. Quoted in Jeffrey Kaplow, *The Names of Kings: The Parisian Laboring Poor in the Eighteenth Century* (New York: Basic Books, 1972), 29. On the poor in general, in addition to the titles cited in the introduction, see Jean-Pierre Gutton, *La Société et les pauvres en Europe, 16e–18e siècles* (Paris: PUF, 1974); Robert Jütte, *Poverty and Deviance in Early Modern Europe* (Cambridge: Cambridge University Press, 1994); and Bronislaw Geremek, *Inutiles au monde: Truands et misérables, 1300–1600* (Paris: Gallimard, 1980).

2. Kaplow, *Names of Kings*, 27.

3. Quoted in Olwen Hufton, *The Poor of Eighteenth-Century France, 1750–1789* (Oxford: Oxford University Press, 1974), 22 (my translation).

4. Quoted in Hufton, *Poor of Eighteenth-Century France*, 11 (my translation).

5. Hufton, *Poor of Eighteenth-Century France*, especially chaps. 3 and 4.

6. Haim Burstin, "Unskilled Labor in Paris at the End of the Eighteenth Century," in *The Workplace Before the Factory: Artisans and Proletarians, 1500–1800*, ed. Thomas M. Safley and Leonard N. Rosenband (Ithaca, N.Y.: Cornell University Press, 1993), 63.

7. Quoted in Fernand Braudel, *The Wheels of Commerce*, trans. Siân Reynolds (New York: HarperCollins, 1986), 308.

8. Louis-Sébastien Mercier, *Panorama of Paris [Selections from Le Tableau de Paris]*, ed. and trans. Jeremy Popkin (University Park: Pennsylvania State University Press, 1999), 73.

9. Mercier, *Panorama*, 96–97, 133.

10. Daniel Roche, *Le Peuple de Paris* (Paris: Aubier, 1981), 73.

11. Burstin, "Unskilled Labor," 68.

12. Mercier, *Panorama*, 71.

13. Mercier, *Panorama*, 72.

14. Hufton, *Poor of Eighteenth-Century France*, 85.

15. Cissie Fairchilds, *Domestic Enemies: Servants and Their Masters in Old Regime France* (Baltimore: Johns Hopkins University Press, 1984), 69.

16. Erica-Maria Benabou, *La Prostitution et la police des moeurs au XVIIIe siècle* (Paris: Perrin, 1987), 328.

17. Mercier, *Panorama*.

18. Benabou, *Prostitution*, 267.

19. Kathryn Norberg, *Rich and Poor in Grenoble* (Berkeley: University of California Press, 1984), 48.

20. James R. Farr, *Authority and Sexuality in Early Modern Burgundy (1550–1730)* (New York: Oxford University Press, 1995), 151.

21. Quoted in Kaplow, *Names of Kings*, 53.

22. Quoted in Roche, *Peuple de Paris*, 100 (my translation).

23. Mercier, *Panorama*, 211.

24. Maurice Garden, *Lyon et les lyonnais au XVIIIe siècle* (Paris: Flammarion, 1975), 161 (my translation).

25. Garden, *Lyon et les lyonnais*, 134.

26. Farr, *Authority and Sexuality*, 151.

27. Quoted in Sarah Maza, *Servants and Masters in Eighteenth-Century France: The Uses of Loyalty* (Princeton, N.J.: Princeton University Press, 1983), 292.

28. Quoted in Maza, *Servants and Masters*, 289.

29. Quoted in Maza, *Servants and Masters*, 124.

30. Richard Gascon, *Grand commerce et vie urbaine au XVIe siècle: Lyon et ses marchands (environs de 1520–environs de 1580)*, 2 vols. (Paris: SEVPEN, 1971).

31. Quoted in Dean Ferguson, "The Body, the Corporate Idiom, and the Police of the Unincorporated Worker in Early Modern Lyons," *French Historical* Studies 23, no. 4 (2000): 564.

32. Ferguson, "Body," 565.

33. Burstin, "Unskilled Labor," 71.

34. Quoted in Arlette Farge, *La Vie fragile: Violence, pouvoirs et solidarités à Paris au XVIIIe siècle* (Paris: Hachette, 1986), 153–54 (my translation).

35. See note 31.

36. Mercier, *Panorama*, 143–45.

37. See Cissie Fairchilds, Sarah Maza, and Jean-Pierre Gutton, *Domestiques et serviteurs dans la France de l'Ancien Régime* (Paris: Aubier Montaigne, 1992; orig. ed, 1981).

38. Maza, Servants and Masters, 281.

39. Fairchilds, *Domestic Enemies*, 19.

CHAPTER THREE

~

Artisans

What Artisans Did

Diversity, Specialization, and "Constant Returns to Scale"

For one with even a passing knowledge of early modern times, the notion of work likely conjures up the activities of craftsmen toiling in shops alongside an apprentice and a journeyman or two, fashioning products from start to finish within the confines of the single shop. The prevalence in the modern imagination of this image of work and of the autonomous artisan is a product of nostalgia (a yearning for the supposed simplicity of premodern life) and the tenacious grip that the assumed equation between work and manual labor continues to exert. Work, however, as I have attempted to demonstrate in this book, was much more complex than mere labor.

The picture of the master artisan flanked by apprentice and journeymen is not so much wrong as limited. Certainly there were thousands of craftsmen who worked in such conditions in cities throughout France (artisans comprised anywhere from 25 to 40 percent of the adult heads of household in urban France), but we would grievously misrepresent the artisanal world of work if we confined our discussion to that type. Rather, it was heterogeneous and complex, characterized by a multiplicity of economic relations. In some places small-scale manufacture in workshops of a master and a handful of workers dominated, while other locales had hot spots of large-scale industries in which large numbers of workers labored under one roof. These shops large and small were knit into a vast commercial and manufacturing sector that absorbed droves of nonspecialized workers.

Generally, artisans produced according to the logic of "constant returns to scale," to invoke the words of economic historian Jan De Vries. This logic assumed that "the growth of output required proportional growth of the inputs of labor and raw materials."[1] Economic growth would thus be marked by increased quantities of labor and raw materials (sometimes swelling shops) rather than a permanent expansion of the physical plant or organization of production into economies of scale. When demand abated, workers were simply laid off and the shop size contracted. Perhaps the most visible results of this logic were a decentralization of the units of production, galloping specialization, and widespread subcontracting. Take coachmaking as an example. The component parts of a coach or carriage were made on spec by specialists in their own shops (as many as seventeen different trades were involved, from ironsmiths making axles, hinges, and springs, to framemakers, to harness platers, to joiners, painters, wheelwrights, and even mirror cutters). Only the final product was assembled in the coachmaker's shop. And this was no small-scale economic sector, for there were fifteen thousand carriages in Paris in 1720.

Such specialization left its footprint on the streets of France's towns and cities. Walking down any one of these, one would be struck by the numbers, variety, and sometimes enormity of signs protruding from buildings and overhanging the street. Such signs became common in the fourteenth century and symbolically announced the type of business inside—a hammer, a key, a horseshoe, a wheel—but sometimes they might invoke humorous puns. For example, in Paris a sawyer (*scieur*) hung a sign depicting three obese men cutting wood with the words *Aux Gracieux* beneath them. Literally this meant "at the graceful one's shop," but also could be read phonetically as "au gras scieux," or "at the fat sawyers' shop." Such signs could be enormous, darkening streets and causing hazard to horse riders. Competition to be seen pushed signs ever farther into the narrow streets, sometimes reaching the center, prompting authorities from time to time to issue ordinances requiring the reduction of size and distance permitted from the building.

Specialization, of course, splintered the division of labor, and a look at tax rolls from the early modern city (which typically listed name and occupation as well as assessment) readily confirms this. Alongside the well-known butchers, bakers, and candlestickmakers were shoemakers, cobblers, tailors, masons, carpenters, wigmakers, goldsmiths . . . the list seems endless. In Dijon in 1556 of nearly 3,000 heads of household, we can count about a thousand artisans distributed across 86 different trades (20 of these had appeared since 1464 and 21 would disappear by 1643), of whom there were 73 tailors and seamstresses, 46 weavers, 39 butchers, 37 shoemakers (and 35 cobblers, or shoe menders), and 36 pastry cooks. There were three lanternmakers, a gearmaker, an illuminator, and even a quivermaker.[2] According to research by Kathryn Norberg, in Grenoble in 1725 there were over 4,500 heads of households and among them we find similar diversity: 239 cobblers and shoemakers, 125 tailors, 90 woodworkers, and 65 bakers. In Paris at the end of the eighteenth century there were more than 30,000 master artisans spread among all the trades, while in Lyon in the same period, according to Maurice Garden, the number of masters in the silk industry alone reached nearly 8,000, over half of all masters in the city (there were about 15,000 of them). The food trades were well represented in the Lyonnais master ranks with nearly 1,700, while shoemakers counted about 1,100 and the building trades, 660.

Labor divided not only among trades, but within them as well. Thus workshops were arrayed in hierarchical fashion descending in status from masters, journeymen, apprentices, wageworkers, and, perhaps surprisingly, women (deemed the most inferior, unless she was wife or widow of a master). It was not uncommon for journeymen to refuse to do tasks they felt were beneath their dignity, leaving them to apprentices, unskilled wageworkers, and sometimes women. Masters were usually the minority. In building trades, for example, typically about one in five were masters. Journeymen and wageworkers were numerous everywhere. Take Lyon in 1789 again as a reliable example. There were nearly 20,000 of them, about 2,700 in hatmaking (under only 157 masters), over 2,100 in construction, and 1,500 in shoemaking. Apprentices were not as prevalent as either masters or journeymen and workers, counting nearly 3,000 citywide, of which nearly 600 were in silk trades and 300 in hatmaking.

Decentralization and specialization undoubtedly were a result of the logic of constant returns to scale, but in some cases they could also result in protofactories. Employment everywhere was uncertain and irregular. As employers sought to keep production in balance with demand, they would hire workers when orders came in and lay them off when the orders were filled. At peak times some shops could get quite large, more like protofactories than traditional workshops. Manufacturing in France's cities, in fact, was a mixture of large and small. In Paris in 1739, for example, about one-third of the master hatters hired half the available journeymen and set them to work in shops of twenty-five to thirty journeymen per shop. In Marseille in1782, to take another example, most locksmith shops had three or fewer journeymen, but 4 percent of the masters hired more than 20 percent of the journeymen who were then put to work alongside about ten of their fellows. We find the same pattern among the joiners of Amiens, where 3 percent of the masters hired a quarter of the journeymen to work in shops of ten or more, while the rest of the town masters employed three or fewer journeymen.

Thanks to the work of historians Michael Sonenscher and Leonard Rosenband, two trades—hatmaking and papermaking—offer a close look at early modern manufacturing.[3] First, they demonstrate the division of labor well. They also show that some production processes had been extensively integrated and, unlike many other trades that remained decentralized, concentrated production in one place. Hatmaking, as Sonenscher shows, involved three dozen processes, starting with the stripping of fur from beaver or rabbit pelts, a task done mostly by women. The fur was then sorted and sent to felters who "bowed" it. Workers stirred in chemicals in closed unventilated rooms to keep the fur from blowing away (with the tragic side effect of progressive dysfunction of the nervous system—thus the expression "mad as a hatter"). Others washed the fur and placed it on a mold (shaped according to fashion), where it was left to dry. The dried hats were then singed by fire, rubbed to raise the nap, then dyed. The whole process ended with women trimming and decorating the hats with ribbons, feathers, or gilt.

Papermaking in the eighteenth century, Rosenband tells us, followed centuries-old artisanal procedures performed in a mill. Like hats, paper was made in dangerous and unhealthy conditions, and involved women in the unskilled aspects of the process. Women were hired at meager rates to pull knots out of old linen (acquired from the ragpickers we met in an earlier chapter) and remove the caked dirt and other foreign matter from this essential raw material of finished paper. The linen was then piled into fermentation vats, where it was left to rot. The rotted linen was then hammered by stamping mallets into filaments and pulp, a process overseen by beatermen. Vatmen then took the pulp and transformed it into paper by dipping a wire-mesh mold into a vat of watery pulp, then "lift[ing] the mold and [shaking] it according to custom so that the fibers of the infant sheet 'shut.'"[4] The coucher then flipped the sheets five or six times a minute onto a "hairy felt," which, with the paper, was pressed. A layman then separated the felt from the paper, a highly skilled and delicate task that was, according to a contemporary who wrote in a book on the art of papermaking, "suitable only for people who have practiced it from an early age and not for . . . inexperienced country-folk."[5] Women then hung the paper on cords of horsehair for drying. The sizerman then collected the sheets and immersed them in an emulsion to close the pores of the paper (to prevent inkblots). Women then sorted the sheets by size, weight, and quality and with the loftsman wrapped them into reams for shipping.

Hierarchy among Artisans: Workers, Apprentices, Journeymen, and Masters

Amid this seeming buzzing confusion a hierarchy within the world of work had long been established. The late-eighteenth-century Parisian police lieutenant general Lenoir wrote in his *Mémoires* of the ideal social order as a "domestic chain," whereby masters were subordinate to jurés (guild officials), journeymen to masters, and apprentices to journeymen, all bound by the subservient relation of servant to master. At the bottom were the wageworkers, mostly hired short term and for a subsistence daily wage or "by the task." Socially marginalized and sharply distinguished from the men associated with the corporations (the apprentices, journeymen, and masters), they formed an enormous pool of unspecialized laborers who had no hope of entering the guilds, the *corps de métiers* (they could never, therefore, ascend to master status). These were the laboring poor we met in the previous chapter, the terminology describing them reflecting their condition: *manouvrier*, *gagne-denier* (penny earner), *journalier* (day laborer). Mostly recent immigrants to the cities, they formed, in Daniel Roche's words, "a gigantic and disparate world."[6]

Within the corporate world, apprentices held an important if numerically small place. Typically apprentices were the select boys who were tagged for eventual rise to mastership. Masters (or senior journeymen) were expected to teach them the techniques and "mysteries" of the trade. This training relationship made possible the transfer of technology through generations, instilling in the boys a sense of status and a skill that enabled the reproduction of the craft. The time in training varied from trade to trade, but for all the trades of eighteenth-century Lyon, for example, the average term was four years (although the goldsmiths required eight). The economic and social importance of apprenticeship was therefore of inestimable value.

The apprentice entered the service of a master by way of a formal contract drawn up by a notary. The signing of such a legal document was a solemn event between the master and the parents of the youth. One such contract read thus: "Before . . . the notaries of the Châtelet of Paris are present Jean-Baptiste Desseigne, bourgeois of Paris and Marie Françoise Régout his wife, who, for the advantage of their son Claude Desseigne, aged 17, recognize to have obligated and engaged him for the time and duration of four entire and consecutive years to le Sieur J. N. Richehomme, master engraver."

Richehomme, like all masters, is bound by contract to teach the apprentice everything "without hiding anything" as well as provide him food, lodging, light, heat, and blankets. The contract demands that the apprentice show unquestioned obedience to the master, and not be permitted to work elsewhere during the term of the contract. Of course, the parents agree to pay the master a stipulated sum of money.

Apprentices, clearly, were a cheap form of labor for masters, but guild statutes often restricted the number of apprentices, usually specified at no more than one at a time. In this way masters hoped to control the pipeline to eventual mastership and thereby regulate the numbers of and competition between masters. Such control became especially pressing in the sixteenth and seventeenth centuries as the urban economy grew. At the current state of research we do not know if Dijon is typical, but the masters of the guilds in this Burgundian city deliberately restricted the growth in the ranks of masters as the economy grew, thereby giving each master a larger portion of a growing pie.[7]

Whereas in the late Middle Ages masters signed up apprentices whose only prerequisite was legitimate birth, by the sixteenth and seventeenth centuries those on track to mastership were increasingly sons or nephews of masters. Those not related by family were confronted with more stringent stipulations (minimum and maximum ages, for example, and longer terms), and increasing numbers remained journeymen for life. In the seventeenth century we find other tactics to restrict the flow of apprentices to mastership. The records of the Paris police reveal that apprentices were frequently bringing complaints that masters were not teaching them the trade. A police ordinance of 1678 noted this, and predicted the troublesome consequence: "[Many] apprentices spend the time of their apprenticeship without ever learning the trade, and what is the most dangerous consequence for them is that they abandon themselves to games, idleness, and debauchery."[8]

After the expiration of their contract, apprentices entered the rank of journeyman. Learning the trade continued, but increasingly in the sixteenth to the eighteenth centuries, these ranks divided between a small core of men (most likely former apprentices) who were, in some cases, tracked for eventual mastership but all of whom remained in permanent employment and learned all aspects of the trade. In the shop they were surrounded by a periphery of journeymen and workers (most of whom did not undergo formal apprenticeship) who were unlikely to ever escape their rank, were hired and laid off as demand dictated, and were taught only certain aspects of the trade. The emergence of such cores and peripheries (and we find them in many cities and many trades) are yet another result of the splintering division of labor that economic growth, increased demand, and the logic of constant returns to scale triggered.

Though often lumped with workers in workshops, the journeyman was fiercely proud of his status as affiliated with the corporation, and ownership of his tools was an important badge of that status. The tools belonged to him, and likely were purchased from a meager inheritance settled upon him at the death of a parent. He took them everywhere, and they were the key to finding work wherever he went. Importantly, such ownership distinguished him from the unskilled wageworkers, who had no tools and were provided them by the masters who employed them.

As far back as the records take us (the late Middle Ages), we can see that the life of the journeyman was a mobile one, marked by constant movement in search of work, advantageous wages, and promising avenues to mastership. Few journeymen stayed put for long, rendering workshops places of constant coming and going. Workers went from master to master, town to town, so that a certain eighteenth-century Parisian furnituremaker who served ten masters in three years was not unusual for the entire early modern years. Records are better from the eighteenth century and allow us to quantify this general phenomenon. The guild employment office of the tailors in Rouen in the late 1770s, for example, shows that one-third of the journeymen hired lasted only a week or less, while 40 percent were gone by month's end. Among the over five hundred journeymen wigmakers registered in the employment office in Rouen in the 1780s, fully 90 percent were gone within a year. And this was for journeymen who, with hopes of eventually entering mastership, had an incentive to remain in the employ of one master. Unskilled workers had no such hopes, and so their mobility was even greater.

Of course, alongside this mobile majority there existed a more sedentary minority, yet another reflection of the core-periphery phenomenon of the workplace. All journeymen began their careers in motion, but eventually some did settle in. This core no doubt comprised those tracked for mastership. A sample of mastership letters in Dijon between 1590 and 1642, for example, shows that sixty-nine journeymen who became masters had spent an average of three years in the service of their last employer. Behind all this flux certain patterns are discernible. In some trades mobility was seasonal. In winter, a slow season for construction, workers returned to native regions (and often families) to eke out a living of expedients, only to trudge back to the city in spring, gathering at the traditional hiring site where they hoped to be employed by a good-paying master with plenty of work.

Finding work was essential for survival, but given abysmal working conditions, long hours, and typical wage rates, even employment could be bleak.

Lack of ventilation plagued all workshops, making dust ubiquitous, especially in textile and carpentry shops. The litany of woes is endless, but consider these: among glassworkers heat and bright light of the fire prematurely ruined their eyesight while the materials they worked with regularly tore, burned, and pierced their skin. Cloth cutters struggled to wield giant shears that weighed up to 100 pounds, and a worker with hands with less than the full complement of ten digits was a frequent sight. Locksmiths and shoemakers destroyed their physique, hunched as they must be for long hours over their materials. Indeed, the hours were long, generally dawn to dusk. Thus in Paris the workday stretched up to sixteen hours in the summer and eight in the winter. Because of the threat of fire, night work was forbidden (although transgression was common).

Wages were notoriously "sticky," meaning they did not float with the rise and fall of costs of living (especially of foodstuffs), and so workers could be badly pinched in times of high food prices. Wages might be paid *à la journée* (a daily rate paid by the week, usually for journeymen who did not live with the master), or *à la tâche* (by the job, the norm for unskilled or semiskilled workers who comprised the bulk of the transient periphery). Many employers paid mixed wages, a combination of cash and *en nature*, usually meaning food. The fluctuation of prices of foodstuffs might make this an attractive option for masters, who would offer food and lower wages when prices for foodstuffs were low, and simply lay off workers when the cost of food was high. Workers were well aware of the fragile security of employment. There were no days without expenses for workers, but many days without work. Depending on the year and the weather, there were between 220 and 260 workable days, a number that hides the reality of seasonal unemployment and surplus labor markets.

At the top of the workshop hierarchy was the master. One arrived at this rank by performing a masterpiece (unless one were the son of a master, in which case the requirement for the *chef d'oeuvre*, as it was called, was waived) that was judged by a jury of masters. The initiate to the guild also was expected to swear an oath to abide by the regulations of the guild, host a celebratory dinner, and depending on the guild, pay certain fees (again, these would be waived for sons of masters). Once the new master entered the ranks of the guild, he was legally entitled to open his own shop and go into business. He was responsible for acquiring the raw materials (or subcontracted products), hiring, training (which he often delegated to a trusted journeyman), firing and paying workers, finding customers, and setting the prices for the products that would be sold.

In varying degrees, all masters (or their wives, as we will see) performed these tasks, but across the trades of early modern cities, vast differences existed among them. Some masters oversaw only a handful of workers, while others employed dozens, even scores, at a time. In the building trades, for example, at the top of the hierarchy were contractors, a master mason or carpenter who would hire workers for specific jobs, often other master masons, carpenters, or roofers, who in turn would bring or hire journeymen and workers. Some of these workers would specialize in a particular task (applying mortar, for instance), while others (not infrequently women) would be put to doing odd jobs on the construction site. Not surprisingly, there was a descending pay scale that corresponded to this hierarchy.

Division of wealth among masters was wide as well. At one pole we find a small group of the wealthiest and best-established masters, usually in large trades, with trade ties that might span the city and even reach beyond it. These masters were also the most likely to be engaged in networks of subcontracting, especially in cities where export was more ready to hand. The wealth of these men might place them on a par with some merchants or lawyers. At the other pole we find poorer, smaller masters who were closer to their workers and whose economic relations seldom stretched beyond their neighborhood. These men hovered dangerously close to the threshold of poverty, and in lean times would slip below it.

Women

Recent research has discovered something about women that earlier generations of historians did not know: they were not simply confined to the household and engaged in what used to be called the "family" or "domestic" economy and were thus sealed off from the male-dominated market economy. We now know that such assumptions are belied by real life, that women were deeply engaged in many aspects of the market economy in early modern France and, furthermore, that they were an integral, if informal, aspect of the craft economy.

Wives and widows were important in this economy. The wife of a master often was entrusted by her husband with managerial tasks in the shop. She therefore hired, paid, and fired workers, imposed discipline on journeymen and apprentices, kept the books, placed orders for raw materials, and received orders from customers. Many also would work in adjunct aspects of the trade. Butchers' wives, for instance, would boil tripe and bones.

Where we find a woman as master (or rather, "mistress") in male-dominated trades, upon closer inspection we usually discover that she is a widow of a deceased master. In Nantes between 1620 and 1650, for example, 10 percent of the bakeries and butcher shops were run by mistress widows. Guild statutes explicitly protected the privileges of widows. Typically they legally sanctioned her maintenance of the shop and her right to guild charitable benefits. She usually would be permitted to keep an apprentice, but she would be strongly encouraged to hire a male worker as an assistant. If this assistant were to marry the widow, he would be granted the same privileges as the son of a master, most importantly, admission to mastership without performing a masterpiece or paying fees. If the widow married outside the guild, she would lose all guild privileges and would no longer belong to the *corps*.

If we left our description of the roles of women in the craft economy to this, we would miss how far reaching female activity actually was. Consider the women in the construction industry in eighteenth-century Brittany. Many unfortunate females slogged across construction sites doing unskilled tasks like hauling buckets of mortar and water, but we also find female wholesalers working on their own account (not their husbands') supplying the site with raw materials. Sometimes they were even contractors who bid for and won large-scale multicraft projects.[9]

If construction seems an unlikely place to find women at work, so too would be publishing. The world of literacy and books in early modern France, at least before the late eighteenth century, was a masculine world. And yet recent research by Susan Broomhall reveals female scribes, illuminators, artists, stationers, papermakers, printers, and publishers in various cities in France, in some cases as early as the fifteenth century when printing was in its infancy.[10] Of course, women were not welcomed by men as equal partners, but some enterprising souls fought hard to carve out a place in this industry. Consider Charlotte Guillard, who spent fifty years as a printer in the sixteenth century. After sixteen years married to one, she continued the business on her own for two years after his death. In 1520 she remarried and ran the business with her new husband, but when he died in 1537 she ran it alone for another twenty years, under her own name. She printed 158 titles. Guillard may be unusual, but she is not singular, for we also find Yolande Bonhomme, Françoise Louvain, and her daughter, Marie l'Angelier, in Paris managing printing businesses that required heavy investments to produce new books.

Of course, the role of women in the economy can easily be overstated, and all historians are aware that during the sixteenth and seventeenth centuries women were gradually losing the formal membership that they had enjoyed in many guilds in the late Middle Ages. And where they did retain guild membership it was increasingly concentrated in cloth and clothing production and sale. A few trades were exclusively female. Such was the case of the ribbonmakers and lacemakers of Rouen, and the linen drapers of Paris. The linen drapers were the oldest female guild in Paris, dating to the fifteenth century. Like male guilds, they had statutes, which among other things regulated apprenticeship (here girls were apprenticed to mistresses). In the late seventeenth and eighteenth centuries the linen drapers rode increasing demand for the undergarments they made, and some of these women organized themselves into a well-heeled group with large networks of suppliers and workers. By the 1780s there were eight hundred mistress linen drapers in Paris employing 1,200 female linen workers (lingères).

Thanks to recent work by Clare Crowston, we know more about seamstresses than any other female trade.[11] The royal government incorporated seamstresses in Paris in 1675 and shortly thereafter in other cities. Even then, this guild was only one of four all-female corporations. Even before incorporation, seamstresses worked France's towns and cities in great numbers, and formed something of a shadow guild. Surprisingly, many formal apprenticeship contracts exist from this earlier period, and though technically illegal (only formal corporations were permitted such contracts), they were notarized in any case. Many of the girls were hired by male tailors, and worked alongside boys in their shops. This appears to have been an accepted norm, despite the laws against it, and seamstresses thus already were developing an occupational identity. When the opportunity arose to formally incorporate (as part of Colbert's broadened system), they were already organized. In 1675, 82 mistresses joined the guild, a number that swelled to 1,000 by 1691 and 1,700 by 1720. In 1776 there were 3,000 mistress seamstresses in Paris, about the same number as master tailors.

Such growth testifies to the seamstresses' important place in a burgeoning consumer economy in the late seventeenth and eighteenth centuries, one led, as Daniel Roche has suggested, by a "clothing revolution." By law seamstresses were permitted to make clothing only for women and children under eight years of age, but this did not restrict their economic opportunity much because women significantly outconsumed men. From darning, hemming, and patching clothing for the lower classes to making fine dresses of silk or velvet for the aristocracy or even the royal family, the activities of the seamstresses were in high demand.

Individual seamstresses usually worked in small shops with a handful of workers, but there were thousands of these—about ten thousand in Paris at end of the eighteenth century.

Within this vast labor force, as in male trades, specialization was the norm, and so there were dress workers, makers of stays, corsets, camisoles,

Figure 3.1. Antoine Raspal, *Atelier de couture en Arles*, 1760, Musée Réattu

and children's gowns, makers of hoopskirts, and makers of hoods. The range of wealth among mistress seamstresses was vast from rich to poor (the latter, naturally, more numerous), and corresponded to the rank of the clientele. The guild itself, like its male counterparts, was dominated by an oligarchy that reproduced itself by monopolizing guild offices, and benefited economically by skimming a share of membership and apprenticeship dues. The rank and file probably was little affected by the guild, aside from structuring apprenticeship contracts, staging an annual inspection of the shop, and, for aspiring mistresses, performing and judging a masterpiece.

Girls learned their skills through formal apprenticeship, typically for three-year terms that usually began in the girls' early teens, a practice apparently more prevalent than among male trades. After 1675, three hundred to four hundred apprentices signed up with mistresses each year. After apprenticeship the girls typically signed a yearly contract with a mistress. These girls might eventually be entrusted with skilled activities like cutting expensive cloth or doing fittings for customers. As in male trades, some of these former apprentices (especially if they were a daughter of a mistress) were tracked for mistress-ship after performing a masterpiece (a requirement waived for daughters). Not all apprentices reached mistress-ship, however, and even those who did usually worked another seven to ten years for a mistress after apprenticeship before becoming mistresses themselves.

Within the labor force of seamstresses, much like among males of many trades, there were cores and peripheries. The workers with annual contracts, of whom there were only one or two per shop and even then only in the more prosperous establishments, formed the core, while the majority of *legal* workers entered the trade through a system of training (and registered in notarial contracts) called *allouage* that, in contrast to apprenticeship, did not allow for eventual entry into the guild. These girls formed the periphery of the legal labor force, and were hired and fired as business dictated (and there were no limits to the number a mistress could hire). Typically the shops swelled with these daily workers in the fall and spring months when demand was brisk (these were the times for buying summer and winter apparel), and shrank to just the core workers in the slower times. Then, as in male trades, there were the *illegal* workers, girls with a skill who were not mistresses but who took on customers as if they were. They were ubiquitous, even comprising an "enormous" population, in Crowston's estimation, that likely outnumbered the mistresses.

One might expect the mistresses to be hostile to these illegal outworkers, and at times they were. But we find that along with male tailors, mercers, and other artisans in the clothing trades, many mistress seamstresses jobbed specialized work out to these women in extended subcontracting arrangements, a practice they also employed with other legal mistresses. This is a point I will return to, but we must guard against viewing the operation of the craft economy only through the lens of the guild, for if we do we will get a very narrow and misleading picture.

The labor market for seamstresses was very informal. Unlike male guilds, this one had no hiring office that would place workers in shops, nor did the trade have a traditional site in the city where workers gathered to be hired by masters, a common practice in many male trades (especially construction). There was no journeywomen association (most male trades had them, as we will see; they were called *compagnonnages*), no tour de France. Instead, girls found work through informal, personal connections—kin, friends, neighbors.

Work and Culture

All of French society was structured by hierarchy, and the world of the artisan was no different. Distinction, discipline, and subordination were preoccupations of artisans no less than their social betters. Status was paramount to an artisan's identity, and thus a keen sense of honor was felt by craftsmen of all stripes. I have argued elsewhere that guilds served an important function in establishing and proclaiming status, and fundamentally served as institutions for ordering the world and making sense of it.[12] Indeed, guilds were likely *more* important to artisans for their social value than for their economic one; guild membership was a recognized and recognizable badge of status and respectability, affirming publicly and legally the artisan's place in the social firmament. With this place came a sense of belonging and an expectation that inferiors (journeymen, women) should be subordinate and obedient. Discipline and subordination were instrumental to patrolling the borders of identity.

But where does work fit in artisanal identity? Did artisans have a pride in their vocation rooted in some notion of the possession of a special skill? Historians disagree in their answers to these important questions. Consider the views expressed by Arlette Farge and Mary Hartman. Farge, writing about the eighteenth-century experience, states succinctly that for most workers, "work is a necessary activity and not a personal investment in a chosen function. . . . For [most], work is decidedly not an expression of self."[13] Hartman counters that the sixteenth through eighteenth centuries were a time of rising status identity among artisans (and others, as we will see, like lawyers): in this period a man's worthiness was validated through his pursuit of any honorable vocation. The notion that work is the measure of worth, according to Hartman, replaces the traditional anchors of a male's identity, the ownership of property and membership in a definable kin group. Population growth, urbanization, and increased social mobility cut the moorings of these traditional anchors, and there were created new ones that grounded identity in socially and gender-differentiated activities, the most prominent being work. Thus for Hartman, men's work was increasingly differentiated from women's, and more and more specified as male activity (this was abetted by an increased division of labor). Predictably, males avoided women's work as a threat to their male identity. Vocations became "badges of manhood," "the chief repositories of male identity."[14]

Can we have it both ways? Perhaps, if we bear in mind that for all artisans life was a ceaseless struggle to earn a living *and* to maintain rank. Most artisans, when viewed against the backdrop of all ranks of society, were poised perilously close to the threshold of poverty. The capitation tax of 1788 in Lyon confirms this picture, one even more pronounced in earlier centuries in other cities like Dijon. The average tax assessment of the Lyonnais silk workers in 1788 was two livres, far below that of the average artisan at nine. From the perspective of the liberal professions (averaging thirty livres) and wholesale merchants (forty), however, all those men working with their hands seemed uniformly poor. For many artisans, even many a master, the specter of unemployment (and rising prices and rents) was ever before their eyes, and all feared falling into beggary. No one wanted to plunge into the mass of workers described by Arthur Young in 1789 thus: "Truly, all those of the town with whom I have spoken represent the state of the [silkworkers] as reaching the most extreme misery. 20,000 people live only by charity, and the distress of the lower classes is the greatest that I have seen, greater than one could imagine."[15] The daily experience of many craftsmen must have been akin to that of the Lyonnais silk worker who knew, in the cold and categorical words of historian Maurice Garden, he must "work or die."

Still, we must guard against viewing the artisanry as an indistinguishable lot, either from the perspective from above, or from its own vantage point. Seventeenth-century elites may have shared the view of de La Roque, who wrote in his *Traité de la noblesse* that artisans were inferior because "the assiduousness of manual labor of artisans and the appetite for gain necessary for their subsistence renders them as slaves, inspiring in them only the sentiments of baseness and subjection," but others knew full well that a hierarchy existed within the artisanry.[16] In the fourteenth century the most affluent *corps* formed a sort of industrial aristocracy and won privileges from the municipality of Paris to be represented in ceremonies as the "six corps" and marched in 1431 in this descending honorific order: drapers, spicers/grocers, money changers, goldsmiths, mercers, furriers, and butchers.

At the other end of the scale we will find litter or chair carriers, who made their first appearance in Paris around 1600 and were dismissed as nothing more than "baptized mules" in the *Dictionnaire de précieuses*. In the late eighteenth century Louis-Sébastien Mercier also commented on distinction among artisans, specifically within a particular trade, shoemaking: "Th[e] prince of shoemakers [he who has the high nobility for customers] wears a black coat, and a well-powdered wig; his waistcoat is of silk; he looks more like something in the legal line than his own.

"His less distinguished colleagues go about with grimy hands and wigs not in their first youth; their linen stinks; but then they have not his clientele, they work for the vulgar, composing in their gross way Visigothic shoes."[17] One can see hierarchy within the artisanry everywhere, and even an intensification of it as the early modern centuries roll on. Note the gradual distinction between artisan and artist, for instance, a development we can trace to the late Middle Ages but that culminated with the establishment of the academy of painting in 1648 and the academy of architecture in 1671; these

Figure 3.2. *Le Cordonnier*, Bibliothèque nationale de France

academies removed these "trades" from the ranks of the artisanry and placed them closer to the liberal professions.

Masters

Hierarchy was crucially important to masters' vision of themselves, and the guild played a central role in it. We can begin to deepen our appreciation of the importance of guilds—after all, they survived for half a millennium!—when we shift our focus from their economic function to the social and moral. The master artisan as guild member was assumed to be a married, financially independent owner of a self-contained business. He thereby had *crédit*, a term that simultaneously had an economic and social meaning. A master who found his honor besmirched by an insult, for instance, would invariably retort, "*Je suis un homme de bien*," which again carried a double meaning—"I am a man of property" and "I am a man of standing," the two inseparable in a common meaning of recognized economic solvency, personal integrity, and social status. He was, in short, a microcosm of the well-ordered polity, and as such possessed honor. As Hans Speier put it when writing about the relation between honor and social structure, "It is inevitable that the process of honoring creates hierarchical distinctions."[18] Guilds, we must recognize, were important not only for their economic role, but also and perhaps even more significantly because membership in them proclaimed status, a publicly recognized place in the social hierarchy that conferred respectability, that announced that the guildsman had the respect of the respected and could demand and expect subordination from his inferiors (apprentices, wageworkers, journeymen, women) while owing deference to his social betters.

Honor functioned not only to support hierarchy, however. It also served as an important glue for horizontal social relations among masters. In other words, it was important to the artisan's sense of community. This, in turn, was important because the conditions of everyday life for artisans generated flux. The buzzing confusion was marked by ephemeral alliances alongside more lasting and permanent bonds—the guild being a fundamental one of the latter. But such relationships were constantly undermined by strife (even within the guild) that threatened to destabilize community. The tension between the fissures that continually threatened to rend the bonds of community and the desire of craftsmen to construct, usually with great attention to ritual and ceremony, bonds of loyalty and solidarity underlies the various nodes of community in artisan lives, the linchpin of which was a shared code of honor that brought an assumption of conformity to agreed upon but unwritten and tacit rules of behavior.

Journeymen

Hierarchy presumed obedience and subordination, and so masters assumed that the proper relation with journeymen should be one structured by labor discipline. The workshop, the fundamental site where work was done and hierarchical authority asserted, however, was constantly in flux. Journeymen coming and going instilled in these young men a sense that mobility was their right, and encouraged them to oppose the master's will to constrain it. Journeymen on the move, of course, disrupted work, and journeymen recognized as early as the fifteenth century that mobility empowered them in their relations with their employers, the masters. They thus fiercely defended this right, and by the eighteenth century equated it with the values of freedom and independence.

The search for better pay, better conditions, and better opportunities for mastership led to a nomadism that marked the lives of journeymen, sometimes even into their thirties. Such mobility was organized by brotherhoods called *compagnonnages* that made their first appearance in the fifteenth century and quickly spread to most trades thereafter. Before the eighteenth century these brotherhoods were organized by trade, and were connected by way stations in towns throughout the realm. These way stations were a certain inn or tavern run by a "mother" (a telling indication that journeymen thought of these organizations as surrogate families of brothers and mothers). A traveling journeyman would know from other journeymen of his trade the name of their inn in the town of his immediate destination. Upon arrival he would be ritually greeted there by other journeymen in the brotherhood (special handshakes, secret slang terms, and the like) who, after testing his skill by having him perform a task of their trade, would help place him in a master's shop or, if the supply of labor in town exceeded demand, urge him to move along to another town. From such a network, journeymen could exert some control over the labor market, and thereby favorably affect wages or conditions. Already by the mid-fifteenth century the fuller journeymen had organized into a "league" that linked forty-two towns, including Paris. This network resembled what would come to be called the *tour de France*, a route that itinerant journeymen traveled to learn their trade and to seek advantageous working conditions.

It was not unusual for journeymen to act collectively by striking, as happened in Lyon in the middle of the sixteenth century in the printing trade. The Griffarins, the name of the journeyman brotherhood there, brought production to a halt by collectively walking out on their masters. The strike lasted four months and forced the masters to concede to some of the journeymen's demands. The Griffarins were not the only journeymen to strike.

The journeymen bakers of Colmar did so at the end of the sixteenth century, as did their colleagues in Paris in 1579. Ten years later the journeymen tailors of Paris walked off the job, as did blacksmiths and hatters in the next century. Between the 1720s and 1780s work stoppages and boycotts became rampant. Over those sixty years or so we find strikes called by journeymen in over sixty towns, and in Paris alone we can count over fifty such incidents where hundreds of workers simultaneously threw down their tools and marched out of the shops. The lieutenant of police in Rouen remarked that "one sees in commercial towns 700 to 800 workers of one trade stop work simultaneously because [their masters] wish to lower the daily wage by a sou."[19] Of course, such brotherhoods were illegal, the police and the crown (and the masters) viewing them as assaults on proper order that was based in subordination and obedience. We need not look far to find town councils issuing declarations condemning *compagnonnages*, as Dijon's did, for example, in 1579, 1585, 1605, and 1619. The authorities saw the unbridled mobility of the journeymen as the cause of insubordination. Over a century later an inspector of manufactures complained that workers were "idlers and drinkers," and that they schemed among themselves to form coalitions to place interdicts on employers who displeased them. In an attempt to slow, or at least regulate, journeyman mobility that seemed to be at the root of the problem of indiscipline, in 1749 the crown demanded that all workers carry a *billet de congé*. This "passport" registered the signature of the previous employer, and so supposedly verified his approval of the journeyman's mobility. Masters were forbidden to hire journeymen without this signature. In 1781 the *billet de congé* was replaced by the *livret*, a more complete record of past employment and the conditions by which the journeyman left work.

Such regulatory methods met little success. By the eighteenth century the *compagnonnages* spanned trades and had become organized into two dominant groups, the *Devoirants* and the *Gavots*. Throughout their existence, journeyman brotherhoods speak to the need for community among itinerant workers. To be alone and anonymous, as Michael Sonenscher points out, was the most dangerous condition that a journeyman could experience. It promised a sure and quick exit from the trades and entry into the world of the beggar.

Just as the masters were keen on distinguishing themselves from their inferiors, that is, the journeymen (one of the prime functions of the guild was demonstration of such status), so too were the journeymen keen on making clear the boundaries that separated them from the unskilled workers below them. The brotherhoods secured community among their fellows, and membership was demonstrated by a host of rituals of inclusion and exclusion.

Many of these rituals were drawn from religious ceremony, the journeymen seeking not to mock Catholic practices (despite what the clergy thought) but to turn it to their own purposes. Thus initiation ceremonies were baptisms, complete with the giving of a new name (a nickname) to the initiate. Journeymen appropriated rites of communion, too, as the bonds of the community were renewed by the sharing of bread and wine. They had their secret and sacred books, their priestlike officials who presided over the ceremonies, and a recognized hierarchy of officers who maintained discipline in the ranks. As in the church, all of these functions renewed and reformed the community, securing its boundaries and defining its members.

Women

As we have seen, women do not appear as prominently as men in the historical records that pertain to work. This, of course, does not deny their presence, but it does make it difficult to do more than sketch what work may have meant to them. Historians like Natalie Davis have suggested that occupational identity of women was "thinner" than that of men because women more readily "shifted into other work channels if the situation demanded it."[20] The primary skill girls learned as part of their upbringing was sewing, but before the mid-seventeenth century they were rarely apprenticed, and so no formal training reinforced a work identity. If she were the daughter of an artisan who was a tailor or a seamstress she might receive a smattering of technical training, but with marriage she would likely move to another trade. Eighty-four percent of daughters of Lyon's artisans between 1553 and 1560 married within the artisanry but only a fourth of them wedded men of the same occupation as their fathers. Similar artisanal endogamy and trade exogamy patterns appear elsewhere, as in Dijon in the sixteenth and seventeenth centuries. Married women and widows, therefore, appear in quite a variety of trades.

It is true that marital interdependency was necessary for the subsistence of the household and the family business, and this often pulled women (both wives and daughters) into men's work, but, very unlike men, most of these women did not see the sphere of work as one in which they had rights or privileges. Outside of the handful of formal female guilds, we find little or no active female involvement in organizational structures like most guilds, religious confraternities, or compagnonnages. Men may have needed their wives to keep the business afloat, but they were also fearful of the "unbridled female," and so hedged the women in whenever possible.

The notable exception where we do find women internalizing a work identity was in needlework. During the late seventeenth and eighteenth centuries seamstresses saw their work recast as essentially a feminine activity. Indeed, by the eighteenth century, men like Jean-Jacques Rousseau or the authors of the *Encyclopédie* naturalized needlework as such, a supposed biologically innate feminine skill. This displayed a general Enlightenment proclivity to see nature behind culture, but it also reflected an accelerating sexual division of labor in the garment trades. This division of labor was formalized by the incorporation of seamstresses in 1675 in Paris and in other cities thereafter, transforming what was a customary affiliation into a legal one. Behind this formality an identity was forming. As Clare Crowston has shown, women producing consumption items for other women had the important cultural effect of producing and reproducing gender ideologies, as clothing increasingly was called on to define femininity. These gender ideologies embedded in work took deeper root than law, it seems, for even the abolition of the guilds in 1791 did not affect seamstresses much because by then they, like everyone else, assumed that they naturally performed this kind of work.

Artisan Ways of Knowing

Artisan identity was embedded in the artisan's work activity in cultural ways, for work activity was ascribed meaning not simply by how it sustained material life but also by how it placed the artisan in society and affirmed and demonstrated status. This was a primary function of guilds. As important as culture is in the formation of identity, however, let's not lose sight of the fact that artisans made things and possessed specific skills to transform the stuff of nature (wood, stone, animal flesh and skin, grains, and so forth) into artifacts useful to, or at least desired by, society. The artifacts he or she produced came from a deep familiarity with the behavior of materials, like a carpenter's knowledge of wood. He knew how to choose, cut, and prepare wood so, for example, it did not warp or twist. Apprentices learned about materials and techniques in their formative years, immersed in a method of constant trial and retrial that produced a kind of cognition that led to a deep knowledge of nature resulting in creation of useful objects. By this training, technology was "transferred" down through generations.[21]

Nature had been the source of artisan knowledge since time immemorial, but until the late sixteenth century there existed a deep chasm between learned and artisanal ways of knowing. Intellectuals disparaged the latter as lowly and inferior to their own because it was not of the mind but of the body, not theoretical but physical, and they expressed their views in written texts that have come down to us. Artisanal ways of knowing, in contrast, are revealed in objects, not books, and so have largely escaped the historian's scrutiny. This kind of knowledge was transmitted through practice, a combination of talking about and showing techniques that were learned by observation and imitation. The learned view that artisanal practice was rote and slavish was distorted by the bias that assumed that the only valuable knowledge was theoretical and textual. But in fact, everyday artisanal techniques were quite complex, often involving mathematical calculation, and were continually adapted to specific situations.

Anthropologists and cognitive scientists recognize that a kind of knowledge is produced by bodily labor, and, as Jean Lave and Etienne Wenger point out, this form of cognition and its "practice . . . [is] inherent in the growth and transformation of identities and . . . located in relations among practitioners, their practice, the artifacts of that practice, and the social organization and political economy of communities of practice."[22] The historian Pamela Smith seizes on this insight and opens up fruitful avenues into artisanal identity by linking the material with the cultural.[23]

In the late sixteenth century the walls between the learned and artisanal epistemologies were partially breached. The maverick medical doctor and alchemist Paracelsus admired the artisan's deep knowledge of the behavior of materials, and he appropriated the epistemology that nature (as opposed to texts) was a primary source of knowledge. Imbued with a religious sensibility, he argued that working with nature was also a form of worship, that craft was a refining of nature for the human needs of God's creation: "To reveal the hidden through human work . . . God wishes that the things that are invisible should become visible. . . . Because God has ordered man to do this, God does not want him to quit working, to be lazy . . . instead He wants him to do daily practice in order to investigate the secrets of nature and all the gifts that God has created in nature."[24]

Bernard Palissey (1510–1590) was another writer who clearly assumed that there was a bodily aspect to artisanal knowledge. It is no accident that Palissey was an artisan himself, a potter, but an unusual one in that he authored three texts (two in 1563 and one in 1580) where he echoed Paracelsus's dictum that knowledge comes not from reading but from doing, not from the word but from labor. As a youth he was apprenticed as a glass painter, then he traveled as a journeyman and eventually settled near La Rochelle and taught himself potterymaking. He is known to us for the works of art he produced for the tables of the highest nobility, called Palisseyware, but a close look at these artifacts reveals a scrupulous rendition of natural objects clearly drawn from close and intense observation.

Smith argues that artisanal epistemology became the basis of the new scientific method of empiricism that took hold among the learned in the seventeenth century, making its first inroads in alchemy and eventually being institutionalized in university faculties of medicine and natural philosophy. Despite Paracelsus's or Palissey's admiration of the artisan, the craftsmen and craftswomen of France found their status not enhanced by such a development but in fact reduced. In the eighteenth century, thinkers and government ministers systematically and methodically sought to appropriate and demystify artisanal techniques. Many articles in the *Encyclopédie* edited by Denis Diderot and the *Encyclopédie méthodique* (an expanded and revised version edited by Charles Josèph Panckoucke) openly aspired to this, explaining in detail the processes of various craft production and disparaging the obscurantism of artisans who tried to protect the "mysteries" of their trades.[25]

Government ministers, such as the director of the Bureau du Commerce Daniel Trudaine, attempted to put this enlightened view of the trades into practice by having the bureau oversee production and regularize and standardize tools, methods, and even know-how. Regulation during the 1750s moved away from detection and repression of fraud and "abuses" in the trades and toward offering improved and standardized technical advice. Men like Trudaine believed that such openness would lead to improvement, to progress. The same spirit of openness partly inspired the Allarde laws of 2 and 17 March 1791. This revolutionary legislation abolished "corporations . . . of whatever état or profession . . . freeing each person to . . . exercise whatever profession, art, or trade that he finds good for him."[26] This frontal attack on guilds, of course, had an impact on artisanal identity, but those transformations are the subject of a later time, and beyond the purview of this book.[27]

What Changed in the Work World of the Artisanry?

The world of work in general and that of the artisans in particular were affected by the three pervasive developments that I highlighted in the introduction and developed in previous chapters—market growth and integration, the intensification of social hierarchy, and the growth of the state. Traditionally, historians have assumed that the institution of the craft guild cramped the craft economy by imposing regulatory proscriptions that stunted economic growth. Recent research, however, challenges this assumption in two ways: first, some historians examining the Low Countries have found that guilds could actually perform as institutions to promote economic growth.[28] No research has yet confirmed this argument for France, but there is ample evidence offering a second challenge to the traditional view of guilds by discovering that the regulatory reach of guilds into the overall economy was incomplete and frequently ineffective, leaving room for the growth and expansion of the market in many sectors.

The Market

Measuring economic growth and market integration precisely, given the state of the sources from early modern times, is impossible, but general trends are nonetheless unmistakable. First, over the early modern centuries sectors of the urban craft economy, much like the rural economy, passed through cycles of growth and contraction. The textile industry, notably in Normandy and Languedoc (wool and linen) and Lyon (silk), illustrates this pattern well. The period from 1470 to 1560 was a time of rising prices pushed by strong demand. The end of the sixteenth century witnessed a depression in manufacturing, but was followed by a period of recovery during the first third of the seventeenth century. Then in the 1630s there was a sharp contraction in textile production (by one-half in Beauvais and three-quarters in Languedoc), a slight recovery in the 1660s and 1670s, another sag in the last years of the reign of Louis XIV, and then strong recovery in the eighteenth century (greatly stimulated by export demand for woolens and the domestic demand for cotton fabrics, which in turn fueled growth in the import of raw cotton).

The economic historian François Crouzet estimated that between 1710 and 1790 the nominal annual production from French industry and artisanry went from 385 million livres to 1,574 million, or a growth of 308 percent, while the growth of exports of manufactured products grew between 1716 and 1787 by 322 percent. We might find the precision of such numbers dubious, but the magnitude of growth is starkly clear. Maurice Garden confirms this picture concerning the master artisans in Lyon: between 1729 and 1788 the property value they brought to marriage increased by 145 percent. Even workers' values jumped 80 percent, ahead of the 60 percent price rise that marked that century.

We have no comparable figures for earlier periods, but there can be no question that nonagrarian growth marked earlier times and places as well. Lyon in the sixteenth century would be a notable example. As we have seen, the silk industry boomed then, but even construction wages went up sharply over the course of that century, for master masons from five to eighteen sols per day. In a growing town there was an abundance of work in both private and public construction. Of course, that century also witnessed a rise in the prices of foodstuffs, but real wages still posted gains.

No doubt an economic history of other craft sectors would reveal such cyclical patterns, but behind this growth and contraction lurked a fundamental change that over the long term had a profound impact on the artisanry—urbanization. As Jan De Vries has shown, France's (and Europe's) cities and large towns continually knit themselves together in market networks as their populations grew (fed by villagers and denizens of towns of fewer than ten thousand inhabitants), and as a result across the kingdom the percentage of the population dependent on the market continued to grow during the early modern centuries, even during cyclical downturns in the economy.[29] In short, even as short-term demand surged and ebbed with specific conditions, the structures of market integration continued to be built. Of course, market integration was uneven temporally and spatially, but its impact on the artisanry was registered in the readily demonstrable and interconnected trends that I have already discussed in this chapter: increased specialization, decentralization of production (notably through subcontracting), and, sporadically but evident in some areas, concentration of production (horizontal combination).

Intensification of Hierarchy

As Natalie Davis has observed, social inequality had increased significantly in the sixteenth century; I would add that it also increased in the seventeenth and eighteenth centuries.[30] The real winners were the enriched minority elite of France's towns and cities, its merchants, nobles, financiers, and royal officials. Wealth was disproportionately concentrated at the top end of the social pyramid, but this does not mean that the craft sector was left out in the cold, for artisans made the products and performed services that the burgeoning elite craved. Not only did the size of this elite grow (the office-holding class in Dijon, for example, grew from about 1.5 percent of the total population of almost 2,400 heads of households in 1464 to nearly 8 percent of the almost 4,700 household heads in 1750), but their consumption habits accelerated beyond their numbers. This consumption was driven by the demands of fashion and the dictates of civility, yet another indicator of an increased emphasis on social hierarchy. In 1644 in the Lois de la galanterie, the vogue for undergarments is underlined: "One must have regard for how one covers the body, and what is not only for hiding and protecting against the cold, but also for ornament. One must have the most beautiful linen and the finest that one can find."[31]

The construction trades were in high demand, too, even in the seventeenth century when parts of the overall economy sagged. Between 1550 and 1650 wealthy urban elites invested large sums of capital in razing old buildings and erecting mansions, or adding stories to existing buildings. One author in 1652 observed that houses had been built so high that it seemed as if two or three towns had been piled on top of one another. Cities like Paris were transformed from wood to stone, and thatch roofs gave way to clay tiles. Half of the building costs of a new urban townhouse in 1673 went for masonry, a quarter for carpentry, and a quarter for roofing and interior finishing.

Naturally, droves of artisans were employed for the work, but employment did not end with the completion of the building. Aristocrats' sumptuous consumption habits kept thousands of artisans employed. In the 1760s and 1770s in Paris, for example, five aristocratic houses alone employed nearly two thousand artisans from two hundred different trades, including painters, sculptors, upholsterers, carpenters, furnituremakers, joiners, jewelers, ironsmiths, and wheelwrights.

Nobles spent lavishly, but they also invested in production. Contrary to popular assumptions, there could be found nobles who invested in manufacturing and commerce without losing their noble status. It has been estimated that 56 percent of France's factories and logging and mining operations in the eighteenth century were owned by men of privilege (especially the landed nobility), who often used seigneurial rights to exploit mines, forests, and quarries. In 1777 the Count of Artois established a factory at Javel to manufacture chemical products, employing one hundred workers. To take another prominent example, the naturalist Georges-Louis Leclerc, Count Buffon, counted 60 percent of his income in 1787 from land and industrial ventures in glassmaking, coal mining, metalworking, and publishing—in each case employing artisans and workers to do the work. He was at once a seigneur and an entrepreneur, typical of the many nobles who took part in commercial capitalism but also clung to political and social ideas that justified their superiority.

The State and the Economy

Another increasingly prominent force in the economy—and in the world of work—in early modern France was the state. Traditionally this role has been viewed in the negative, as a millstone around the neck of the economy that through its regulatory apparatus choked the economic growth that supposedly would have occurred otherwise. There is no question that actions of the state did retard economic growth, but this was due more to its burdensome taxation policies than its regulatory apparatus. Colbert's program for textile inspection, which we will return to in a later chapter, was intended as a stimulus for growth, and the licensing of privileges to many manufactories served the same goal. Colbertian *dirigisme* got its bad name, so argues Philippe Minard, only after liberal economists of the eighteenth century touting free-market ideology were ascendant.[32]

As far as artisans were concerned, the state-endorsed corporate regulatory system was expressed, of course, in the guild. As early as the fifteenth century, in most cities a regulatory apparatus was firmly in place. Each guild had its statutes, or bylaws, sanctioned by the royal government that vowed, among other things, to protect monopolies and permit workshop searches to enforce quality control. The guilds received these privileges from the crown in exchange for making and selling products in the public interest—quality goods at a fair price. Guilds and corporatism grew together, with Colbertism the high point. In 1673 a royal edict ordered the incorporation of all previously unincorporated trades throughout the kingdom's cities and towns where guilds were already established. The idea was to protect the consumer from shoddy goods and the producer from freelance and therefore illegal and unsupervised workers. And, because each guild was assessed a fee, the system would raise revenue for the crown. As a result, between 1673 and 1714 the number of incorporated guilds increased dramatically (in Paris, for example, they lurched from sixty in 1669 to 129 in 1691).

At the same time a flood of royal regulation washed across the guilds. During these years the royal government issued 450 rulings (*réglements*) on manufacturing, and another 500 on policing the trades and the jurisdictions between them. The government, strapped for funds, also practiced venality in the guilds. It not only sold mastership letters (previous kings had engaged in this practice, whereby the purchaser became a master without performing a masterpiece or paying to the guild the requisite fees normally charged new masters), but in 1702 Louis XIV ordered (and sold) a new office created for each guild, the treasurer and bursar (*trésorier et payeur*). In 1704 he added controllers of weights and measures (*contrôleurs visiteurs des poids et mesures*), and clerks for the registration of guild contracts (*greffiers pour l'enregistrement des brevets d'apprentissage, lettres de maîtrise*, etc.). In 1706 came controllers of guild registers (*contrôleurs des registres*), and in 1709 guild archivists (*gardes des archives*). Often guilds purchased these offices themselves, a practice that caused widespread indebtedness among corporations.

Let me be clear. I am not trying to argue that the guild system was economically irrelevant. Regulation may have had a stultifying effect on economic growth in some places and at some times, but the more research that is done into the overall operation of the early modern urban economy, the more we realize how much was happening *beyond the purview and reach* of the guilds and of government regulation. In other words, prescription (guild regulation) should not be equated with practice (what was actually happening). Guilds were legal administrative units and thus kept records of their activities, while the men and women engaged in the economy beyond the guilds did not (many of their activities were illegal), so we must be on our guard against assuming that the official records (in which prescription dominated) reflect the total reality. Historians have debated, and continue to debate, these fundamental questions: Did guild regulations affect the economy, and if so, how much and in what way? Does the existence of a regulatory regime mean that it was extensive, efficient, or punitive enough to impede economic activity and stifle economic growth in general? When we consider the magnitude of violation, we begin to see how inadequate the regulatory apparatus was to actual production, distribution, and consumption.

Recent research strongly suggests that the regulatory reach of guilds was short and incomplete, the magnitude of violation of the normative guild bylaws enormous. Everywhere we look we find masters operating multiple shops and thereby flouting explicit guild bylaws, as well as journeymen illicitly setting themselves up in their own shops and taking on apprentices, customers, and clients (something legally permitted only to guild masters). It was not even uncommon for these workers to get subcontracted business from the masters themselves! Spot markets popped up in response to accelerating demand, drawing artisans of all stripes—guild members or not— into them. Some artisans speculated in purchasing letters of mastership (the crown was more than willing to sell them), like the eighteenth-century wigmaker Lacouture from Bordeaux. He bought seven of them, keeping one for himself and then selling off the other six at a profit. Sometimes entire guilds ignored their own statutes, as did the goldsmiths of Paris. Their bylaws stipulated that only three hundred shops could operate in the city, but in fact by the eighteenth century there were eight hundred such shops, the excess being enterprises run by nonmasters who often received subcontracted work from masters in the guild. Bakers were doing this too, renting out bakeries to nonguild artisans and even having their illegal lease contracts notarized!

The consumer revolution beginning in the late seventeenth century no doubt stimulated these developments, fueling what Michael Sonenscher called a "bazaar" economy that operated on a day-to-day basis according to rules more akin to the spot market than the tightly regulated guild world prescribed in statute and legislation.[33] The eighteenth-century Parisian glazier Jacques-Louis Ménétra amply demonstrates this in his inimitable journal.[34] Here he describes masters employing masters, journeymen working on their own account for private individuals, masters forming partnerships with other masters and even merchants, and journeymen employing apprentices, all often coming together in complex networks of subcontracting.

Indeed, government regulatory action, by its repeated invocation of the same transgressions, often indicated an economy it could not control. In 1581, for example, King Henri III issued an edict similar to the Colbert-inspired one of 1673, calling for the incorporation of all trades in the kingdom. It was a dead letter. Such an inclusive guild system, despite its regulatory intentions, was immediately recognized by the crown to be inadequate to actual production and distribution. What follows into the seventeenth century are countless ad hoc royal patents and privileges exempting the artisan recipients from guild regulation and surveillance, legitimating a preexisting de facto unregulated market that hummed along parallel to, and was perhaps even larger than, the licit market regulated by the guilds.

Illicit workers were ubiquitous. The Dijonnais master blacksmiths' complaint to the city authorities in 1596 speaks for many a trade: "Many abuses are committed in the exercise of [this] art, because a great number of vagabonds are drawn into this town and are practicing the blacksmith trade."[35] Illicit "roomworkers" (called *chambrellans*) posed similar threats. Drawn into their work by demand, these illicit workers were periodically arrested by the authorities, but the frequency of the discussion of the problem by municipal authorities and the complaints about these workers by masters, as well as the numbers occasionally hauled in, gives the distinct impression that we are simply glimpsing the tip of an enormous and uncontrollable iceberg.

The state may have been ineffective in regulating much of the craft economy, but its influence could be felt in other ways. It appears to have been effective in stimulating economic growth in some sectors, specifically through the industries it directly sponsored. The first royal manufactory in France was established by Louis XI in Lyon in 1466, the second in Tours in 1470, both for silk production. Henri IV forbade all foreign importation of silks, and then ordered the planting of twenty thousand mulberry trees and the cultivation of silkworms in the Tuileries outside the royal palace in Paris and elsewhere, and a year later sixty thousand more trees were planted in Languedoc.

Royal manufactories were quite different from normal workshops. These were built for display and the demonstration of prestige as much as for efficient production. First, consider their size. The royal ropeworks (called *La Corderie*) built in 1666–1667 housed hundreds of workers in a building 370 meters long. Royal manufactories also boasted quality building materials, a rational layout, and elaborated facades. All proclaimed status. Indeed, they looked more like palaces than workshops.

A royal cloth manufactory was set up in Abbeville in 1665 on Colbert's initiative by the Dutchman Josse Van Robais. By 1708 a mixed-gender workforce of three thousand was employed, all recruited locally. Initially the workshops were dispersed around town, but in 1710 most were brought into a large building called *Les Rames*. The spinsters (all women) continued to be dispersed around town, but inside Les Rames was a central hall for the masters (positioned so they could keep an eye on all operations) and two wings for the weavers and cloth cutters. The building was surrounded by hedges and moats, creating a small world unto itself. Inside, the workers were strictly disciplined; none, for example, were permitted to drink alcohol on the premises. A division of labor was quite pronounced, with 52 different processes in the manufacture of fine cloth. By 1728, 3,500 male workers and 400 females (supervised by mistresses and working separately) went about their monotonous tasks to the sound of a drum.

Notes

1. Jan De Vries, *The Economy of Europe in an Age of Crisis, 1600–1750* (Cambridge: Cambridge University Press, 1976), 91.

2. James R. Farr, "Consumers, Commerce, and the Craftsmen of Dijon: The Changing Social and Economic Structure of a Provincial Capital, 1450–1750," in *Cities and Social Change in Early Modern France*, ed. Philip Benedict (London: Unwin Hyman, 1989), 156–57.

3. Michael Sonenscher, *The Hatters of Eighteenth-Century France* (Berkeley: University of California Press, 1987); Leonard N. Rosenband, *Papermaking in Eighteenth-Century France: Management, Labor, and Revolution at the Montgolfier Mill, 1761–1805* (Baltimore: Johns Hopkins University Press, 2000); and Rosenband, "Hiring and Firing at the Montgolfier Paper Mill," in *The Workplace Before the Factory*, ed. Thomas M. Safley and Leonard Rosenband (Ithaca, N.Y.: Cornell University Press, 1993).

4. Rosenband, "Hiring and Firing," 227.

5. Quoted in Rosenband, "Hiring and Firing," 227

6. Daniel Roche, *Le Peuple de Paris* (Paris: Aubier, 1981), 74 (my translation).

7. James R. Farr, *Hands of Honor: Artisans and Their World in Dijon, 1550–1650* (Ithaca, N.Y.: Cornell University Press, 1988).

8. Quoted in Alfred Franklin, *Dictionnaire historique des arts, métiers et professions* (New York: Burt Franklin, 1968; orig. pub. 1906), 29.

9. Elizabeth Musgrave, "Women in the Male World of Work: The Building Industries in Eighteenth-Century Brittany," *French Historical Studies* 20, no. 1 (1993): 30–52.

10. Susan Broomhall, *Women and the Book Trade in Sixteenth-Century France* (Aldershot, UK: Ashgate, 2002).

11. Clare Haru Crowston, *Fabricating Women: The Seamstresses of Old Regime France (1675–1791)* (Durham, N.C.: Duke University Press, 2001).

12. James R. Farr, *Artisans in Europe, 1300–1914* (Cambridge: Cambridge University Press, 2000).

13. Arlette Farge, *La Vie fragile* (Paris: Hachette, 1986), 128.

14. Mary Hartman, *The Household and the Making of History* (Cambridge: Cambridge University Press, 2004), 198.

15. Quoted in Maurice Garden, *Lyon et les lyonnais au XVIIIe siècle* (Paris: Flammarion, 1975), 227–28.

16. Quoted in Franklin, *Dictionnaire historique*, 559 (my translation).

17. Louis-Sébastien Mercier, *Panorama of Paris [Selections from Le Tableau de Paris]*, ed. and trans. Jeremy Popkin (University Park: Pennsylvania State University Press, 1999), 214.

18. Hans Speier, "Honor and Social Structure," in Speier, *The Truth in Hell and Other Essays on Politics and Culture, 1935–1987* (Oxford: Oxford University Press, 1989), 55.

19. Quoted in Farr, *Artisans*, 198.

20. Natalie Z. Davis, "Women in the Crafts in Sixteenth-Century Lyon," in *Women and Work in Preindustrial Europe*, ed. Barbara Hanawalt (Bloomington: Indiana University Press, 1986), 169.

21. See S. R. Epstein, "Crafts Guilds, Apprenticeship, and Technological Change in Preindustrial Europe," *Journal of Economic History* 58 (1998): 684–713.

22. Jean Lave and Etienne Wenger, *Situated Learning: Legitimate Peripheral Participation* (Cambridge: Cambridge University Press, 1991).

23. Pamela H. Smith, *The Body of the Artisan: Art and Experience in the Scientific Revolution* (Chicago: University of Chicago Press, 2004).

24. Quoted in Smith, *Body of the Artisan*, 84.

25. Denis Diderot, ed., *Encyclopédie, ou dictionnaire raisonné des sciences, des arts, et des métiers*, 28 vols. (Paris: 1751–1766); Charles Josèph Panckoucke, ed., *Encyclopédie méthodique*, 206 vols. (Paris: Panckoucke, 1782–1832). See William Sewell Jr., "Visions of Labor: Illustrations of the Mechanical Arts before, in, and after Diderot's *Encyclopédie*," in *Work in France: Representations, Meaning, Organization, and Practice*, ed. Steven L. Kaplan and Cynthia Koepp (Ithaca, N.Y.: Cornell University Press, 1986), 258–86; and Cynthia Koepp, "The Alphabetical Order: Work in Diderot's *Encyclopédie*," in Kaplan and Koepp, *Work in France*, 229–57.

26. Quoted in Philippe Minard, *La Fortune du Colbertisme* (Paris: Fayard, 1998), 351.

27. See Farr, *Artisans*, epilogue; and Farr, "The Disappearance of the Traditional Artisan," in *A Companion to Nineteenth-Century Europe, 1789–1914*, ed. Stefan Berger (Oxford: Blackwell, 2006), 98–108.

28. Maarten Prak, Catharina Lis, Jan Lucassen, and Hugo Soly, eds., *Craft Guilds in the Early Modern Low Countries: Work, Power, and Representation* (Aldershot, UK: Ashgate, 2006); see especially the articles by Bert De Munck, Piet Lourens, and Jan Lucassen, "The Establishment and Distribution of Craft Guilds in the Low Countries, 1000–1800," and Catharina Lis and Hugo Soly, "Export Industries, Craft Guilds and Capitalist Trajectories, 13th to 18th Centuries."

29. Jan De Vries, *European Urbanization, 1500-1800* (Cambridge, Mass.: Harvard University Press, 1984).

30. Natalie Z. Davis, *Society and Culture in Early Modern France* (Stanford, Calif.: Stanford University Press, 1975), 188.

31. Quoted in Franklin, *Dictionnaire historique*, 697.

32. Minard, *Fortune du Colbertisme*.

33. Michael Sonenscher, *Work and Wages: Natural Law, Politics, and the Eighteenth-Century French Trades* (Cambridge: Cambridge University Press, 1989).

34. Jacques-Louis Ménétra, *Journal of My Life*, ed. Daniel Roche, trans. Arthur Goldhammer (New York: Columbia University Press, 1986).

35. Farr, *Hands of Honor*, 60.

CHAPTER FOUR

~

Merchants, Large and Small

What Merchants Did

In a little book that has become a classic, Pierre Jeannin wrote that "it would be rather difficult to define the archetypical merchant, to characterize accurately the ways of thinking, behaving, feeling, and living of a social stratum as unstable as the merchant class . . . [but] one can attempt to delineate the salient features of a merchandising 'style' common to all levels of the business world."[1] What Jeannin wrote about merchants in the sixteenth century can, in fact, be extended to most of the early modern period. To be sure, there were significant changes in France that would greatly affect the mercantile population, but some salient characteristics that remained constant throughout the period can be identified.

Europe experienced a "commercial revolution" in the High Middle Ages, and despite the economic downturn of the fourteenth and part of the fifteenth centuries, a considerable residue of that revolution, above all in business techniques and organization, was inherited by the early modern world. Fundamentally, merchants remained the linchpin of important sectors of the commercial economy—long-distance and local and regional trade, and the circulation and use of money and credit. As we will see, they also dramatically expanded their operations in the early modern period into government finance, land acquisition and management, and manufacturing. For all of these men (and a few women), their world was one of complex calculation. Small merchants (called *marchands*) and large wholesalers (called *marchands*

111

de gros before the seventeenth century and *négociants* thereafter) were the same in this regard, and all relied on money and credit in all its multifarious forms. The free circulation of monetary instruments was an absolute necessity to attain their goal, which was to generate surplus from trade transactions. What merchants did with these profits varied from trader to trader and over time, but to reach their objective they had to be acute observers, capable of analyzing and using productively whatever information came their way. Indeed, the restless search for profit defined how merchants conceived of time and distance as well as the nature of their social relations.

Business Techniques, Organization, and Training

Uncertainty was constant in the life of the merchant. Communication and transportation were at the mercy of unpredictable weather, poor and at times impassable roads, and pirates and bandits. Risk and chance defined the mercantile life, and obstacles to profit were compounded by distance. For profit to be attained and loss avoided, merchants large and small employed varieties of business techniques to minimize risk and maximize predictability.

First and foremost, in nearly all mercantile transactions credit was central. This was true of the small trader in local and regional agricultural products as much as of the merchant engaged in precious goods in long-distance trade. Scattered evidence suggests that wives and widows of merchants may have been active in urban and rural credit markets, serving as "deputy husbands," in Mary Hartman's words, in these transactions.[2] The retail trade of towns and cities became utterly dependent on small-scale credit agreements. For example, in Parisian marketplaces and above all at the famous and enormous one known as Les Halles, money was loaned short term, usually weekly or less (thus such loans were called *à la petite semaine*) and at high interest. The rates were high because the risks were high, the borrowers hailing from the poorest sectors of the populace, truly a trading proletariat. The borrowers had no choice but to accept the high rates as a necessary condition to earn a living.

Cash payment occurred only at the liquidation of final balances. In very complex trading arrangements the bill of exchange was widely used. This monetary instrument can be traced back to use by the Italians during the Commercial Revolution of the High Middle Ages (borrowed from Muslims who employed it before that). Basically, these bills enabled paper to be converted into cash (redeemed), traded with other bills, or be a source of profit in itself if the merchant speculated on exchange rates between currencies. In rudimentary usage, the bill of exchange was employed in monetary exchange between currencies, or for the direct settlement of a loan. During the early modern period it gradually became negotiable, and thus greased the wheels of commerce dramatically. A considerable amount of trade could occur with a negligible transfer of actual cash. For example, by using a bill of exchange a merchant who was owed money could retire his own debt to another by transferring what was owed him to his creditor. No cash would change hands in such a transaction, which could be continued indefinitely among other traders and creditors. Of course, the security of the financial circuit that these bills traveled on was essential, and this security depended on effective communication as well as the personal integrity of the correspondents.

Credit was convenient in that it accelerated business transactions, and merchants knew then what they know now, that profit increases with the velocity of transaction. Credit was invaluable in another way, though, for it reduced the risk of transferring actual strongboxes of money from one merchant to another. Thus bills of exchange were a crucial instrument. Consider this typical example of a bill of exchange sent from Antwerp to Rouen in 1576:

> Praise be to God. For the sum of 853 livres, 4 sous tournois. Pay by this first [bill] of exchange, [we] having paid by the second [bill] a week after presentation to Sr. François Delobel the sum of 853 livres and 4 sous tournois in good currency that is in circulation among merchants, in exchange for 100 livres de gros here received from Sr. Steven Ractret. Make good payment and charge to our account as stated in letter of notification. Issued in Antwerp the 18th day of April in the year 1576. Jehan de Voss and company.[3]

Merchants also used other techniques to minimize risk besides the bill of exchange. In the fifteenth century the Letter of Marque appeared in response to the rampant piracy on the Mediterranean Sea. When a merchant was robbed on the high seas, what recourse did he have? First, he could appeal to the political authority of the perpetrators for compensation. For example, if a French trader was robbed by Venetian pirates, he could appeal to the Republic of Venice for redress. If compensation was not forthcoming, he might appeal to his own political authority, in this example, the king of France. The king could then issue a Letter of Marque to the wronged merchant; the letter would grant the merchant the authority to compensate his loss by seizing goods from compatriots of the perpetrators (in this case, Venetians). Of course, this could and did lead to a spiraling of confiscations, thus encouraging more piracy, so eventually reprisals were transformed into taxation on trade to generate funds to compensate victims.

Maritime insurance, which was increasingly used among French merchants from the fourteenth century on, also was a hedge against risk (including piracy) on the high seas. A rule of business was (and is) that merchandise was attracted to high prices, and the longer the distance goods traveled, the higher their value but the higher the risk—thus the value of insurance in long-distance trade. *Le Compagnon ordinaire du marchand*, published in 1698, describes how a merchant might use maritime insurance. A contract *à la grosse aventure* was an investment contract for long-distance trade where an investor would lend money on a voyage at 30 to 50 percent, depending on length and perceived risk. Once the loan was made, the investor would then immediately "hedge" it by purchasing insurance covering the amount of principal plus interest, with up to a 6 percent premium. If the ship were lost, then the investor would collect the insurance, and even with the premium deducted, he would still come out ahead.

One thing remained constant throughout the early modern period among merchants, and that was the centrality of the family in their operations. In this regard again they copied the Italians and changed little during the early modern years. Distance and trust posed enormous problems for traders, and involvement of the family in the firm was seen as the best way to overcome these problems. To be sure, merchants had to trust fellow traders, and sometimes would employ one another as commissioned agents in distant markets. Such arrangements allowed one to take a small percentage on deals negotiated for the other. These were not partnerships, but simply reciprocal services offered within the mercantile community. Still, the family was the preferred institution of trust. Even by the eighteenth century the vast majority of mercantile firms were family owned and only rarely corporate. Merchant fathers usually brought their eldest son into the business (placing subsequent sons in royal or municipal office and the church, thus linking the family to every level of the power structure in France).

It was essential for firms in long-distance trade to have direct links with financial centers and markets (first fairs and later exchanges and large cities), and merchant houses reflect the salience of the family in these arrangements, often in the very names of the firm. Fraissinet Son, for example, was a branch of one firm that was managed by a son, while the home office was run by the father. Pellet Brothers of Bordeaux, to take another example, set up a branch in Amsterdam, and did it through marriage. One of the brothers married Jeanne Nairac, and her brother Guillaume was set up to run the Amsterdam office. Indeed, the principal merchant families of every French city were linked together by a multitude of interlocking alliances, and as the Pellet-Nairac marriage suggests, women were very important in this regard. We have only sketchy evidence on their business activities within the firm, but there is no doubt that their roles in marriages that were arranged with an eye toward the success of the family enterprise were fundamentally important.

In many ways French merchants adopted Italian practices. The Italian *commenda* was another institution employed by the French. It was basically a partnership where one partner remained at home and the other sailed with the cargo-laden ship. The arrangement usually was for one voyage only, and was unequal in that the partners' share of profits was commensurate to their investment. The lesser partner usually was the mobile one, buying cargo and insurance on site, traveling aboard ship with the goods, and then writing up a "faithful account of the handling and the negotiation of the entire transaction," as the contract for a partnership between Jacques Guillmard of La Rochelle and his lesser partner, Jehan Bouet of Montpelier, put it in 1599.[4] Partnerships could be more complex, with more investors, but the principle remained the same in that profit (and loss) was commensurate with investment. Indeed, many commercial and financial relationships crossed confessional lines, even during the strife-torn sixteenth century. In the 1570s, for example, twenty-five Catholic and Protestant merchants pooled capital to launch a ship, the *Henry*, on a voyage to Africa and South America—and shared in the loss when pirates plundered it.

As these examples of partnership demonstrate, trust was essential. And as the Guillmard-Bouet agreement illustrates, such trust rested in part on the faithful writing up of the venture. Most merchants could read and write, an essential skill for success. Access to information has always been a key factor in business success, and early modern merchants knew this well. Merchants succeeded or failed by knowing where commodities, cash, or credit were scarce or plentiful, for there lay profit or loss. Access to such information was crucial, and so, too, was communication. The daily life of a long-distance trader, then, could largely be consumed in letter writing, inquiring about prices or credit rates in distant markets, or arranging transactions with other merchants there. As the wholesale trader André Ruiz of Nantes wrote to his brother Simon in 1576, his work consisted of "writing letters and more letters all day long."[5] Similarly, the comte d'Avaux, Louis XIV's ambassador to the United Provinces, reported in 1688 about a wholesale merchant named Monginot, noting that he was "someone with a great deal of business; he writes day and night."[6] Manuals written for merchants all emphasized the importance of correspondence. Early Italian ones and later French ones like Jacques Savary's *Le Parfait négociant* (*The Perfect Merchant*), first published in 1675 and reprinted many times into the eighteenth century, differed little in this regard. Letters were full of political news, military news, harvest news. And letters always ended with a list of prices and exchange rates in various markets.

Because most merchants composed their own correspondence, handwriting and letter composition were important skills taught by private instructors to sons of merchants destined to join the family business. Such skills were also taught in the emerging municipal schools of the sixteenth century that many a merchant's son attended. Merchants in training also learned arithmetic, including the local current system of weights and measures, and then, because these were far from standard anywhere, how to calculate conversions from one system to another. From basic math and abacus computation followed more advanced instruction in computation of prices, interest, exchange rates, and what was called "the reduction of coins," meaning, determining the value of various currencies and the amount of alloy therein. Instruction, as is amply evident in the proliferation of books written for the edification of merchants, was always based on learning rules about merchandising with practical, utilitarian examples. This was not an education in the abstract science of numbers.

Apprenticeship reinforced this type of education. Apprentices would accompany their master merchant everywhere, from daily tasks to long-distance travels, observing and learning by experience. Jacques Guillmard of La Rochelle actually stipulated in a contract with his lesser partner Jehan Bouet of Montpelier in 1599 that Bouet was to take his apprentice along on the impending journey "so as to give him an opportunity to learn and to see distant lands."[7]

The apprentice learned quickly that manual labor had no part in becoming a merchant. Although his activities were concerned exclusively with negotiating, he nonetheless found out that the daily routine could be exhausting. With apprentice trailing behind, the merchant was constantly running back and forth between his cellars, sheds, and attics and his counter, or office, where he kept his books, paper, and money locked up in closets and strongboxes. He kept his own inventory and his own books (sometimes aided by his wife, but only in the largest firms do we find secretaries or clerks). Indeed, bookkeeping was crucial because of the use of credit and the ubiquity of bills of exchange. Most merchants simply kept a chronological record of transactions and noted credit arrangements. Sometimes, however, these books were more systematic. For example, a merchant might organize his books by debtors, on one side listing the name and date of the loan, and then on the opposite page making note of the payment. Like so many business techniques eventually used by early modern French merchants, double-entry bookkeeping was invented by the Italians during the Commercial Revolution of the High Middle Ages, but it spread only slowly into France and was still not widely used even in the sixteenth century. Not until an edict in 1716 was double-entry auditing introduced into public finance.

Investment: Commerce, Manufacturing, Land, Office, and Rentes

Merchants in early modern France had a rather narrow range of investment opportunities. Once they had generated profit from a commercial venture, they could reinvest in commerce, redirect investment to manufacturing, buy land, purchase public offices, or fund private or public loans. Many successful large merchants did all of these in varying degrees, but even small traders sought to buy a parcel of land or make a personal loan when enough capital could be saved to do so.

Of course, merchants began their careers and, if fate smiled on them, made their fortunes in commerce. All merchants, large or small, had one thing in common: as Braudel wrote, "At the end of the day, the goods traveling towards him, in sailing ship, cart or pack-saddle, had to fetch a price which would not only cover incidental expenses, purchasing price and transport costs, but also the profit the merchant hoped to obtain from the whole operation."[8] Everything, then, relied on a circuit that determined profit or loss. The value of whatever flowed in had to exceed the amount invested in what flowed out. If the circuit were broken (loss of cargo, default on credit, or what have you), all was lost. Not surprisingly, merchants labored constantly and painstakingly to work out networks across which goods, credit, and information could flow efficiently.

Some merchants, obviously, were better at this than others. Tax rolls like the Capitation of 1788 in Lyon (based on a more or less progressive system where assessment correlated with wealth) show the average assessment of the négociants at forty livres (contrast that to the silk workers at two or even the artisans at nine). Dowries in the same city in the eighteenth century show négociants to be among the very richest inhabitants in town (although as a whole below the noble officials). They comprised about 6 percent of the population. These figures, however, obscure life stories like that of Jean Pellion, an eighteenth-century master silk winder in Lyon who saved up some capital and tried the jump to the world of commerce. He became a mercer, but he soon found that he had too little capital to cover his debts. When his business collapsed, he took flight from his creditors with his eldest son, leaving his wife and four other children in Lyon. Pellion's sad fate was not unique, for bankruptcy records reveal many others like him and show the fragility of petty commerce.

Successful or not, wholesale grain, wine, wood, and hay merchants would cluster near the wharves on rivers that invariably flowed through the cities and towns of the realm, overseeing the unloading and transporting to markets around town the goods they had purchased from nearby regions.

Figure 4.1. Pierre Landry, *Les heureux fruits de la paix par le rétablissement du commerce*, 1700, Bibliothèque nationale de France

These substantial businessmen, like those who thronged the Quais de Grève in Paris, traveled into Brie, Beauce, or Champagne buying grain, timber, or wine, and arranged for shipment to Paris, by cart or by boat or barge. Water transport was preferred, of course, because it was much more efficient (the same animal-powered energy could pull 100 tons of cargo on water but only 1.5 tons on land), but whether by land or water, the quantities moved could be substantial. For instance, in 1649 a grain merchant bought 400 sétiers of wheat in one transaction in Vitry-le-François, while another in 1654 purchased 60,000 bundles of wood and 4,000 logs for shipment to Paris where they were broken up into small lots and sold, usually on credit, to small retail traders, carpenters, joiners, even bakers and pastry cooks.

This may sound straightforward, but in practice many merchants running large enterprises diversified their operations in remarkably complex ways. For example, Nicolas du Renel, a merchant from the Mediterranean port city of Marseille, shipped soap and oil to the Norman port of Le Havre on the Atlantic in 1587. His Norman operations invested the profit in the purchase and sale of herring and English pewter. The herring he sold locally, but the pewter, of which he purchased large quantities, was shipped along with woolen cloth and paper to Alexandria and Syria in the eastern Mediterranean. The proceeds from sale of these goods were then spent on spices that were, in turn, sent back to Marseille for sale. About a decade earlier he was already trading in the Atlantic through his associate in Rouen. He assumed half the cost of fitting out and supplying a vessel sailing from Dieppe bound for Brazil, where it would take on a cargo of brazilwood, pepper, cotton, and birds for sale back in France. Merchants like du Renel scanned their world for profitable opportunities, and seized them when they spied them. In 1593 du Renel imported wheat from Brittany into Marseille, and then reexported some of it to Genoa in Italy. No matter that a wheat shortage had hit the Marseille markets; he could fetch an even higher price in Genoa, so that was where it went.

A contemporary of du Renel's, Dominique de Laran from Toulouse, diversified his operations as well, and in greater scale than du Renel. Laran traded in iron, wheat, horses, pastel, and above all woolen, silk, and linen fabrics. He would purchase large lots and then resell them in smaller ones. He bought and sold in every major city in France, relying on dozens of factors carrying bills of exchange and even some cash to make purchases, and another extensive team of associates to handle the sales.

Trade in the Atlantic basin boomed from the sixteenth century on, and drew many French merchants into this long-distance commerce. Often the circuit of operations was "triangular." For example, in 1743 Captain de La

Roche Couvert was hired by the merchants who owned the ship *Saint-Louis* to sail from France to Canada laden with supplies for the inhabitants of the French colony of Quebec. Once there the captain was to load a cargo of cod caught in the prolific Grand Banks off the coast of Newfoundland, and this cargo was then to be shipped to and sold in the French colony of Guadeloupe in the Caribbean Sea. The proceeds from the sale of the cod were to be spent on a load of sugar, which was then to be brought to Le Havre for sale, thus closing the circuit and, hopefully, returning a tidy profit to the merchants who sponsored the entire venture.

Merchants were not just traders. As we have seen in a previous chapter, they also became involved in textile manufacturing, in both managerial and investment capacities. Wool and woolens had been put out to workers since the late Middle Ages in towns, suburbs, and nearby countryside, and though the rural work would come to dominate, we still find some cities bustling with textile production throughout our period. Half the artisans in seventeenth-century Amiens, for example, were engaged in textiles somehow, and of course, Lyon was the center of silk production. Indeed, when dealing in higher-quality fabric, merchants tended to keep the work in cities, and this for two reasons. First, merchants could keep a closer eye on the manufacturing and their materials there, and second because urban workers were better trained and thus presented less risk in ruining valuable materials through shoddy workmanship. Coarser fabrics, in contrast, had been put out to rural workers since the sixteenth century (rural labor was cheaper than its urban counterpart, in some places by as much as half).

In some places like Lyon, manufacturing occupied all the merchant's energies, and paid handsomely. The silk industry in Lyon was dominated by an aristocracy of *négociants*. About fifty families commanded one-half of the total production of the Grande Fabrique, the silk monopoly. They controlled the raw material and credit markets; this was typical of textile merchants everywhere. Indeed, merchants were well positioned to manipulate the protoindustrial system because they were aware of market conditions. Supple and adaptable, the merchant employed workers commensurate to demand. During times of slack demand he simply did not provide his rural workers with raw material, and did not pay them, but when demand was brisk he exploited a plentiful labor supply by paying piece rates, the lower the better (for him).

Commerce and manufacturing were not the only sites of merchant investment, as important as they were. Whenever a merchant amassed enough capital he invariably bought land. The return from land was less spectacular than that from commerce, but it had two advantages: it was less risky than commerce and it carried social prestige. As we will see, merchants aspired to leave commerce behind when they could, for that was prerequisite to climbing the social ladder. So merchants bought land when they could, and conditions of the sixteenth and early seventeenth centuries were decidedly in their favor. Commerce boomed and generated capital that could then be spent on acquiring land from a peasantry that, as we saw in a previous chapter, was increasingly pushed into poverty and debt. Peasants had little choice but to sell to raise cash to survive. Landholding merchants then rented out their plots, seldom reinvesting in agriculture but rather using the land rent to fund a lifestyle necessary to demonstrate they had departed the inferior status of merchant.

Upwardly mobile merchants also invested in public offices. We will have more to say about venality of office in the next chapter, but a boggling array of public offices—from customs officials to supreme court judges—were sold by the crown, which was perpetually strapped for revenue. Offices could be lucrative, often more for the fiscal privileges they conferred (in some cases tax exemption) than for the capital they generated, but the greatest incentive was status and access to power. Ownership of office enhanced social prestige, and merchants, avid for prestige, were eager buyers. Office did not necessarily confer nobility (although the number of nobility-conferring offices expanded greatly in the sixteenth and seventeenth centuries), but climbing the social ladder across generations was the ultimate goal of all affluent French families, many of which had their roots and the beginnings of their wealth in commerce.

Merchants tended to buy financial offices more than judicial ones, largely because these were more available (there was much more growth in these types of offices) and because merchants already possessed a knowledge and expertise about finances. Indeed, the first inroad into officialdom made by merchants often occurred in tax farming. Tax farming attracted many merchants, large and small. A merchant would bid with the public authorities for the privilege of a monopoly on collecting a given tax in a given area for a stipulated length of time. The successful bidder would pay the king in advance an agreed-on sum, and then would collect the tax, which included a certain extra sum for the collector's efforts. Tax farms ranged from excise taxes in local markets to customs duties and royal tolls, to the truly enormous farms on the national taxes like the *taille* (the royal tax on personal wealth), and, in the late seventeenth and eighteenth centuries, the capitation and the *vingtième* taxes (also income taxes). The bids ranged from small farms of less than one thousand livres to huge ones of several hundred thousand. Tax farming was a profitable business, in some cases enormously so. In the eighteenth century, the largest tax farmers, associated in the Ferme générale, were fabulously wealthy—among the richest men in all of France.

Successful merchants were keen on leaving commerce behind, and another route out and toward greater respectability was investment in annuities, called *rentes*. Indeed, given the volatility and risk inherent in long-distance trade especially, some *négociants* left commerce not simply for status reasons, but, like men of the fabulously wealthy Depont family in the eighteenth century, for the relative security of land and *rentes* investment.

Private *rentes* (called *rentes constituées*) were effectively perpetual loans to individuals at a specified interest, while public *rentes* were bonds purchased from the crown, the clergy, or the provincial estates, again earning an annual interest. In exchange for the cash up front, the seller guaranteed an annual and perpetual payment in interest. The result, of course, was a mounting debt. Royal *rentes* were begun by Francis I in 1522, and by 1663 payment to rentiers (the holders of *rentes*, or creditors) constituted one-third of the royal budget. *Rentes* offered by the clergy were an even sounder investment than those offered by the state, because the church tended to be a more reliable payer. Obviously, many French people considered the purchase of *rentes* (which paid as much as 6 percent, but which could be substantially lower) an attractive investment option, and, because they were backed by royal revenues or church property, a relatively sound one. This financial technique offered the advantages of low capital investment and a steady return. An investor, called a *rentier*, with enough *rentes* could live on the returns without working. Like land, *rentes* were more secure than commerce, especially long-distance trade, and were favored by merchants who were just beginning careers and had only modest investment capital available.

Work and Culture

With the growth of the market economy came an increased division of labor, and so it is perhaps misleading to speak of the merchants as a coherent group. A hierarchy among traders emerged. At the top were the large, long-distance traders, and at the bottom poor peddlers who carried, often on their backs, a meager stock. In between were hordes of petty wholesalers who stocked the countless urban marketplaces with goods bought in and brought from the countryside. Then there were retail merchants called *merciers* who, according to a French proverb, "sell everything, make nothing." What all of these traders had in common, though, was a calculating mentality with an eye toward turning a profit.

This profit-seeking mentality is likely as old as trade itself, but in a Christian culture it was problematic, giving rise to ambivalent attitudes within the church toward the merchant and his work. In his compilation of canon law in the twelfth century, Gratian said succinctly that "the merchant cannot please God, or only with difficulty," while the tremendously influential theologian of the thirteenth century Thomas Aquinas added that "commerce, in and of itself, has a certain shameful character."[9] The problem for churchmen was that merchants avid for profit run counter to the fundamental Christian teaching that the fruits of this world are not to be enjoyed for their own sake, for this draws the good Christian's attention away from his proper mission, the preparation of the soul for salvation.

Profit-seeking merchants had another problem with the church, for theologians equated the taking of interest with usury, and thus forbade credit. Of course, charging interest was central to the entire credit mechanism and essential to commerce itself. Indeed, it was inherent in the very notion of profit. Still, the church condemned it. Aquinas put it this way: credit and the charging of interest are effectively selling time, and time belongs only to God and cannot be sold. Interest, or earnings on time, is illicit because it is theft from God. A merchant is selling what does not belong to him.

Such religious strictures, if effectively applied, would freeze commerce in its tracks, for credit, as we have seen, was the grease that allowed the trading world to operate. History shows that the church was powerless to enforce its views and, moreover, made accommodations with merchants and commerce. Effectively, it turned a blind eye to the merchant's use of subterfuge to charge interest. For example, interest was sometimes paid as a voluntary "gift," other times as a "fine" assessed when accounts were settled.

The church accommodated commerce in more theoretical ways, too. With the recovery of Roman law in the twelfth century, the powerful concept of public utility and public good was introduced, and Aquinas explicitly accepts commerce as public utility in that it provides the things necessary for existence and not as an end in itself. When conceived this way, commerce becomes remuneration for labor, which for Aquinas and others influenced by his thought was acceptable. Burchard of Strasbourg pointed out, for instance, that "merchants work for the benefit of everyone and serve public utility by bringing merchandise to the fairs."[10] From there it was an easy step to see commerce as a necessity wished by God, and the merchant's work a service to the common good.

Merchants undoubtedly were deeply concerned about their salvation, but increasingly it became apparent that the rhythms of commercial life were not those of the church, and this can be seen most clearly in perceptions of time. Church time was demarcated by the sacred services that punctuated the day, and so time was reckoned by the periodic and regularly organized prayers, or "clerical hours," like vespers, compline, and so on. For the merchant, time was conceived in an entirely different way. Indeed, commerce imposed a different notion of time. What mattered to the merchant, for example, might be the duration of a voyage, or, if the merchant is involved in rural industry, how long it might take a laborer to fashion a certain product. Attention to duration suggests, in turn, that merchants were conceiving of time as an object of measurement, and as it was related to profit, it had a price and a value. In short, time was becoming a commodity.

The merchant's perception of time reveals to us a pragmatic mentality given to calculation and quantification. This is amply evident in late medieval commerce manuals (*Pratiques du commerce*) that some merchants kept and that have come down to us. Here we find the detailed enumeration and description of all sorts of merchandise, of varieties of weights and measures, of coinage, of customs duties. These books are not theoretical manuals about commerce, but rather practical compendiums full of technical information. As Jacques Le Goff notes, they are based, like the merchant mentality itself, in "the concrete, the material, and the measurable."[11]

Even treatises on bookkeeping or on nautical science, both of which increased in number and quality in the sixteenth century and were collected by merchants, were practical and utilitarian. They reflect the merchant's desire for exactitude, and his constant activities involving counting and calculating display an increasingly quantitative mentality. This propensity to think in quantitative terms, in turn, contributed to the elaboration of a mathematical worldview that would assume fundamental importance beyond the world of the merchants. As Jeannin puts it, "Numbers were tools in the service of practical interests, before they became a means to greater understanding of science."[12]

Jacques Savary, author of the *Perfect Merchant* in 1675, refers to "the mercantile profession" and points out that this "profession" was knit together culturally by a common education. For him, education is on-the-job training, and the key requirements in this training are understanding arithmetic and, in his words, "knowing how to write well." He warns merchants against educating their sons at the *collèges*, however, for there they are likely to imbibe a classical education disdainful of commerce. More insidious still for mercantile families, Savary cautions, these sons are likely to form friendships with sons of nobles (*gentilhommes*) who are destined for court or magistracy; in either case, these boys will be culturally predisposed to hold a repugnance for commerce and for merchants. His advice fell on many deaf ears, however, for more and more *négociant* families sent their children to these colleges, precisely because it was seen as an avenue away from commerce and toward the more socially respectable world of officeholding.

How did this mercantile, empirical, quantitative mentality leak into the general intellectual culture? The answer may have had something to do with social history and with the meaning of work, for recall that merchants abhorred manual labor and as soon as commercial success permitted it, they escaped the world of trade altogether. Thus, as they left the mercantile world, they brought with them to the world of refined taste this quantitative mentality. It seems no accident that music (so close to mathematics), judging from the many books in after-death inventories of many former merchants, comprised an area of great interest to merchants. By the eighteenth century the upper crust of the commercial world was moving socially among nobles and royal officials. Masonic lodges, which became quite widespread and popular among France's upper classes in the eighteenth century, were a place where *négociants* and courtiers encountered one another and shared a common discourse focused on wide-ranging affairs of the day.[13] Entry into this culture was further smoothed by reading, and these wealthy merchants were increasingly acquiring books as they broadened their scholarly interests. They read about politics and economics and read newspapers, novels, and plays; in short, they read for both utility and recreation. They tended to be men of pragmatic tolerance, and so religious reading materials are not in much evidence.

Much has been written about the "modern" work ethic that supposedly appeared on the historical stage in the early modern period. This mentality, so the argument goes, prized hard work as its own reward, or in a variation on this theme, such industriousness found expression in a new attitude toward accumulation and so spawned new thinking about profit. Not only was profit sought and desired (it probably always had been, as long as trade existed) but now the maximization of profit became the objective, and efficiency in economic transaction became the guiding principle. Few would question that these characteristics have become central to modern capitalism, but few agree on where, when, why, and even among whom they came to the fore in economic thinking. Were they uniquely Western, or did merchants in other parts of the world also develop them? Did they fully emerge in the early modern era, or earlier or later? And who first began thinking this way? Was it intellectuals who first formulated this mentality that eventually spread to the commercial classes, or the other way around? Max Weber famously associated this new mentality with Calvinism, and though this strain of Protestantism made inroads into France in the sixteenth century, its adherents (called Huguenots) never counted for more than 10 percent of the population, and in the seventeenth century saw its numbers dwindle to almost none. In other words, it cannot be the primary cause for a new, calculating, quantitative, and industrious attitude toward the economy and toward work.

There is no question that by the seventeenth century many educated men were disparaging the idleness they saw all around them, and focused their scorn mostly on workers. Idleness gave rise to libertinage and wastefulness, all loath to a man like Savary, who contrasts them with the proper values of hard work and rigorous accounting that were required in business. The "perfect merchant," for him, clearly already espouses key elements of the modern work ethic.

Current research in other parts of the world finds entrepreneurialism everywhere, and where we used to link the single-minded drive for the *maximization* of profit, the preoccupation with extracting the greatest return from any and every economic transaction, *uniquely* to European capitalism, today scholars are less likely to do so. It is clear, however, that this attitude took deep hold in Europe's (and France's) mercantile classes (and curiously, as far as we know, *not* among the men who worked with their hands), probably among long-distance traders first, and then later found theoretical expression among intellectuals (like Adam Smith). A word of caution, however. Merchants were pragmatic, not theoretical, and guided their actions by a general sense of what worked and what did not.

What Changed in the Work World of Merchants?

It is undeniable that France's economy grew from the late fifteenth century to the end of our period, and after 1550 it is equally clear that increasing amounts of capital were being mobilized in long-distance trade. It is true that rural merchants specializing mostly in agricultural products in short-distance domestic trade represented the bulk of mercantile activity, but, as Braudel has shown, there can be no doubt that in terms of large-scale profits, trade returned more than either manufacturing or agriculture, and overseas shipping profits led the way. This growth, of course, transformed the lives of merchants in myriad ways. The growth in the volume of trade and the reach of the market economy triggered an increase in specialization of mercantile activity. The numbers of urban shopkeepers exploded in the seventeenth and especially the eighteenth centuries, reflecting the expansion and greater organization of the distribution network from the wholesale to the retail level.

More and more goods were finding their way to fixed points of sale, and were purveyed to increasing numbers of consumers during more regular business hours.

The increase in the division of labor in the mercantile world, in turn, exacerbated inequalities among merchants. Indeed, again according to Braudel, a "trade hierarchy" became increasingly pronounced, with high finance "the ultimate development in this direction."[14] Just below the financiers (who were not really merchants at all, and will be dealt with in the next chapter), at the top of the pyramid was a new class of extremely wealthy merchants engaged in long-distance trade. This class could already be glimpsed as early as the thirteenth century in the port cities of Bordeaux, La Rochelle, Nantes, and Rouen, but their visibility would increase dramatically with their numbers and wealth over the next five centuries. The *négociant* became the aristocrat of trade. As such, he looked down on the retail merchant and the shopkeeping artisan. Listen to Charles Lion, a rich wholesaler in 1676: "Do not call me a retailer . . . I am no fishmonger but a commission agent," selling on commission being a distinction that characterized the wholesale merchant.[15] Following the logic of inegalitarian hierarchy, retail merchants, in their turn, looked down on artisan shopkeepers because they worked with their hands. At the bottom of the pyramid swarmed innumerable peddlers, street criers, hawkers, and regraters (petty merchants who bought and sold cheap victuals; many of them fanned out into remote pockets of the countryside looking for cheeses, eggs, vegetables, or an odd sack of grain to haul into the city for sale). This was a trading proletariat (we have already met these folks in our previous chapter on the *menu peuple*), and one that was flanked by a multitude of cashiers, carters, errand boys, packers, porters, loaders, and what have you.

The Expansion of the Market Economy

Before cities became the fixed points of market activity, fairs were the hubs of the European and French economies. Fairs existed everywhere, and in the thirteenth century the fairs of Champagne were the most important market locale in Europe. Held in four different locations and covering most of the year, the fairs served as a quasi-permanent market and a clearinghouse for settling of accounts. A fair, in Champagne or elsewhere, was a "privileged market," and participating merchants from all over Europe enjoyed the security of their person and their property guaranteed by the local political authority—in the case of Champagne, its counts. Special tribunals heard grievances and enforced contracts, but the principal allure of a fair for the merchant was the promise of tax exemption, a privilege offered by the local authority to attract merchants and trade. Fairs were wholesale markets where dealer met dealer for purposes of large-scale long-distance trade and were the meeting places of great merchant houses. Thus, both commodities and money (usually as bills of exchange) were traded. The fair was like a pyramid. At the base we find multitudes of minor transactions in local, usually perishable and cheap, goods, but as we move up we encounter luxury goods that traveled greater distances and were more expensive. Perched at the top was the money and credit market, without which no business could take place at all.

The fairs of Champagne declined in the 1300s as a result of a shift of mercantile activity to cities. The sedentary merchant gradually superseded the itinerant trader, and merchant firms, as we have seen, increasingly established home bases linked in networks of commissioned agents, associates, and factors in branches in other cities. Recent research suggests that the decline of fairs in the early modern period may be overdrawn, however, for despite the increase in the number of urban markets and the development of a transport network, privileged markets were still quite robust in some areas and in some commodities into the nineteenth century. Fairs were still active in eighteenth-century Beaucaire, just across from Tarascon in southern France, drawing products shipped down the Saône and Rhône rivers, especially leathers, hides, and iron. In Guibray-Caen in Normandy there was a fair that drew manufactured goods from the entire western region. Fairs, then, did not entirely disappear; they did, however, gravitate toward cities. For example, thirty-two separate localities near Paris held fairs in the early sixteenth century, while the fairs of Lyon in the 1520s were among the major ones of Europe. The Lyon fairs drew woolens and low-quality cheap linens from all over France, imported in both large and small quantities (the merchant Léonard Arnoux, for instance, brought a single cartload of cloth to the great fair of Lyon in 1509). These textiles were then exported across the Mediterranean to the Levant, where they were exchanged for goods from the East, like spices, that were brought back to Lyon—usually by Italian merchants.

Lyon and its great merchants profited handsomely from the fairs. The value of all trade in Lyon in the year 1523, for example, was about ten million livres, which, as a point of comparison, was greater than all royal revenues in that year. The Lyonnais merchants capitalized on the shifting tastes of France's aristocracy that increasingly defined its status in terms of refinement demonstrated by consumption, comportment, and sartorial splendor. Thus there was a boom in the importation and sale of luxury products, especially Italian silks, a trade that was balanced by the export of wheat, salt, wine, and as we have seen and above all, woolens and linen. As one of the key functions of the fair was as a money market, so too did Lyon become a banking center, financing both trade and, as we will see in the next chapter, the rising fiscal needs of the crown. In 1547, for example, the bankers of Lyon (many of them Italian families that had settled there) floated loans totaling six million livres. Also illustrating Lyon's prime position in long-distance trade, the city became an important market for maritime insurance, merchants purchasing coverage for ventures sailing to such distant markets as London, Amsterdam, Narva in Muscovy, Constantinople, Alexandria, Sicily, Seville, New Spain in the Americas, and St. Domingue in the Caribbean.

Lyon's fairs, just like those in Champagne before them, were fated to decline in the seventeenth century, victims of the shift to sedentary merchant houses, warehousing, and stock and commodity exchanges. Cities became the sites of better-organized distribution networks, and warehouses well served the merchant's needs. As Braudel pithily observes, "The Europe of fairs was turning into the Europe of warehouses."[16] It was also becoming a Europe of exchanges (*bourses*), and merchants in these entrepôts handled every kind of business transaction. Like fairs before them but now in permanent session, exchanges were at once commodity markets, financial markets, and maritime insurance markets. In 1681 Samuel Ricard defined the exchange in his *New Merchant* (*Le Nouveau négociant*) as "the meeting-place of bankers, merchants and businessmen, exchange currency dealers and bankers' agents, brokers and other persons."[17]

The market economy expanded and extended in the early modern period, built up step-by-step. Cities were at the heart of it, and merchants its linchpins. Cities had to be supplied to grow, and grow they did. This means that the regions around cities, their catchment areas, were organized in ways to supply the urban masses and to allow merchants large and small to turn a profit.

Predictably, Paris's catchment area was huge. A traveler on his way to Paris from the Atlantic coastal town of Dieppe wrote in 1728, "We meet nothing but catches of fish, [but it is impossible] to get hold of any of this fish which follows us on all sides. . . . It is all bound for Paris."[18] A traveler from Meaux might say the same thing about cheese from Gournay or butter from Isigny. And this mountain of consumables was carried to Paris (and every other city) by armies of transporters. These hordes of small-time merchants scoured the countryside looking for produce to buy and bring to the city, some just to hawk from temporary stalls on street corners, others, like livestock traders en route to the multitude of stock markets that ringed France's cities, to purchase animals on the hoof to deliver to urban butchers. Some of these markets could be huge, and no wonder, when we consider that in 1707 Paris consumed on a weekly basis 1,300 oxen, 8,200 sheep, and 2,000 calves.

Such commerce put pressure to forge more efficient avenues of transport, and transportation networks did improve in the seventeenth and especially the eighteenth centuries. Road-building programs under the direction of royal intendants and the royal engineers were widespread (the labor provided by peasant workers).

On overland routes innkeepers and haulers were key figures, as Jacques Savary noted in *The Perfect Merchant* in 1675. Innkeepers were often commission agents for haulers, greasing the wheels of commerce by collecting fees from merchants that they then advanced to the haulers.

River traffic had always been more efficient than overland, and that remained the case in the seventeenth and eighteenth centuries, but rivers were still clogged with toll stations. Dozens, for example, dotted the Loire until well into the eighteenth century when the crown, not entirely successfully, tried to eliminate the ones that had been established recently. But because the royal government had to pay compensation to abolish these "privileges," it had less success against the well-established and lucrative ones. The crown also sponsored the digging of canals to facilitate inland commerce, like the one linking Sète with Toulouse that permitted the export into the Mediterranean of cereals from the entire province of Languedoc.

As Braudel observed, "The sea was the gateway to wealth."[19] All along the coasts scurried countless small craft—from little ships to open boats—all engaged in local traffic and thus the counterparts in sea traffic to the haulers and carters on land. Braudel, however, was referring more to long-distance traders than these small-scale merchants. And small wonder, for France's export trade—despite high risk—burgeoned in the seventeenth and eighteenth centuries. Take Bordeaux's export trade in quality wine. Around 1550, twenty-one million liters of wine were shipped out of this Atlantic port. By 1640 that volume had jumped to fifty-one million, joined by 720,000 of brandy. In 1700 the volume had swelled to seventy-five million liters of wine and fourteen million of brandy. Growth continued throughout the eighteenth century. Indeed, between 1710 and 1789 the total commerce of Bordeaux increased twentyfold, much of it with the Americas. Bordeaux, of course, was not alone. Commerce was growing rapidly in all the major ports. Nantes, Marseille, and Rouen joined Bordeaux in commanding 90 percent of France's Atlantic trade (wine, fish, sugar, and slaves were staples). And because the exterior commerce of France quintupled in volume between 1715 and 1789 (recall that prices were up 60–70 percent), the leading *négociants* who controlled this trade joined the ranks of the wealthiest men in France.[20]

Given the attention French men and women gave to distinctions in social status, and the fact that merchants sought to leave "degrading" commerce as

Figure 4.2. Claude-Joseph Vernet, *The Construction of a Road*, 1774, Musée du Louvre

quickly as possible, it may be surprising to find many nobles in the seven-teenth and eighteenth centuries deeply invested in trade. Of course, some opposed such activities as threats to the existing legal and social system of or-der, but many others joined *négociants* in commercial ventures. It seems that the stigma of trade, so quickly shed by rising merchants in the sixteenth and early seventeenth centuries, was less derogatory as the mercantile economy grew. Molière's famous *bourgeois gentilhomme*, so memorably characterized in the 1670 play by Monsieur Jourdain, may well be an avatar of former times. He was ridiculed for his clumsy behavior and despised for his social preten-sions, but behind them lurked a serious challenge to the royally sanctioned social hierarchy. This social construct, however, was an ideology, and busi-ness practices and the creation of wealth were undermining its tenets.

Indeed, the crown itself was complicit in this. In 1627 the king issued an ordinance that permitted nobles to participate in maritime trade without losing rank (an act that had the practical effect of raising the status of the merchants involved in it), and it would not be long before the high nobil-ity was investing (usually silently, for they were not required by law to at-tach their names to the contracts) in all sorts of maritime business ranging from colonial companies to plantations and the slave trade. We know that those who attained nobility in the late seventeenth and eighteenth cen-turies through the purchase of a royal secretaryship (there were over three thousand *secrétaires du roi* in the eighteenth century) were under no legal obligation to cease their business activities. Not one ennobled *négociant* from Nantes, for example, closed his business upon assuming his title of *secrétaire du roi*.

By the eighteenth century, nobles were involved not only in maritime trade, but also in local commerce. The high Parisian nobility invested heavily in large capitalist enterprises, while the *robe* nobles from Toulouse were deeply involved in the grain and wine trade in the region. Their coun-terparts from Bordeaux were equally invested in the profitable Bordelais wine business, as owners of quality vineyards and as shippers overseas of the cherished product. Daniel Roche thus perceives the formation of a single group of commercial capitalists (that included commoner *négociants* and many nobles) that was "the predecessor of the notables in nineteenth-century bourgeois society."[21]

As we have seen, throughout the early modern period, merchants were in-volved in rural manufacturing, an activity that accelerated in the seven-teenth and above all the eighteenth century. Textile protoindustrialization was amply evident in many regions. If we take a slice in time in the Beau-vaisis in the seventeenth century, we find merchant families like the Danses and the Mottes deeply involved in textile manufacture. They owned no looms, and they did not manufacture anything, but they controlled the industry. These merchants knew the markets and the tastes of their clientele, and so they instructed clothmakers to produce the types of cloth in demand. They would supply peasant cottages in the countryside with wool to spin (by the wives) and weave (the husbands); this was wool that they had acquired in Soissonais, Brie, Beauce, or Berry. The merchants would then pay the spinners and weavers for the bolts of unbleached cloth they produced, and the merchant would then take the cloth for finishing to fullers, shearers, and dyers.

Little had changed a hundred years later. In Léon in the mid-eighteenth century, nearly 2,500 peasants wove for 600 merchants. Similarly, around the town of Mans in 1764, we see a dozen *négociants* controlling the manufacturing of textiles in the surrounding countryside. These men lived in town, but controlled 2,000 cottage workshops in three provinces (Maine, Anjou, and Touraine), producing 18,000 pieces of cloth, two-thirds of which the *négociants* exported abroad. Farther to the north, in Roubaix in 1781 we find 40,000 peasant workers (including 8,500 weavers) in the employ of urban merchants who controlled the textile industry.[22]

These operations were organized in the classic protoindustrial way, the putting out system, but rural industry could be organized in other ways, too. Small-scale merchant-manufacturers in seventeenth-century Beauvais, for example, would have a workplace filled with looms, spinning wheels, bales of wool, combs, warping frames, presses, shearing tables, and so forth, and they would hire weavers, beaters, shearers, combers, and so on to make the cloth on-site. These same merchant-manufacturers, however, also would likely "put out" such operations to cottagers, lending or selling looms in the process.

Centralization of operations was not as foreign a concept as we once thought. In the mid-eighteenth century Christophe-Philippe Oberkampf, a Protestant, German-speaking entrepreneur with only a halting command of French, tapped the urban feminine fashion market for printed linens (called *indiennes*). With an eye toward worker discipline and thus improved efficiency, he constructed a factory in the rural village of Jouy-en-Josas, where he employed over a thousand workers, a proletariat of worker-peasants recruited from the countryside surrounding the wall-enclosed factory (which covered over twelve hectares). Paris was the prime market, and Oberkampf raised capital from such places as Rouen and Caen, and imported raw linens from London or as distant as the Levant in the eastern Mediterranean. He was ennobled in 1787 by a king appreciative of his activities.

The Merchant and the State

Measuring the impact of the expansion of the market economy on work in early modern France has been one of our fundamental concerns. Gauging the impact of the growth of the state has been another. As we have seen, the state provided investment opportunities to merchants in the form of annuities (*rentes*) and offices. We will have more to say on these matters in the next chapter when we discuss financiers and royal officials, but here we need to explore the interactions between the state and the merchant in terms of commercial activities.

Commerce and the affairs of state have never been distinct, and the commercial activities of merchants demonstrate amply throughout the early modern period that merchants knew well that fortunes could be made through business relations with the state. The life of Jacques Coeur (ca. 1395–1456) is a very illustrative place to start. Historians have debated whether this fifteenth-century man was a merchant (so argued Michel Mollat) or a royal official (so argued Jacques Heers). In fact, making such a distinction is anachronistic because he was both—and saw no contradictions in his hybrid role (so, most recently, argues Kathryn Reyerson).[23] He was a very active trader and made a personal fortune in commerce, but much of his funding was provided by King Charles VII (1422–1461) and he turned tidy profits for His Majesty.

Coeur was the king's bursar, called an *argentier* then (tellingly, the word *argent* means both "money" and "silver" in French). During his tenure in this office Coeur was instrumental in organizing the royal finances more efficiently, Charles being in constant need of evermore funds (the costs of war were escalating dramatically at this time, and until 1453 the kings of France were locked in the seemingly interminable Hundred Years' War with the English). Coeur reformed the royal tax system, notably in the production and taxation of salt (with extremely lucrative results), and he was closely involved in stabilizing the royal currency by supplying precious metals to royal mints. But the task that was to open avenues of vast wealth for Coeur came with his duties to supply the royal household, especially with greedily coveted luxury goods, silks, and spices. Coeur thus became an international financier and a Mediterranean merchant, and he mixed his private and official public roles seamlessly. The *argenterie* moved with the king's court (until Coeur established it at a permanent location in Tours) and the closeness to the royal entourage meant a ready market of potential commercial clients. Coeur created a vast commercial network that supplied them. His operations were similar to the Italian firms of the Bardi and Peruzzi in the fourteenth century, resting on a far-flung network of enormous scale, with trading operations coordinated by trusted agents and factors (many of whom were from his home region of Berry, and most of whom were either family by blood or marriage, or clients bound to him by loyalty and debt).

In the 1440s his enterprise expanded as he built up trade on the king's behalf and his own. He sought to reduce costs by eliminating the mostly Italian middlemen who sat between his French markets and the source of the desired luxury products in the eastern Mediterranean and Asia. He did this by going directly to the supply markets in the Levant, and setting up a base of operations in Alexandria, Egypt (which was held by Muslims who were more friendly to trade with Europeans than the Ottoman Turks were). He established a network of agencies staffed by his people in France and abroad, counting as many as three hundred factors and agents employed in his enterprises. Indeed, the bishop of Laon remarked that Coeur "has all the merchandise of the realm in his hand and everywhere has his factors."[24] Around Europe he purchased woolen cloth, furs, metalwork, weapons, and rugs and moved them to the East for spices, silks, and other luxuries.

Coeur further reduced his reliance on middlemen by increasingly hauling his and the king's cargo aboard his own ships. Indeed, ships and shipping became a fundamental part of his enterprise. In the 1440s he built up his fleet to at least seven ships, four of them galleys, impressive numbers for the time. He established his shipyards in the Mediterranean port town of Aigue-Mortes (though due to its silted harbors it now is landlocked), and based his French commercial center in Montpelier. Although he would eventually move his operations to Marseille, while he was in Montpelier he established a commercial exchange, attracting merchants who came to make contacts, strike deals, trade bills and exchange money, and share news and information.

Coeur and Charles shared in the profits of these Mediterranean enterprises, the king granting his bursar privileges like tax exemption on imports and even the authority to conscript rowers for his fleets. Coeur, of course, became enormously wealthy, and ready capital and social and political connections opened other opportunities for Coeur to make more money, notably in financial transactions. He often was asked to extend credit to his cash-strapped king and the nobility, in effect providing the means to purchase the products that he himself was providing. He thus made money on both ends.

With such success and influence, Coeur inevitably incurred envy and made enemies, and given the fact that he was of nonnoble origin, the social stigma of trading stuck to him and incurred further hatred from his social "betters," the court nobility (many of whom were in debt to him). Since the thirteenth century royal officials were required to present and justify their accounts to the royal Chamber of Accounts, and Coeur was no exception.

With the mixture of private and official business in Coeur's enterprises, it was hardly possible to separate them, and this rendered him vulnerable to accusations of graft. Coeur had been protected by the king and above all the king's mistress, Agnès Sorel, but when Agnès died in 1449, the king, renowned for his fickleness and mental instability, shifted his favor to another faction at court that included many of Coeur's enemies.

Coeur's fall from grace began with his arrest in 1451 for embezzlement, and after lengthy proceedings he was convicted in 1453 of high treason. A sentence of death was commuted to banishment after the intervention of Pope Nicholas V, but Coeur was still ordered to pay the astronomical sums of 100,000 écus to the royal treasury and 300,000 écus in fines to the king. Whatever was left of Coeur's estate would then be confiscated. He was imprisoned, but in 1454 he escaped, finding religious asylum in several monasteries as the king's men pursued him. He eventually made his way out of France, but not before several close calls. With the aid of his extensive personal relations who had remained faithful to him, he ultimately found refuge in Rome at the papal court and died in exile there in 1456.

State and merchant joint enterprises like those Coeur and Charles VII had forged seem to have fallen out of favor (no wonder, given Coeur's fate), but the state continued to have an active role in commerce. First, as the costs of governance and especially of warfare continued to skyrocket, merchants purveying goods to the crown tapped into a seemingly infinite growth industry. Indeed, consumption by the state was a huge and growing market through the eighteenth century, yielding steadily increasing profits to merchants meeting the demand. But the state as consumer was not its only role in the early modern economy. As the market economy expanded, especially in the Atlantic basin in the sixteenth century, commercial techniques and organization of trade were based largely on private initiative and independent voyages. In principle, wholesale trade, maritime trade, banking, and money changing were all "free" (that is, free of government regulation), although the state got its substantial cut in customs duties and taxation.

It was not long, however, before state-sponsored commercial joint stock companies appeared on the stage. In the late sixteenth century Henri IV chartered a state-sponsored and royally controlled overseas trading company called the Company of the Indies (*Compagnie des Indes*) and in the 1620s the prime minister of Louis XIII, Cardinal Richelieu, did the same. These ventures were short lived, unlike the East India Company and West India Company established in 1664 on the initiative of the royal controller-general (the chief financial official in the kingdom), Jean-Baptiste Colbert. Colbert urged merchants, nobles, and high-ranking judges (called *parlementaires*) to invest in the new companies by purchasing shares, following the crown's initial capital investment of 20 percent. These companies were corporations, and so officially they were charged with fulfilling a function for the common good of the kingdom. In return for this contribution to the public good, the companies were granted exclusive privileges, most notably a monopoly on trade in specified goods and regions, as well as exemptions from customs duties. A general assembly of shareholders elected directors, mostly wholesale merchants, who then ran the company in profit-seeking ventures.

These enterprises were an important aspect of a more general group of economic policies and practices launched by Colbert. Customs policies of the state were totally protectionist, but within France the controller-general envisioned a more unified market and encouraged competition between regions and producers. In terms of labor, Colbert promoted policies that ideally would result in full employment (a requisite for optimal production and thus economic growth). These ideas are already evident in Antoine de Montchrestien's *Treatise on Political Economy* (*Traité de l'économie politique*, 1615), but Colbert extended, systematized, and implemented them. Central to Colbertism is the idea that the public welfare will benefit and national interest be served from a robust economy that in turn requires active government involvement. An archetypal institution of Colbertism that is also very germane to a history of work is the Inspection des Manufactures. The men who staffed this institution (established in 1669), about whom we will have much more to say in the next chapter, were dedicated to Colbert's vision that it was in the national interest to have a well-regulated economy.

Merchants and *négociants*, for their part, were not "free traders" in principle, and to assume they were would be anachronistic. They were not given to abstract doctrines, but rather were entirely practical men bent on making profits as best they could. Certainly they complained bitterly if they perceived inspection and regulation to be detrimental to their trade, but they also recognized benefits that would come with Colbertism. They were immersed in a world of corporatism and privilege, and fully supported regulatory policies when it suited their interests. Indeed, merchants and *négociants* were well represented in the corridors of power, and the antechambers of the royal palace of Versailles were haunted by men representing mercantile interests and lobbying for royal favor.

Small wonder, for royal favor could create fortunes. Consider, for example, the silk industry in Lyon and its leading merchants. The Grande Fabrique, an association of large-scale merchants in the silk industry, completely controlled the industry there and by extension in the kingdom, and had the full support of the royal government. Deemed in the national interest by the crown, the Grande Fabrique was granted a monopoly on all imports of raw silk into France. This gave the silk merchant-manufacturers an insurmountable advantage in the making of silk garments (this industry remained urban, merchants putting out the raw material to dispersed households of weavers, but within the city), severely reducing the competitive position of Tours and Nîmes.

Merchants embraced corporatism and privilege when it suited their interests, and constantly demanded regulation of their workforce. Merchants who were engaged in rural industry were especially vociferous, largely because of the independence that came with workers in dispersed and often remote locations who easily escaped surveillance and inspection. Pilfering of raw materials by workers was especially vexing to merchants. Merchants complained that the materials they "put out" to their cottage workers were not entirely being converted to finished products. Instead, workers would accept the raw material from the merchant and then sell some of it on the black market. For example, in the mid-eighteenth century at Sedan, an important center of production of woolens made from high-quality and expensive imported Spanish wool, weavers would peddle some of the raw wool to soldiers in the nearby garrison; the soldiers in turn sold it in Verviers or Limbourg—to competitors of Sedannaise merchants! In 1773 an inspector estimated the loss from this "ruinous brigandage" at fifty thousand livres a year.[25]

Not only were merchants in favor of governmental protection to control theft, but they also wanted regulation to stabilize the workforce by preventing unlicensed mobility. Indeed, disciplining the workforce was a primary concern of merchant employers, and the notion that employment rested on a contract between free wage labor and the employer was a concept quite foreign to them. Surveillance and subjection of workers geared to limiting their mobility had become a heightened concern for employers, especially in rural manufacturing like textiles or papermaking in the eighteenth century, and merchant-manufacturers pressed the government for legislation requiring workers to carry *billets de congé*, or documents certifying by the signature of the former employer that the worker had left his previous position in good standing (and with the permission of the former employer). As we have seen, this regulatory measure met with resistance by workers and only qualified success in the eyes of the merchant-manufacturers.

Regulatory policies and practices of the government, what historians generally call Colbertism for France (or mercantilism more generally), sprang from the ideology of corporatism. Corporatism, however, was challenged in the eighteenth century by another ideology called liberalism, which espoused a view that regulation was inimical to economic growth and "progress."

Liberalism was an ideology issuing from Enlightenment thought, not from the mercantile community, but as its principles infiltrated government circles, we find a shift in government policy that affected merchants. Between 1749 and 1776, the Council of Commerce, the body within which the Inspection des Manufactures operated, was headed by Daniel Trudaine, his son Trudaine de Montigny, and then Jean-François Tolozan, all dedicated to a liberal policy of "economic improvement." We will have more to say about this movement when we discuss royal officials in the next chapter, but the net effect of the movement on merchants and commerce was a freeing of trade from restrictions on growth and an increase in fraud in mercantile transactions.

With the Revolution, liberal policy ultimately triumphed, and in 1791 a trilogy of laws passed between March and September suppressed the corporate and regulatory regime. With the abolition of inspections went quality control, and for some merchants this was bad for business because it gutted confidence in the marketplace. In the words of Flavigny, a well-known textile merchant-manufacturer in Les Andelys, "Commerce had become a shameful brigandage" in the wake of the "Grand Suppression."[26] In the Year VI the Directory ordered that all fabricants had to put their mark on each piece of cloth they produced, but fraud still reigned nearly unchecked into the time of the empire in the early nineteenth century when the Napoleonic prefects had to take up the regulatory challenge anew.

Scaling the Social Ladder

Throughout society, individuals belonged to ranks, and these états, as they were called, were arranged according to a stratified, vertical hierarchy. This order was an essential element in corporatism. Within general ranks more specific ones held sway, and this was certainly true among merchants. In every city one's official classification by rank went according to the presumed "dignity" of one's function. In Paris, to take a prominent example, there were six corporations that perched at the top of the merchants' (and artisans') social world. They in turn were ranked in descending order thus: the drapers, the wholesale mercers, the hatters, the furriers, the grocers, and the goldsmiths. Behind what appears to be a blending of merchants and artisans lay an internal hierarchy that, not surprisingly, placed merchants at the top of each corporation. For centuries the wholesale wine merchants sought official recognition as one of these superior corps, testimony to the perceived importance of such classifications.

As a group, merchants ranked below the nobility, officially because merchants were engaged in the degrading activity of commerce (never mind that, as we have seen, in practice many nobles were also engaged in commerce, with the blessing of the king!). Merchants, in turn, were loud in their proclamations of difference from and superiority over ranks below them (artisans, shopkeepers)—and signaled the chief mark of distinction as the freedom from working with one's hands. Such a distinction was, in their mind, a badge of honor, and the official recognition of it was announced in the very titles attached to them in official documents, like *honorable homme, marchand* ("Honorable man, merchant").

In 1702 a group of *négociants* petitioned the Council of Commerce to purge their profession, "distinguishing once and for all between the merchant and any manual worker—apothecary, goldsmith, furrier, bonnet-maker, wine-seller . . . second-hand clothes dealer, and also a thousand other trades [practiced by men who are] workers (*ouvriers*) and yet [claim] the status of merchants. . . . The status of merchant [should only be granted to those] who sell merchandise without either making it themselves or adding anything of their own to it."[27]

Within and beyond the mercantile community, then, hierarchy reigned supreme. Wholesale merchants (*marchands de gros*, or *négociants*) were keen to distinguish themselves from lesser traders (especially retailers). Consider this description of a *négociant* by one of them in 1775:

> Let no one judge the superior and distinguished men of this profession by those who are its artisans and who, accustomed to filling orders that, like needs, continually recur, are condemned to live in narrow-minded ignorance. Incapable of broadening their views or perceiving causes other than prosperity or fate, they creep, labor, obey, and all their lives perform a necessary duty that does them little honor. The trader of whom I am speaking, whose status is not incompatible with the most ancient nobility or the most noble sentiments, is the one who, superior by virtue of his views, his genius, and his enterprise, adds his fortune to the wealth of the state. . . . While his vessels, laden with our foodstuffs and the products of our factories, travel in search of goods from the most varied foreign climes, his ministers follow him everywhere, keeping him informed and carrying out his orders. His agents transmit his orders to all the markets of Europe. His name on a circulating note causes funds to be disbursed and multiplied. He orders, he recommends, and he protects.[28]

Indeed, as this quotation expresses, the highest reaches of the merchant community over time could infiltrate that of the nobility. And this, clearly, was the aspiration, albeit the ultimate achievement for only a small minority, of every merchant family. Many families reinvested in commerce and industry only until they amassed enough wealth to leave commerce altogether.

Over the course of the seventeenth century in Amiens, to take but one example among many, the composition of merchant families was almost entirely renewed, with less than one-sixth of the families in commerce at the start of the century still in commerce or industry at the end. Similarly, an eighteenth-century inspector of manufactures wrote in his report about commerce in Cambrai that "the best [merchant] houses having made their fortunes have established their children in public office or the church, or are content to peaceably enjoy their fortunes; not one of them has taken the route of commerce."[29]

This desire to climb the social hierarchy marked merchant aspirations throughout the early modern period. The first step was to amass wealth, then, if possible, to "live nobly," then to have official recognition of the status of nobility conferred by the crown. Rouennais merchants in commerce with the Americas, to take an example of a general pattern, were among the most upwardly mobile merchants in Rouen in the sixteenth and seventeenth centuries.[30] Once commercial wealth was acquired, they would invest it in the purchase of land and office, hopefully launching their descendants toward nobility. Rich merchants like these Rouennais might display their status in appearance, "clad in silk costume and cloak of plush," as a document in 1622 described one.[31] Indeed, the richest Parisian merchants aped the highest aristocracy in luxury display. François de La Rochefoucauld remarked in 1783 that among the wealthy mercantile elite luxurious display was prominent: "The way of life of the merchants of Bordeaux is extremely luxurious. Their houses and commercial premises are on a very grand scale. Great dinners are often served on silverware."[32] Other provincial merchants might be outwardly more sober, but still they poured much of their wealth into resplendent domestic interiors of their elegant townhouses or even more in their nearby country residences. Such were the demands of "living nobly."

In the seventeenth century a reaction against wealthy and upwardly mobile merchants was led by the established nobility of the robe and sword (no matter that many, perhaps most, of the former were descendants of trading families). In their desire to close their ranks, they gained an ally (at least for a time) from the king, who saw such mobility as undermining the social order whose stability he believed rested on an immutable hierarchy. In the 1660s Louis XIV endorsed investigations into the backgrounds of families to determine whether the official requirements of nobility had been met (called *recherches de noblesse*). Pretenders simply "living nobly" and surreptitiously claiming the status were to be ferreted out.

Such royal policy was short lived, however, for before long Louis himself reversed course and was easing the path to nobility for successful merchants.

Again, we see clearly the pressure that an expanding mercantile economy (and the creation of wealth) could exert on social ideologies, exposing the contradictions that lay beneath. Among those who were "living like nobles" and were candidates for ennoblement were wholesale merchants, the *négociants*. An edict of 1701 defined them as "all those who carry on their business in warehouses, selling their goods by bales, crates, or entire pieces, and who have no shops opening on the street or any displays or signs on their doors or houses."[33] The king was now keen on encouraging this kind of commercial activity, and so also exempted from derogation nobles (*gentilhommes*) in wholesale trade. Indeed, the Sun King's father, Louis XIII, had issued an edict in 1629 (though it never took effect because the Parlement of Paris refused to register it) that would have conferred the privileges of nobility, but not nobility itself, to persons who had maintained for five years a trading vessel between two and three hundred tons, and would continue to enjoy these privileges as long as they maintained such a vessel.

As the crown recognized that commerce served the national (and royal) interest, the theoretically rigid boundaries between the rank of nobility and high commoner were further undermined. Royal secretaries (*secrétairies du roi*) and treasurers (*trésoriers de France*), among the most available ennobling offices to upwardly mobile commoners, were allowed by law to continue their business without losing noble status. A wholesale merchant, in other words, could become a noble while remaining a *négociant*—and some did.

The pressure to bring the wealthiest *négociants* into the ranks of the privileged estates was unrelenting. In 1767 an order (*arrêt*) of the royal State Council (Conseil d'état) had this to say:

> His majesty wishes and intends that they [the *négociants*] shall be regarded as living like nobles and that they shall be given rank and precedent in this quality in municipal and other assemblies and enjoy all the honors and advantages that are associated particularly with exemption from militia service for themselves and their sons, that they shall have the privilege of wearing swords. . . . His majesty reserves the power to grant each year two special letters of ennoblement to those of the said wholesale merchants who have distinguished themselves in their profession and, preferably, to those whose fathers and grandfathers have exercised this profession with the honor that it demands and who continue to distinguish themselves in it.[34]

Not surprisingly, after this *arrêt* was issued, letters of ennoblement became numerous. Those most favored, predictably, were the wealthiest, and the wealthiest wholesale merchants were those who sailed the most numerous vessels. The nature of the cargo mattered not a whit, for the slave-trading *négociant* Laffon-Ladébat was ennobled in 1773, his letter specifying that his "honor" resulted from the "transport of more than 4,000 [Negroes to the West Indies], in fifteen shipments" since 1764.[35] Another ennobled *négociant*, a man named Gourlade, could count thirty ships in the port of Lorient that were his, a fleet that imported or exported goods exceeding forty million livres in value. Customs on this cargo alone sent four million livres to the royal treasury. Small wonder the king would favor such a contributor to the national interest with nobility!

As all of these examples make clear, wealth was essential to upward mobility, and fabulous wealth the key to the door of nobility. But how did one gather such wealth? Even in the early modern period, it took money to make money, and so the primary precondition for economic success was a good start in life, and then an advantageous marriage as one entered adulthood. Because of the centrality of credit to commercial transactions, merchants needed backing to float loans, and creditworthy families were essential.

We can find family dynasties in nearly every important commercial city in France. In seventeenth-century Amiens the Morgan family established veritable monopolies over the wholesale trade in dyestuffs, spices, and textiles, amassing huge fortunes in the process. Jacques Morgan possessed ten thousand livres in 1646, a fortune that grew to eighty thousand by 1688. His son Jean-Baptiste commanded a total worth that dwarfed that of his father, however, reaching four hundred thousand livres by 1695. The son was ennobled in 1709 as a *secrétaire du roi*, but he continued in business. Merchant families dominated rural industry as well, like the Danses and the Mottes in the Beauvaisis in the seventeenth century. These families amassed prodigious fortunes. Indeed, one of the Danses had a total wealth of over a million livres at the turn of the eighteenth century.

Securing family financial success meant advantageous marriage, and the wealthy tended to marry the wealthy. Of four hundred marriage contracts between *négociant* families sampled in Bordeaux between 1782 and 1784, over half of the new couples had more than two hundred thousand livres when they married (combining the bride's dowry and the husband's contribution), this at a time when a laborer's wage was about two hundred livres a year. Turned to commerce, ample dowries provided the necessary capital for large-scale ventures. Marriage also cemented a kinship community that was of inestimable importance. As we have seen, in-laws, uncles, and nephews became business partners and associates, essential for business confidence and contacts. Indeed, the bonds of kin forged through marriage were nearly impossible to sever. Not even the occasional open confessional split within a family of Protestant and Catholic would fracture the kin solidarity in business ventures.

Notes

1. Pierre Jeannin, *Merchants of the Sixteenth Century*, trans. Paul Fittingoff (New York: Harper and Row, 1972), 79.
2. Mary S. Hartman, *The Household and the Making of History* (Cambridge: Cambridge University Press, 2004).
3. Jeannin, *Merchants*, 51.
4. Quoted in Jeannin, *Merchants*, 44–45.
5. Quoted in Jeannin, *Merchants*, 94.
6. Quoted in Fernand Braudel, *The Wheels of Commerce*, trans. Siân Reynolds (New York: Harper and Row, 1986), 410.
7. Quoted in Jeannin, *Merchants*, 89.
8. Braudel, *Wheels of Commerce*, 169.
9. Jacques Le Goff, *Marchands et banquiers du moyen âge* (Paris: PUF, 1969), 70.
10. Le Goff, *Marchands et banquiers*, 80.
11. Le Goff, *Marchands et banquiers*, 104.
12. Jeannin, *Merchants*, 112.
13. Dominique Julia, "L'Education des négociants français au 18e siècle," in *Cultures et formations négociantes dans l'Europe moderne*, ed. Granco Angioline and Daniel Roche (Paris: Editions de l'EHESS, 1995), 221.
14. Braudel, *Wheels of Commerce*, 376.
15. Quoted in Braudel, *Wheels of Commerce*, 377.
16. Braudel, *Wheels of Commerce*, 96.
17. Quoted in Braudel, *Wheels of Commerce*, 97.
18. Quoted in Braudel, *Wheels of Commerce*, 38.
19. Braudel, *Wheels of Commerce*, 361.
20. Daniel Roche, *France in the Enlightenment*, trans. Arthur Goldhammer (Cambridge, Mass.: Harvard University Press, 1998), 159. On merchants and merchant culture in general, see chaps. 4–6.
21. Roche, *France in the Enlightenment*, 418.
22. See Jonathan Dewald, *Pont-St-Pierre, 1398–1789: Lordship, Community, and Capitalism in Early Modern France* (Berkeley: University of California Press, 1987), and Liana Vardi, *The Land and the Loom: Peasants and Profits in Northern France, 1680–1800* (Durham, N.C.: Duke University Press, 1993).
23. Kathryn Reyerson, *Jacques Coeur: Entrepreneur and King's Bursar* (New York: Pearson Longman, 2005).
24. Quoted in Reyerson, *Jacques Coeur*, 68.
25. Philippe Minard, *La Fortune du Colbertisme* (Paris: Fayard, 1998), 296.
26. Minard, *Fortune du Colbertisme*, 361.
27. Quoted in Braudel, *Wheels of Commerce*, 383.
28. Quoted in Roche, *France in the Enlightenment*, 167–68.
29. Minard, *Fortune du Colbertisme*, 191.

30. Gayle K. Brunelle, *The New World Merchants of Rouen, 1559–1630* (Kirksville, Mo.: Sixteenth Century Journal Publishers, 1991).

31. Quoted in Braudel, *Wheels of Commerce*, 382.

32. Quoted in Roland Mousnier, *The Institutions of France under the Absolute Monarchy, 1598–1789: Society and the State*, trans. Brian Pearce (Chicago: University of Chicago Press, 1979), 238.

33. Quoted in Mousnier, *Institutions of France*, 229.

34. Quoted in Mousnier, *Institutions of France*, 230.

35. Mousnier, *Institutions of France*, 231.

CHAPTER FIVE

∽

The Professions
Medical Practitioners, Men of the Law, and Government Officials

Early modern French people tended to think of work in physical terms, and framed their conceptions of status according to who worked with their hands (a sign of social inferiority) and who did not. The situation became more complicated than this simple dichotomy suggests, for increasingly we find men (and some women) involved in nonphysical activity describing their actions as "work." This was true of medical practitioners, men of the law, and government officials. As we will see, the conceptualization of intellectual work was closely related to the historical process of professionalization (however incomplete during the early modern period).

What the Men and Women of the Professions Did

Medical Practitioners

Medical practitioners in early modern France were men and women who offered a wide range of health services. Perhaps surprisingly to modern eyes, educated physicians were only a small group among a variety of healers, any of whom could be consulted in time of sickness. Formally trained barber-surgeons and apothecaries were also consulted for healing, but the medical world included legions of untrained and noneducated male and female practitioners. True, as Laurence Brockliss and Colin Jones point out, the core of the medical world were the physicians, surgeons, and apothecaries, but outside this core was a "penumbra" of popular healers. Brockliss and Jones hasten to add, however, that both the core and the penumbra occupied a unitary world. Since at least the sixteenth century they shared a medical discourse derived from Galen, the medical authority from antiquity, and a surprising amount of cultural exchange flowed among them.[1]

Physicians, Surgeons, and Apothecaries
What distinguished the core from the penumbra was, first, the law: the core was "sewn into the fabric of the early modern state." The crown legally granted this core corporate privileges (which encompassed teaching and training, either at a university in the case of physicians, or by apprenticeship in the case of barber-surgeons and apothecaries) that it upheld in public law. The second distinction, although not watertight, was that the core was clustered in towns and cities, while the penumbra worked the villages and hamlets of the countryside.

The legal incorporation of physicians, surgeons, and apothecaries created a tripartite hierarchical division within the official medical community, with the physicians at the top. These doctors claimed to master the arts of diagnosis and prescription, and treated internal ailments (they rarely operated on patients, leaving that to the lesser surgeons). Physicians were university educated and literate, and moved in higher social circles, associating with urban and sometimes even courtly elites.

Surgeons came next in the hierarchy, and straddled the worlds of intellect and craft. On the one hand, they claimed an "art" to the performing of operations (and so associated their trade with the intellect), but, on the other hand, there was no escaping that part of what they did was deploy manual skill, for they often cut into patients with a knife. Unlike physicians, they mostly treated external maladies, primarily bone fractures and flesh wounds.

Apothecaries were like surgeons and artisans in that they were usually organized into guilds that supervised standards and the training of apprentices, but they also had a foot in the world of commerce. They claimed that their practice of preparing drugs and medicine was an "art" as well, but law required that they could dispense medications only when directed by a physician. Society ranked apothecaries beneath physicians and surgeons (but higher than barbers once barbers were separated from surgeons), although apothecaries themselves were keen to assert their dignity and elevate their status by emphasizing their place in the world of medical arts rather than the more lowly mercantile and artisanal world. From the sixteenth century we see them increasingly stressing a textual basis for their knowledge and a simultaneous separation from the openly commercial spicers and grocers while they increasingly excluded women from their ranks.

The above description of the "core" of medical practitioners is more precise than the reality of the delivery of health services in early modern France. The kingdom had no uniform standard of qualification in the three branches of medicine (there was considerable geographic diversity), and sharp distinctions between some corporate members and noncorporate practitioners are actually difficult to sustain. We need not look far, for instance, to find surgeons encroaching on the privileges of physicians, or apothecaries dispensing medicine on their own. Moreover, within the "penumbra" we find practitioners often claiming "privileges" to engage in medical work. Sometimes these were even legal—a license granted by a municipal government, for example. Or they were rooted in tradition, as when a religious house had a hospice and dispensary and justified medical practice as a form of Christian charity.

Folk Healers, Empirics, and Charlatans

If we confined our view of the medical world to its core, we would miss most of its practitioners, for the world beyond the core was populated by multitudes of folk healers, empirics, and even charlatans. Folk healing was rooted in the popular culture of the countryside, and its practice (and its effectiveness) depended on a set of values and beliefs that were shared by the community. Like saints and the local priest, folk healers were often regarded by villagers as a kind of protector of people, animals, and even crops. The folk healer—whether a man or a woman, for females were prominent practitioners—was not an outsider, and usually worked not for fees but for "gifts." That is to say, his or her work was not integrated into the market economy. The folk healer passed his or her skill, knowledge, and special gift (often assumed to have been granted by God or a saint to some distant ancestor) to a carefully chosen successor. Sometimes little books of healing secrets were kept and passed down through generations. Healers mixed empirical remedies (herbs, salves, potions, and the like) with rituals that mingled religion and magic (signing the cross, invoking saints, laying on of hands, using sacred objects, and so on). Many healers, perhaps surprisingly, were literate and had exposure to popular texts like the *Grand Albert* or the *Petit Albert* from which they might glean formulas. These manuals originated in learned circles in the Middle Ages, but by the early modern centuries they were circulating widely in rural popular culture.[2]

Many villages and small towns had sedentary empirics practicing medicine alongside the folk healers. Where folk healers usually claimed some special gift for their knowledge and craft, sedentary empirics usually gained their expertise through practice. Usually part-time practitioners, these men and women were frequently artisans, shepherds, or farm laborers, and occupied a stable place in the medical marketplace. Most rural empirics were generalists, engaging even in veterinary medicine (the blacksmith was the most common village veterinary empiric). In towns, however, we find evidence of greater specialization, above all in bonesetting. In 1726 a certain Bellet, a master roofer in Paris, was prohibited from practicing bonesetting, a trade he had carried on for some time and in which he had developed enough renown to threaten the established surgeons. His ready clientele were other roofers, for whom broken bones were an ever-present occupational hazard.

As this example illustrates, the practice of unlicensed empirics was often denounced in law and by the "core" practitioners. One might at first suspect that such denunciation was based in a concern for malpractice, and it is true that we readily find examples of medical intervention gone badly awry. Historian Matthew Ramsey recounts the grim story of a young man from the village of Sainte-Reine in eighteenth-century Burgundy who had an inflammation in his abdomen. He consulted a priest who also enjoyed a reputation as a healer. The curé diagnosed a fire consuming his patient's intestines, and to cool it he applied a bellows to the patient's rectum. The effect was deadly.[3] Examples like this were not uncommon, but we would be mistaken if we assumed that physicians and surgeons condemned such practices only because of the results (licensed medical practice was not much more effective in curing, after all). True, they found the practice of empirics as ignorant and lacking in science, but they were as much concerned about encroachment on their privileged sphere of operation and the monopoly of it that was at the heart of their social identity and status.

We find empirics in the historical record throughout late medieval and early modern times. As early as 1352 King Jean II described empirics in a royal ordinance as "many persons of both sexes, women and old wives, monks, rustics, some apothecaries and numerous herbalists, besides students not yet trained in the faculty of medicine or coming from foreign parts to the town of Paris to practice, ignorant of the science of medicine."[4]

Later, educated observers often suspected empirics and folk healers of witchcraft. In the early seventeenth century, Pierre de Lancre, the renowned demonologist and witch-hunter, wrote of four kinds of healers whose work was ignorant of the art and science of medicine. Two he saw as innocent (those who had divine grace and enjoyed the gift of healing, and others of extraordinary sanctity who could heal through prayer). He condemned, however, the impostors who faked the divine healing gift, and magicians, enchanters, and witches who used spells and incantations that worked only through the power of the devil. Not surprisingly, large numbers of healers, especially women, were swept up in the witch hunts that plagued France for a hundred years after the middle of the sixteenth century.

De Lancre may have been partly right in perceiving impostors among the rural healers, for some were frauds, tricksters engaged in an elaborate confidence game. Thomas Courval de Sonnet, a sixteenth-century physician from Rouen, wrote of some empirics he saw as being more interested in "external appearance" than in "doctrine and experience." He described one healer "dressed in superb and magnificent clothes, wearing at his neck chains of gold." Courval may have been troubled by an appearance of fraudulence, but he was equally insulted by such garb mimicking that of the true physician, who typically was recognized by his distinctive robes, gold rings, long cloaks, yellow gloves, ermine collars, and special hats.[5] In the eighteenth century the *Dictionnaire de Trévoux* defined *charlatan* (and the feminine form, *charlatanne*) as "empiric, false physician, who gets up on a stage in the public square, to sell theriac [an elaborate antivenin and panacea] or other drugs and who gathers the people by magical tricks and clowning, to sell his drugs more easily."[6]

Winnowing out the frauds is nearly impossible for historians, however, for we have no way of gauging effectiveness. We do know that all itinerant empirics behaved in the same way. They came to villages amid a carnivalesque atmosphere, singing and dancing, then selling their wares or performing operations from makeshift benches. They claimed to treat the entire body and so sold emetics and purgatives as well as soaps, cosmetics, and sundries. Their products did not come cheap, and they generally charged even more than a local surgeon or apothecary (if one were in the vicinity). It might cost a farm laborer more than a day's wages for an oral consultation, and a week's worth for a written one. Itinerant empirics were the most visible medical figures in the French countryside throughout the early modern period, and, as they bought their goods in the cities and sold them in the villages, they contributed to the emerging market economy that was urban based but reached its tentacles into the countryside.

Female Medical Practitioners

The sixteenth-century physician Jean de Renou complained that " there is no miserable village in which one cannot find some old witch who meddles in setting dislocated bones, raising . . . the wombs of women, and I hardly dare say it, the paralytic organs of men, by means of I know not what muffled words that they gnash between their teeth."[7] Typically, Renou is as much concerned about boundary transgression (females in male preserves) as malpractice, but he does signal the prevalence of women in medical care. More reputable was the work of religious women, such as those who nursed the ill in the Hôtel Dieu in Paris, but significantly their work was not deemed medical by male commentators. The work was administered and governed by women, and these men allowed no clear recognition of nursing as a vocation or a profession. Regardless of whether men recognized the women's activities as properly medical, some townswomen, like those in sixteenth-century Tours, were the sole medical practitioners treating the illnesses of foundlings and abandoned children. Their duties went beyond breast-feeding, for they were expected to have knowledge of how to treat everyday childhood ailments—and were paid by the town council to do it.

Next to folk healing, and certainly overlapping with it in many instances, the most common female medical practice was midwifery. Midwives were supposed to treat patients only in childbirth, but in practice they were consulted on more general matters, especially by women about medical conditions of a female nature. We find women practicing midwifery throughout the early modern years, but we also see incursions by men into this sphere. By the late eighteenth century we hear male observers like Louis-Sébastien Mercier opining about how this came about, once again revealing the male bias against female capacity. "At the beginning of the last century," Mercier wrote, "such a profession was unheard of among men. . . . But the women charged with these duties, being ignorant or careless, maimed or crippled some of the children they helped into the world, besides adding to the number of imbeciles by compressing one or two heads; and the end of it was that propriety yielded to common sense, and the race of *accoucheurs* [male obstetricians] came into being."[8] As we will see, the masculinization of obstetrics would only slowly take hold, for as late as 1708 there was published in Paris a book by P. Hecquet with a title that clearly reveals the author's sentiment: *On the Indecency of Men Birthing Women* (*De l'indécence aux hommes d'accoucher les femmes*).

Men of the Law

Lawyers and Notaries

When we examine what lawyers did in early modern France, we first must make the important distinction between barristers (*avocats*) and attorneys (*procureurs*). The attorney handled the procedural aspects of a case. He was the first lawyer consulted by a litigant, and was called on to steer cases through courts, taking care of procedural matters like filing motions or gathering evidence. The barrister might be consulted by the attorney or client for legal advice, and he had the sole right to plead either written or oral arguments before the court, and then only in civil cases (by the royal Edict of Viller-Cotterets of 1539, accused criminals lost the right of legal counsel). Barristers were formally trained in jurisprudence at a university and earned a degree as doctor of law, while attorneys received their training in long apprenticeships, serving as clerks for as many as ten years. Moreover, unlike barristers, attorneys had to purchase their office from the crown before they could practice.

Not surprisingly, much like surgeons relative to physicians, attorneys were perceived to hold an inferior status to barristers. Officially confined to the "mechanical" tasks of the law, they were akin to artisans, and due to the cost of purchasing their office (which increased sharply in the sixteenth century) and the modest income they derived from their practice, they were often seen as rapacious, similar to the reputation of merchants. They were constantly squeezing their clientele for payments, all the more abominable when barristers charged no fees, instead simply receiving "honoraria" for their work. Until the middle of the seventeenth century most served as legal counsel to nobles, religious houses, municipalities, and the like, or held positions in courts or royal, civic, or seigneurial administration. Indeed, especially in provincial towns and cities with royal courts like Rennes, Douai, Besançon, or Toulouse, barristers dominated city government. Relatively few barristers practiced courtroom defense.

Notaries, like attorneys and court scribes (*greffiers*), were men of practice rather than theory. They were trained in a kind of apprenticeship where they gained knowledge and skill through practical training, much like artisans or attorneys, paying fees to masters and remaining in their service for stipulated periods. In an effort to distinguish themselves from the lowly artisans, however, notaries never tired of pointing out that their work served the public good more than that of artisans and merchants (stained by the drive for economic gain). Its importance, therefore, placed them in the upper echelon of the corporate order. Indeed, they called themselves a "company" rather than a "community," a further effort to distinguish themselves from guildsmen.

Notaries were not only recorders of legal records, but, responding to the expansion of the market economy, they also became important brokers of credit. The use of credit grew rapidly in the early modern era, and the crown required that any loan (*rentes*) of more than 100 livres had to be notarized. This meant business for notaries. In mid-eighteenth-century Paris, over 40 percent of notarial acts involved credit transactions. Notaries were well placed not only to record such transactions, however, but also to arrange or broker them. As brokers, they brought borrowers and lenders together. Sometimes, as Hardwick has discovered in Nantes, they even served as bankers, holding cash provided by a lender until a suitable borrower could be found. During the sixteenth and seventeenth centuries such credit brokering became commonplace, and was an essential component in the credit networks at the lowest levels (as we will see, large-scale credit networks were dominated by financiers).

Officials

Did France have a bureaucratic state in the early modern era? It is true that if we look at the eighteenth century, we can see a technical corps of royal administrators. Philippe Minard has revealed in meticulous detail how such a bureaucratic body—the inspectors of manufactures—emerged under Controller-General Jean-Baptiste Colbert in the seventeenth century and operated until the Revolution. Clearly these men, and others like those trained in the Royal School of Roads and Bridges, were the first bureaucrats (*fonctionnaires*) in the modern sense of the term. As Philippe Minard writes, "The public function [of these corps] is defined by statute, by precise rules of recruitment, by career trajectory, by hierarchy and obedience."[9] These men held royal commissions and thus answered directly to the state and were recruited based on technical competence.

When we speak of government officials, however, we must be careful not to impose assumptions about modern bureaucratic structures on the administration of governance in early modern France. Surrounding the emergence of a bureaucracy so well charted by Minard was a world of officialdom dramatically different from it. In short, we must be attentive to the multitudes of types of office men held in government administration. It will be helpful first to distinguish between royal officials (those working in the direct service of the crown) and seigneurial officials (those staffing the offices of lordships that, as we will see, had much to do with local governance). Yet even within these two general categories we must also distinguish between a center and a periphery, the former closer to the center of power (the king) than the latter (those who worked in the provinces, and though they might be royal officials, their interests and tasks would be firmly tied to the locale). The numbers of men working in all these categories grew over the early modern years, driven by the growth of the state that was marked by an expansion in the ranks of officials both near the center (the royal administration focused on the court) and in the provinces.

Let's begin with the center. The primary business of kings was twofold: making war and attempting to maintain order among their subjects. Thus the warfare state and what historians call the judicial monarchy marched arm in arm throughout the early modern centuries. Kings built their power in part on the administration and distribution of law (to maintain order) and the collection of taxes (to pay for war), and so kings gathered around themselves specialists in justice and finance. Vast sums of money were required to wage war, and because taxes proved inadequate to the need, kings beginning in the fifteenth century struck on the useful expediency of venality of office—the selling of government posts. The result was a swelling class of government officials of dizzying variety, but also a group of men who had a private, proprietary stake in public power. As we will see, the farther from the center, the less effective was royal control of this mass of officials. As a result, in matters of law royal sovereignty was deeply compromised by provincial interests and privilege.

Close to the king we find officials who defined their tasks in terms of service to the king and the public welfare he represented. The primary duty of office, then, was an unswerving loyalty to the person of the king. By the fifteenth century these men were emerging as a significant element in the judicial monarchy, and a fundamental characteristic of public power from 1450 onward would be that of the royal office. Those staffing offices closest to the king—chancellor, controller-general, royal councilors, masters of requests— were at the top of the pyramid. A degree of expertise was required of these royal servants (although by modern bureaucratic standards the various duties of these men were elastic in the extreme), but by the sixteenth century a professional caste dominating the most important offices at the center of power had emerged. Most of these men were trained in the royal household, usually as masters of requests (*maîtres des requêtes*), in a form of apprenticeship, and we find examples of offices passing through three or even four generations of the same family.

Radiating from the center and descending hierarchically were provincial royal offices. At the apex of the provincial hierarchy were the judges of the royal judicial courts, the Parlements, of which there were twelve by 1700. Five had existed since the fifteenth century (Bordeaux, Dijon, Paris, Toulouse, and Grenoble), three were added in the sixteenth (Aix-en-Provence in 1501, Rouen in 1515, and Rennes in 1554), and the other four in the seventeenth (Pau in 1620, Metz in 1633, Besançon in 1676, and Douai in 1686). Each of these courts, of course, was staffed by hundreds of venal officers—from judges down to tipstaffs, ushers, sergeants, guards, and jailors. Add to these "supreme" courts the hundreds of first instance bailiwick courts (called *bailliages* in the north and *sénéchaussées* in the south), and the Présidial courts that were created in 1552 as an intermediate appellate jurisdiction between them (there were initially thirty-two of these, but their numbers swelled to sixty-five by 1600 and a hundred by 1764), and we have a picture of a judicial administration teeming with venal officials.

There would be little point in multiplying this list of royal offices, for the clear picture that emerges is a mushrooming venal royal officialdom. It was also one that was only partly responsive to royal intentions. Many formed companies that, like all corporations, were granted self-regulative privileges from the crown and thereby had significant control over their own affairs. Even in Paris at the dawn of the Revolution we find 48 commissioners at the Châtelet who were organized thus, as well as 113 notaries and 237 attorneys at the Châtelet. Each body had its common treasury, regularly electing officers to manage business and finances, and a flourishing social life with regular meetings, masses, and feasts. In 1665 there were about 8,500 royal judges in France for a population of 17 million, but that is merely the tip of the iceberg of officialdom for we need to add to this number the men who worked the 20,000 to 30,000 seigneurial jurisdictions. This quadruples the number of judicial officials across the kingdom.

For judicial officials of whatever stripe, royal or nonroyal, the key function was the ordering of civil society, and the key element here was the preservation and devolution of property. As Zoe Schneider has recently written, "Justice was designed to provide good order in the public sphere, and to protect the interests of property and households in the private sphere."[10] Royal officials in theory represented the king's will embodied in legislative sovereignty, but in day-to-day workings in ordinary courts throughout the realm we find thousands of these men deeply immersed in defending and advancing private interests, frequently their own. The cash-strapped crown may have desperately wanted to extract resources from its subjects with no opposition, and certainly wished to have an officer corps that would carry out its will, but it ran up against local elites who expended much energy defending their property from royal predation.

The most effective way for the elites to resist was to occupy the place where the boundaries between public law (royal will) and private law (property) met, and to police them. They did this by dominating local offices—both seigneurial and royal—and invoking age-old, royally sanctioned customary law. Provincial customary law codes were overwhelmingly concerned with private property rights that former monarchs had recognized as legitimate, and there were well over three hundred such provincial and local codes operative in early modern France. Local officials constantly invoked this law to counter new royal edicts, ordinances, and regulations that were often designed to tap the wealth and property of French families. As men trained in the law, these officials navigated a complex course between crown law (as Schneider points out, by the late seventeenth century royal law amounted to "a haphazard collection of well over a million ordinances, edicts, arrêts, and declarations"),[11] customary law, and even unwritten local traditions.

Monopolizing knowledge and practice of law was an indispensable means to local power, but equally important to dominating the localities was the common practice of cumulative officeholding. The same man might simultaneously occupy such posts as mayor, alderman, judge, receiver of taxes, lieutenant of police, subdelegate of intendants, president of salt warehouses, treasurer of parish churches, or overseer of hospitals. Moreover, such cumulative practices often spanned royal and seigneurial offices, rendering the local judicial system effectively a single one operated mainly by the same groups of families. France's provinces, therefore, were dominated politically by a local governing class fused together by marriage, legal education, and offices that concentrated much of local administration in its hands. Economically calculating as well as politically powerful, this class used its offices as a mechanism for acquiring land, cash, and more titles—that is, authority and prestige in the locality that allowed them "to wade deeply in the revenue stream."[12]

Financiers

No less than the judicial state, the financial administration was venal, expansive, and complex. There were the royal Chambers of Accounts, courts responsible for auditing the collection of royal finances (there were eleven by 1715), the Courts of Aids, charged with adjudicating financial disputes (there were twelve by 1715), the Bureaus of Finances (staffed by royal treasurers, among others, who oversaw tax collection), and salt tax courts (the greniers à sel). In 1542 King Francis I created sixteen généralités (staffed with receivers, etc.), units of tax collection that subsequently would become intendancies (intendants were an oddity in the royal administration for their office was nonvenal, and they answered directly to the king's inner circle of royal officials). In the first half of the seventeenth century there were twenty-two of them, and by 1700, thirty.

Throughout the early modern era, the expenditures of the crown always ran ahead of income. Kings tried various ways to raise revenue, most notably venality, borrowing, and taxation. Indeed, all three were intertwined, as venal officeholders were responsible for the taxation system, and credit and debt were at the heart of its functioning. As in the judicial sphere, thousands of venal financial offices were sold, yet despite these offices and officials, France had no centralized system. As a result, control of the flow and forecasting of the revenue stream was almost impossible. The tax system was not systematic, and was complicated in the extreme. Comprising a mixture of direct and indirect taxes and dues, as Controller-General Jacques Necker put it at the end of the Old Regime, "at most one or two men each generation can come to fully comprehend it."[13]

The venal royal office of receiver general was created in 1542 and charged with controlling direct taxation, at that time essentially the *taille* (a tax on personal wealth). Originally there were sixteen receivers general, but their numbers grew to forty-eight in the eighteenth century, and scores of receivers particular were added along the way. They enjoyed great independence and amassed private fortunes through their public capacities. Each had his office, his strongbox, and his employees whom he hired and paid. His only obligation to the state was to render his accounts for auditing by the Chamber of Accounts. The receivers general advanced to the king agreed-on sums of money that they then recuperated from the *taille*, allowing for an extra cut for themselves. By the eighteenth century the direct taxes of the *vingtième* and the capitation also came under their purview. The venal treasurers general did the same in the *pays d'état*, the regions of France where, because of provincial privileges, *généralités* were not established.

As the example of the receivers and treasurers general illustrates, as in its judicial system, private interests were deeply embedded in France's financial system. Royal finances depended on intermediaries, seen no more clearly than in the operation of the financiers (among whom we count the receivers and treasurers general). These men (in the seventeenth century it was a pretty small circle—about a thousand) would draw investment money to themselves, then loan it to the state at rates favorable to themselves. Good credit in private credit markets was essential to attract funds to channel to the king (after all, they had to stand guarantor to the monies advanced to him), and so we should not be surprised to find them involved in whatever profitable ventures they could find, public or private. We therefore find them provisioning for war (a handsome return came from providing the king's military with food, horses, weapons, clothing, boots, and so on), and investing in land, textiles, and above all commerce and banking.

Tax farmers, or *traitants*, worked in a similar way as the financiers described above, but they would be directly involved in the tax system, especially the gathering of indirect taxes. The tax farmer would bid for a contract with the king that would grant him the sole privilege to stand guarantee to the state for collection of a certain amount of tax in a certain district or region. He would pay the king a specified sum in advance, collect the tax, and then pocket the difference between the bid and the amount actually collected. As a result, as the great French historian Fernand Braudel wrote, "A fantastic share of the nation's wealth remained in the hands of the tax-farmers who levied tax on salt, tobacco, wheat, imports and exports of every kind."[14]

Much of the front money to the tax farmers was put up by an aristocracy generally forbidden to engage in such degrading actions directly. According to legislation, their names did not have to appear in the contracts (only the name of the responsible party did—the tax farmer himself), but by silently channeling revenues from land or office, they were, albeit indirectly, among the most important and influential investors in the king's finances.

Work and Culture

Gauging the meaning of work among doctors, lawyers, notaries, officials, and financiers brings us up against the concept of professionalization. Because the meaning and history of professionalization has been much debated of late, and because its history in early modern France has much to do with our central themes of social status, state, and market, a few words about it seem in order here. As Toby Gelfand has written, "Modern concepts of professionalization emphasize the formation of a fairly homogeneous elite, which established authority over a given occupation by virtue of acquired knowledge and consequent expertise. Uniform standards of training and certification reinforce the collegial nature of modern professions and foster a high degree of competence, autonomy, and social prestige."[15] The characterization of a profession in modern society has at its center an unequivocal delimitation of a specific occupational competence, a freedom in disciplining the exercise of the occupation, and an autonomy in its relationship to its own clientele.[16]

When invoking these definitions of professionalism in our study of work in early modern France, we must guard against the danger of essentialism, the practice of defining concepts prior to empirical research and then imposing them upon that research. Instead we need to observe and explain how men come together historically to form what would become professions given the specific contexts within which they lived and worked. It would be best, then, to start with an inquiry into how knowledge and skill were used by its owners. Clearly knowledge systems can lead to prestige and power, and can have symbolic value. When shared by individuals and expressed by a common discourse not shared by others, they create distinction and quite often associate occupation with honor. Knowledge systems can, therefore, help form status groups with a shared consciousness that take their place in the overall division of labor. The use of knowledge and its association with a certain social status, in turn, contributes to a production of social inequality (hierarchy) through organizational closure and exclusion. Practitioners gain control of their training, admission to practice, and evaluation of standards of performance, sanctioned by education and credentialing. The honor associated with occupational status then contributes to a sense of esteem about the kind of work performed, and denies it to proscribed "others."

Professionalization has more than a social and symbolic face, however, for it also may be related to public authority (often certified or sanctioned by the state, and/or incorporated into the functioning of the state) and, because it is informed by the organization of work, it always pertains to the market in some fashion. As we have seen most vividly among medical men, occupational groups sought control over the market by controlling the supply of practitioners and the fields of their practice, often by driving off and delegitimizing competition. These exclusionary strategies are called *expertise*, and they assume a monopoly over the knowledge system they express.

Medical Practitioners

In the contemporary West we have grown accustomed to thinking of work in terms of an ethic, an activity that gains value by the effort put into it. Before the eighteenth century we rarely hear medical practitioners describe their occupation that way. The sixteenth-century doctor André Du Breil hints at the future when he describes his medical knowledge as acquired through "labor, work, and study."[17] When we place those words in context, however, we discover that he is pointedly contrasting it with diabolical knowledge, and his sense of work identity is rooted in a concern for distinction from unlicensed practitioners, especially women. The eighteenth-century surgeon Jean Bernier is no different from Du Breil in the obsession for distinction, for he described unlicensed practitioners as ignorant, dirty, uneducated or ill educated, socially déclassé, and morally suspect, the opposite of the upright surgeon who possessed "studies, principles, and character."[18]

Indeed, "professional" work identity throughout the early modern period is inextricably bound up with personal honor, social esteem, and hierarchy. Victor Lamothe, to take a well-studied eighteenth-century example, was a medical doctor from Bordeaux, and he was fiercely proud of the title *médecin* attached to his name. It was a badge that was an essential component of his personal and professional identity, and it was a sign of the status and respect that was supposed to come with it. He wrote that "when one is in the position to choose a profession, one must make a choice that is not only honorable, and estimable, but also honored and esteemed." Indeed, in Bordeaux physicians as well as barristers were classified *nobles hommes*. Part of the "esteem" that Lamothe wrote about, and his identity, too, rested in his conviction—a typically "enlightened" one—that medical science contributed to bringing progress to humanity. Professional duty and public service were inseparable, however, from his drive to "fulfill the duties of his rank (état)."[19]

The emergence of empiricism in the formation of knowledge no doubt also contributed to the sense of worth that medical practitioners, first surgeons and later physicians, had for their work. Ambroise Paré (1510–1590), like his contemporary Paracelsus, emphasized the importance of experience as much as texts in the formation of knowledge. He told his fellow surgeons that "thou shalt fare more easily and happily attaine to the knowledge of these things by long use and much exercise, than by the reading of bookes, or daily hearing of teachers. For speech how perspicuous and elegant soever it be, cannot so vively expresse any thing, as that which is subjected to the faithful eyes and hands."[20] Such a view was a social and intellectual threat to learned physicians in the sixteenth century who saw experience as socially degraded because of its association with manual labor. By the eighteenth century, however, empiricism had shed its association with artisanal labor, and for many physicians (though certainly not all) had become an essential means of knowledge formation.

Lamothe and men like him had a strong sense of professional, social, and personal worth associated with what they did, but it was not always shared by others in society. Lamothe himself voices concern that the "medical profession" is neither honored nor esteemed, a view echoed by Mercier when he writes of medical science "to-day [as] nothing more than a brazen and accredited charlatanism; its practitioners know its emptiness, uncertainty and confusion, but hold to it none the less for their pocketbooks' sake. . . . The doctors owe much to the empirics who waste no time in philosophy, but set to work to observe the reactions of the human body. These are less fruitful in argument, possibly, than the Faculty, but the cures they accomplish discredit the learned experts."[21]

Views like Mercier's may reflect resentment about the cost of medical care (beyond the means of many, for surgeons and physicians charged the equivalent of a daily wage of a prosperous artisan), and no doubt many licensed medical men did earn enough to occupy a place in the socioeconomic hierarchy generally on a par with men of the law. Although we can find the very rich and the very poor in their ranks (especially among surgeons), according to the capitation tax in Lyon in 1788 the average assessment of the "liberal professions" may have been only three-quarters of that of the wholesale merchant, but it was over three times that of the artisan and over ten times that of the average silk worker.

Sadly, we know far less about how female medical practitioners identified with their work. Much of their work, as we have seen, was associated with charitable nurturing of the ill or attending to births, clear indication of cultural assumptions about the natural or spiritual inclinations of females. These are male presuppositions, of course, and there is little indication if and how women may have thought differently. The historian Natalie Zemon Davis has suggested that women had a "joint work identity" with their husbands, revealed by their actions in widowhood.

The case of the widow Clément Bardin in 1551 seems to confirm Davis's point, a flash of light briefly illuminating a dark landscape. Bardin sued in court in Lyon for the right to continue to practice her deceased surgeon husband's craft. She claimed that she had an *intellectual* right (based in her learning the craft alongside her husband) as well as a material "property right" (she possessed the shop and tools) to do so. The Corporation of Surgeons countered her suit and lost. The court ordered Bardin to pay nine livres for a mastership that would admit her to the corporation and allow her to practice as a surgeon. The "joint work identity" signaled by Davis seems to have infused Bardin's thinking about her work.[22]

The example of Jeanne Lescallier suggests another medical woman with a professional work identity. Once again court records are our source, and once again we find men opposing females engaged in medical practice. Lescallier was tried in various courts in the 1570s for infringing on the work of the male medical community. The physicians claimed she did not have university medical qualifications, and so labeled her an unlicensed and illegal "empiric" who was paid for her work. In her defense the views of her patients of twenty years were summarized thus: "They have received infinite commodities from Jeanne Lescallier . . . who, for having watched them and knowing their temperament and complexion, has so dextrously aided their children and their families in all their illnesses . . . and even a larger number of poor people that she treated by charity." Amazingly, Lescallier described her own work as that of a doctor, saying in court that "it is not the title nor the profession, but the operation, in such a way that he who knows well how to medicine and cure is the true doctor."[23]

These are sixteenth-century examples. We could point to the work and writing of Louise Bourgeois in the early seventeenth century as further evidence that women medical practitioners possessed a work identity. The cultural assault of males on female work in the seventeenth and eighteenth centuries, however, signals a masculinization of medicine and points toward gender distinction being a fundamental characteristic of emerging professionalization. In short, medicine in particular and professions in general were becoming male preserves.

Historians debate whether medicine became a genuine profession during early modern times. Toby Gelfand holds that medical professionalization emerged during the revolutionary period and was "the result of an abrupt and definitive break with the past rather than an evolutionary process."[24] Perhaps this is true, if we opt to answer the question by looking for a full-blown profession with all its modern attributes. More satisfying and less essentialist, however, is the gradualist perspective of Brockliss and Jones. The medical world may have been organized along different lines from its modern counterpart, but the medical men of the early modern age were increasingly defining their work as distinctive.

Lawyers and Notaries

The debate about professionalization applies to men of the law as much as medical practitioners. Barristers, in contrast to physicians, surgeons, and apothecaries, were never officially organized into *corps*. If we follow Matthew Ramsay's definition of a liberal profession "in terms of a loose set of simple criteria, particularly a distinct identity as a professional group, an established body of theory taught in institutions of higher learning, uniform standards for training and performance, an independent governing body, and a monopoly on certification and practice," then by the eighteenth century barristers fit the bill.

Gradually in the late seventeenth and early eighteenth centuries barristers began to regulate themselves, the Parlement and the crown relinquishing their formerly active role. By 1696 barristers had attained the rights to distinguish themselves from other legal practitioners (notably notaries and attorneys), to oversee recruitment into their ranks, and to disbar members. The leaders of the Order of Barristers summed up the regulatory stance by announcing that "those who are at the head of this Order have considered that, since it is founded on honor alone, this honor cannot be maintained except by an exact discipline upon all those who compose it. Every year this body elects one of its elder members according to the order of the Tableau to the title of Standard-Bearer [*bâtonnier*], who for this year is its head . . . and whose function is really the maintaining of discipline among lawyers.'"[25]

But how did the order impose its discipline? It had no written rules, and there exists no record of appeals to state authorities to back it up. It is true that at the turn of the eighteenth century there had appeared a didactic literature that spelled out the various rules and responsibilities of barristers (including rigor of internship and training), but none of these works were official. What they do reflect, and this is the important thing, is a cultural orthodoxy among barristers characterized by shared assumptions about and values of their work.

The historian Robert Nye recently wrote that the "French bourgeoisie" of the nineteenth century sought honor through their work and believed that diligence in a profession like law or medicine could ensure that honor and secure social standing.[26] We can see this sentiment already in the early modern period, especially among lawyers. Barristers molded a professional self-conception that was based on social status as much as career definition, on a way of life more than a function. They displayed a homogeneity in life styles. Not all barristers were wealthy, but most hailed from propertied, cultivated, often legal families; their median tax assessments in the latter half of the eighteenth century placed them below financiers and the high magistracy but comfortably above artisans and tradespeople. Usually barristers were more sober consumers than the aristocracy, and often dressed in subdued colors of black and maroon. Their *état* also dictated where they might live. In Toulouse, for example, they clustered in two distinctive and distinguished parishes with judges and high municipal officials. The uniting factor among barristers, Berlanstein writes, "was not a common type of work but rather a participation in the honor of the profession."[27]

From at least the mid-sixteenth century, legal practice became more exclusive as lawyers became more conscious of their status and took measures to protect it. As we have seen, this prompted a growing distinction between barristers and attorneys, the latter falling in status, and the former ascending the scale signaled by the possession of a university doctorate degree (which could take six to eight years to earn). Throughout the seventeenth and eighteenth centuries barristers continued to consciously set themselves apart by establishing standards of conduct and even appearance for their members, and enforcing them with draconian discipline. When one joined the Order of Barristers, one assumed not only a title but an identity. As David Bell notes, the oath of membership emphasized legal practice as "a vocation, a public service that demanded a degree of self-sacrifice."[28] By the eighteenth century the barristers were defining their worth in terms of utility, as usefulness to public welfare. They also stressed their independence, grounded in a pride in their disinterestedness and their refusal to charge a fee for their services. These men self-consciously situated themselves in the shift to the politics of public opinion that marked the second half of the eighteenth century, often referring to themselves as the "voices of the nation." The lieutenant general of Paris, d'Argenson, was not far wrong when he reportedly called the

Paris bar "a sort of absolutely independent little republic at the center of the state."[29]

Barristers also shared the value of hard work as part of their identity, a clear reflection of the emerging work ethic that penetrated the minds of medical practitioners as well as lawyers. The Bordeaux barrister Delphin de Lamothe wrote to his brother Alexis in 1755: "Many things are necessary for success in this profession: health, taste for work, and what work! Hard work, continuous work, engrossing work."[30] This sentiment can be found in many eighteenth-century handbooks for barristers where one need not look far to find a description of law as a burdensome and laborious profession. Hard work and diligent application along with a sense of public utility became essential aspects of a barrister's identity. He was convinced of the elevated purpose and public worth of his calling. Barristers like the Lamothes of Bordeaux proudly held a professional creed that emphasized their calling, their honor, and their independence. What emerges in the eighteenth century is a shared value system that binds the culture of lawyers together. Cultural conformity was further fostered by a sociability focused on the Palais de Justice, or courthouse, a shared physical space that was at once the common site for work and a symbolic space where legal ritual (and thus a display of belonging) was played out. Here were channeled the social relations of the whole profession into a dense network of sociability.

In Chalons-sur-Marne in the first half of the sixteenth century, 40 percent of notaries were also attorneys, but as costs of the offices rose in the seventeenth century the two practices diverged. In the sixteenth century they occupied a similar place in the social hierarchy (on par with master artisans) and shared similar social origins (petty legal officials, like court clerks or bailiffs, and the artisanal elite), but during the seventeenth century we find attorneys rising above the notaries. Both notaries and attorneys, however, remained distinctly inferior to barristers. In the eighteenth century the author of a legal treatise, Claude de Ferrière, described the profession of barrister as "noble and independent" but dismissed that of the attorney as "vile, abject, and degraded."[31]

As in most emergent professions, an increasing self-awareness of the specificity of their work marked notaries and attorneys. Identification with their work deepened as they increasingly defended their privileges as a group. We know relatively little about attorneys, but studies of notaries demonstrate that even in the sixteenth century "the principal care" of the corps of notaries was to protect its members against competitive encroachments and to maintain the privileges granted them by law.[32] In 1561 the royal Ordinance of Orleans stipulated rules for the trade, including requisite age, examinations, and so forth, and in 1583 the crown formally granted heritability of office and writings to notaries. Notaries likely underwent technical training akin to that of scriveners. Among the latter the apprentice's body posture and each finger of the hand holding the pen were strictly regulated by a master to arrive at uniform letter formation. The result was an expertise based in a "technology of the hand."[33]

Like doctors and lawyers, a notary's honor was bound up with his work. He authenticated formal acts, and so his good name and credit were paramount and associated with the integrity of the documents he produced. Not surprisingly, we find in notary manuals as early as the sixteenth century the ideal notary described as sober and serious, with a quiet and dignified devotion to duty. His function was to secure public confidence by guaranteeing the integrity of private transactions, and as such, as Furetière wrote in his dictionary in the late seventeenth century, the notary was a "keeper of public faith." Throughout the early modern period, notaries thought of themselves as safeguards of public order who contributed to social and political stability and maintained civil society.

Officials

Although there was no strict juridical definition of nobility in the fifteenth and sixteenth centuries (it was acquired through common consent), the prestige of the traditional nobility was increasingly challenged by the emergence of another form of nobility with a different set of values, not so much replacing the traditional warrior nobility but certainly competing with it in terms of social prestige. We find this new nobility first among judges of the royal courts. Dressed in long gowns that became their symbol, they differentiated themselves from the ideal of the traditional nobility and countered the chivalry and largesse of the warrior with measure, compunction, and competence acquired through education, often in a university. Indeed, a university education gave these men the taste for a certain kind of work based in intellectual study that rendered a specific competence and convinced them of the value of it. In the sixteenth century some offices, the most elevated of the "robe" (as the high magistracy was called) like masters of request, presidents and councilors in the Parlements, tax courts, and chambers of accounts, and the treasurers of France, were recognized by the crown as noble by customary and "gradual" means; that is, it took three generations to arrive at full nobility.

This new class of high officials tended to adopt self-defining attitudes and comportment that centered around a devotion to the king and a sense of duty to the public welfare that the monarch embodied. As such, royal service was the source of the officers' prestige and social rank that was displayed through association with the monarchy in public ceremonial. A collective identity took hold and, especially among judges, was reflected in an emphasis on the dignity and seriousness of their office.

In 1610 Charles Loyseau penned a *Treatise of Orders and Plain Dignities* that expressed this value system; this was a work that would remain influential throughout the seventeenth century. In it he defined an office as "a dignity with public function," the "public function" referring to the office-holder's service to the king and the "dignity" of the status that the official gained from such service. The king, of course, was considered divinely chosen and his missions assigned by God, so officials, especially royal judges, likewise viewed their tasks as divinely sanctioned. This ethos of public duty to a sacralized state embodied by the king marked the identity of magistrates for much of the seventeenth century. As we move into the eighteenth century and see the gradual desacralization of the monarchy, however, we find officials purging their persona of its religious elements yet retaining the notion of public duty.

An identity inspired by public service seems to have taken hold in nascent *fonctionnaires*, or bureaucrats, of the Old Regime, men like the inspectors of manufactures, royal engineers, and other men of the various technical corps of the royal administration. They held commissions from the king to comport themselves faithfully in his service, but their modernity is heralded by their oath to work diligently in the public interest by employing their knowledge. As Philippe Minard writes, "The unity of an administrative corps is . . . the product of a work of identification and interiorization, of an adherence to shared values and beliefs."[34]

One of the values these men shared was the association of their activities with hard work and social status, if Michel Huet de Vaudour is any indication. A subinspector of manufactures in Rouen in 1751, he even describes his work as a *métier*, and one marked by endless toil: "I am at work like a galley slave . . . I work night and day like a slave in order to earn the approval of my superiors and to be able to advance myself in my rank."[35]

Public service, hard work, and social status are associated in the lives and attitudes of the Depont family of La Rochelle as well. Over the course of the eighteenth century men of this clan made the step from commerce to officialdom, leaving the insecurities and risks of commerce for the security of investment in land, annuities, and office. Across the transition, they retained the mentality of valuing work. We read in their abundant letters, so astutely studied by the historian Robert Forster, how they abhorred sloth and self-indulgence, favoring moderation and diligent effort. When Paul-François

Depont came of age in the second half of the eighteenth century, his family had amassed riches suitable to the noble lifestyle, but simply living nobly was not for him, for he was driven to have some occupation. He became a royal official and viewed this group as a corps apart from the landed nobility, one that viewed itself, in Depont's words, as a "service elite."[36]

Paul-François' son Jean-Samuel followed in public service, eventually rising to the office of intendant. Prior to this he had served seven years as a councilor in the king's privy council, the Conseil d'Etat Privé, and ten years before that as a master of requests. Jean-Samuel's long apprenticeship was not exceptional, nor was his gaining of administrative expertise and a sense of public service that all future intendants were expected to have. As a master of requests Jean-Samuel "had been carefully trained as a professional who understood the business of government, the range and complexity of its functions, and the responsibilities of power."[37] As he rose through the ranks of public service, Jean-Samuel continued to embrace the values of his clan and of other public officials: hard work and a moral condemnation of idleness.

Officials like Depont or the *fonctionnaires* who shared his work ethic may have served the public, but they were no men of the people. Indeed, they viewed their *état*, or rank, as socially superior to the multitude. Jean-Samuel Depont, like most high officials, was very wealthy (the family fortune was based above all in land, but he earned a tidy sum from loans and tax farms as well), and judging from his writings he felt he was far above the people. He was eager to claim esteem and respect, and in the hierarchical world of early modern France, this meant distancing himself from those below him.

Not every official, of course, was so high minded. We know surprisingly little about the world of lesser officialdom, but a recent study by Zoe Schneider casts some light into this dark corner. She finds that the men of this "class" comprised a distinctive brotherhood, a "community of the mind." University trained, they knew the law—royal, but even more importantly, customary and local—a knowledge that gave them power and influence in their locales. And they used this position of influence to achieve wealth; this allowed them to acquire more offices as well as land and annuities. Their ambitious social aspirations did little for their reputations among the populace, however, all the more troublesome when we consider the "breathtaking rate" of increase in the number of venal offices in lower tribunals. Schneider finds in some Norman jurisdictions that the number of royal offices in the ordinary courts increased fivefold over the course of the seventeenth century.[38]

There is an irony here, for men like Depont, or Huet de Vaudour, or no doubt the ordinary officials in the provinces, claimed their status and esteem from public service but held themselves aloof from the public they supposedly served. Moreover, this was a public that had historically despised the very existence of the royal official. Already in 1452 Jean Juvenal II warned the king: "God grant . . . that those who serve you may be as attentive to the common good . . . as they are to their own advantage."[39] At the Estates General of 1484, the Third Estate (the commoners) complained to King Charles VIII of the "malice and covetousness" of certain "perverse and wicked officials" and urged the king to relieve his subjects of the "multitude of officials . . . and their wages."[40] The contemporary Christine de Pizan is no less critical when she writes that officials should be appointed for their virtue and intelligence, but she concedes that usually they advanced through favor or the aid of friends and patrons. Concern about venality undermining quality in royal officialdom had been voiced since the beginning of the sale of offices. The Third Estate at Tours in 1484 reminded the king that "if anyone is promoted to offices through [venality], virtue and knowledge will be of no account . . . the most 'expert' are not appointed, and those who are, seek to recover the price of the office through extortion."[41]

Public sentiment had not changed significantly by the eighteenth century, although now the world of public officials had grown such that the negative connotation of bureaucracy as redundant and useless government employees had emerged. Mercier writes that "bureaucracy" is "a word recently coined to indicate, in a clear and concise manner, the overgrown power possessed by simple clerks who, in the various offices of the administration, make up and push forward all sorts of projects, which they find most often in dusty drawers in the offices, and which they favor for reasons of their own, good or bad. . . . These ministerial offices have such great power, and power that is so generally felt, that the people have created a new word to describe it."[42] He continues elsewhere in the same vein: "When one considers with a philosophic eye the idlers and the useless people . . . such as . . . the court clerks, ushers, bailiffs, paper-shufflers, and thousands of other personnel who live off taxes . . . you realize how few are occupied with bringing forth from the earth things that are really valuable."[43]

Financiers
The public perception of financiers was negative as well. Mercier calls them "crocodiles," a "ravaging and detestable group," an opinion that was evident in the seventeenth century as well. No doubt this sprang from the same soil that fed their own positive self-perception, for like officials, they saw no contradiction in being dedicated to the state (as all public officials claimed to be) and profiting from it.[44] Much like Jacques Coeur in the fifteenth century, they all felt that their service to the king should be profitable, even if their

critics saw this profit as theft. As Françoise Bayard pointedly writes, "It is un-deniable that they are very attached to the state; it is no less incontestable that they are interested as well in the means from which they can enjoy its riches."[45]

In the seventeenth century the big financiers formed a close-knit group of trusted friends and families, a network that was linked often by marriage. They formed a nearly closed caste, with the existing ones controlling the ap-pointments of their replacements. A high degree of professional competence was demanded, and promotion was reserved for the most capable. The Ferme générale, the greatest institutional expression of this network, in the words of Braudel, "was like a mighty clan, with a network of marriages and old or new blood ties."[46] The wealth of the great financiers gave them entry into high society, and during the seventeenth and especially the eighteenth cen-turies they socialized with the high nobility, sharing their culture expressed in forms of leisure and education.

The *fermiers-généraux*, perched at the apex of this class of financiers in the eighteenth century, attended the best salons. They graced their estates with exquisite gardens, their homes with collections of tapestries and sculptures, and their tables with luxurious faience. By the eighteenth century they were placing their sons in the military or in royal administration (some even be-came intendants or ministers) and were marrying their daughters into the nobility—that of the robe much more than sword as the latter was more re-sistant to the penetration of a moneyed class into their ranks.

What Changed in the Work World of the Professions?

Medical Practitioners

Change marked the world of early modern French medical practitioners, and, as with all the groups we have studied so far, it was characterized by the three salient developments we have highlighted in this book: (1) the increase in hierarchy marked by the advance of corporatism, (2) the expansion of the state, and (3) the growth of the market. These developments reflect three different visions of medical organization. The supporters of traditional hier-archy gradually constructed a corporate medical community of surgeons and physicians over the sixteenth and early seventeenth centuries, a system that reached its apogee in the seventeenth century but still remained legally in-tact until 1791.

Alongside the corporate system of organization emerged what Brockliss and Jones call the "statist" form, one based more on bureaucratic than cor-porate principles. Royal ministers increasingly advocated a rational, state-directed administration of public health under the authority of the crown. In this essentially eighteenth-century development, we see the emergence of public health practitioners, above all in serving the military but gradually in public hospitals as well; these were men who were salaried by the state and operated outside the corporate system of surgeons and physicians.

The third development that altered the organization of medical practice was the expansion of the market for health services. The commercialization of health delivery accelerates dramatically in the eighteenth century, marked by a growing demand in some quarters for an unregulated market. This vision directly opposed the more heavily regulated corporate and statist visions. At the outbreak of the Revolution all three visions had their supporters, but the statist and commercial views were ascending toward dominance.

Surgeons and Physicians

Throughout France, the corporatization of the world of work gathered speed in the sixteenth century, and this clearly affected the medical practitioner. From the perspective of the crown, incorporation was a way to exert control over subjects, but in such a way that corps would regulate themselves in accord with legally defined and royally sanctioned rules. Such licensed bodies not only theoretically granted their members certain privileges, above all the monopolization of their practices in a given locale (usually a town or city), but they also recognized a certain social rank, a visible display of honor and social status. As such, these privileges were jealously guarded. Physicians, surgeons (who gradually expelled the lowly barbers from their ranks), and apothecaries were all organized in corporations, but this prescriptive system did not preclude these practitioners from encroaching on one another's terrain. In practice, in other words, uniform monopolies were very difficult to enforce, especially as the demand for medical services grew.

The surging demand was partly met by more apothecaries, physicians, and above all, surgeons, but as we will see, the numbers of empirics, or unlicensed medical practitioners, grew as well. Empirics are impossible to count, but one historian estimates that the numbers of physicians and surgeons increased in the early modern years, from about 400 physicians and 2,000 surgeons in the 1530s to nearly 1,800 and 8,400, respectively, by the 1650s. The eighteenth century saw truly voluminous growth, for Brockliss and Jones suggest that by the 1780s there may have been as many as 25,000 surgeons working in France. Not surprisingly, surgeons were nine times more prevalent in cities than in the countryside. Physicians were not nearly as numerous as surgeons, perhaps only 5,000 in all of France in 1789 (and unevenly distributed—they were most prevalent in the south, least in the west, and always concentrated in cities and towns).[47] Overall, it is unmistakable that growth marked the medical world. In the city of Caen alone between 1750 and 1792 the entire licensed medical population of physicians, surgeons, apothecaries, dentists, midwives, and so on increased by nearly 40 percent amid an overall demographic surge of about 25 percent.

Throughout the early modern period, surgeons were widely distributed, with nearly four hundred corporations by the second half of the eighteenth century. Almost half of these were in towns with fewer than four thousand souls. Until the eighteenth century, unlike those of the physicians, surgeon communities were classed with those of artisans, called *arts et métiers*, and as "mechanical" trades they trained their practitioners by apprenticeship (rather than in schools and hospitals) and journeymanship (which, as with many artisan guilds, included a *tour de France*). Also like artisans, master surgeons evaluated apprentices and journeymen for promotion to mastership by examination of their skill as well as their morals. There thus emerged a group identity, one that distinguished surgeons from artisans at one end (despite the similarities) and from physicians at the other.

In the late seventeenth and eighteenth centuries changes set in that would alter the world of the surgeon irrevocably. As we have just seen, this was a time of numerical expansion of surgeons. The corporations remained legally intact, but their authority and autonomy was undermined. In 1692 Louis XIV legislated a common, kingdomwide system of apprenticeship. Statist organization was further propelled in the late seventeenth and early eighteenth centuries when local surgical communities found themselves increasingly tied to an elite group of Paris surgeons, led by the king's own. The corporate structure remained (apprentices and journeymen remained explicitly beneath masters in legal status, and surgeons retained monopolies over practice), but gradually royal appointees were placed in local corporations. These appointees were point men in the application of royal legislation that established for all surgical communities a common framework that standardized licensing, granting of mastership, examining and certifying not only surgeons but also midwives, bonesetters, dentists, and so forth. The king also established a school for surgery in 1724 and an academy in 1731, both with the goal of creating educational standards for surgeons. Surgical schools were then set up in provincial cities, and gradually such training began to challenge and then to supersede apprenticeship. In 1730, royal legislation required all surgeons, even at the village level, to be masters. A royal declaration in 1743 required a university arts degree for master surgeons and formally forbade them to work as barbers. In 1772 the crown legally abolished apprenticeship and elevated surgery to the level of a liberal profession and ended its historic association with the manual trades.

These changes for surgeons spelled a growing separation from physicians who traditionally had had a close hand in the affairs of the surgical corporations. Before 1650, colleges of physicians (corporations in their own right) had increasingly asserted control over the knowledge content and certification of all three branches of trained medical practitioners, and had thus reduced the autonomy of surgeons and apothecaries. Corps of physicians, however, would be no less immune to statist intervention than were those of the surgeons. Traditionally diplomas from the medical schools of Paris and Montpelier granted the licensed physician the right to practice anywhere in France, although other, lesser faculties carried only local authority. Developments in the eighteenth century rendered this no longer the case. By 1700 there were nineteen faculties of medicine, and their licensed practitioners were fanning out across the kingdom. In 1707 a royal edict required all physicians in cities and towns to hold the degree of *licencié* from one of the medical faculties. The numbers were still much fewer than surgeons (in Brittany in 1786–1790, for instance, there was only one physician for every ten thousand inhabitants), but they were increasing in numbers, and so was competition.

The growing emancipation of surgeons from the physicians, spearheaded by the crown, was a cause of great concern to physicians (and apothecaries), for they saw surgeons increasingly practicing physic and pharmacy, and thereby encroaching on traditional monopolies. Moreover, surgeons further signaled their rising social status by increasingly employing the language of "utility" and public good to justify their practices. By the late eighteenth century the traditional hierarchical organization of medicine had become "nonsense," according to Brockliss and Jones, the instability of the corporative community baldly exposed.[48]

During the Revolution, medical regulation collapsed along with corporatism in general. The anticorporate laws of 1791 that destroyed the guilds also swept away the medical corps and allowed any man to practice medicine if he paid a tax called a *patente*. A 1793 decree abolished all *collèges* and *facultés* in France, including those of medicine, and so these institutions lost control over certification of doctors. Further legislation reduced the official medical world from three to two: doctors (physicians and surgeons converged officially in 1794 legislation on medical education) and pharmacists. Only in 1803 was a law passed that required state certification of physicians as a protection against incompetence or outright charlatanism. Then a Napoleonic bureaucracy promoted a uniform system of state control that licensed individuals rather than privileged groups, created the title of doctor of medicine or surgery, and required a degree from a medical school and examination by a departmental medical board.

Folk Healers, Empirics, and Charlatans
Although we have no way of actually counting the number of empirics, folk healers, and charlatans, historians are confident that their numbers increased in the early modern centuries. This was especially true in the eighteenth century as commercial demand for medical goods and services expanded a marketplace fed by a growing and increasingly diverse medical penumbra. Handbills hawking medical services and advertisements in the increasingly ubiquitous newspapers witness a growth in market networks and medical entrepreneurialism. In Versailles on the eve of the Revolution, for example, we find individuals retailing secret remedies; in addition to a few surgeons and apothecaries, these retailers included a musician, a cobbler, three grocers, a perfumer, a lemonade seller, and an enameler.

The growth of this penumbra was impossible for either corporations or the state to control, despite repeated attempts. In 1598 we find a typical *arrêt* (legal ruling) issued by the Parlement of Paris referring to nonlicensed medical practitioners as "empirics," and renewing "the prohibitions made formerly against all empirics, not approved by the Faculty of medicine, to practice the art of healing."[49] This reflects a mobilizing of physicians and a collective sense of identity against a proscribed "other," a group of illicit competitors.

Behind this proscription was another development equally serious to licensed practitioners: the grounds on which they condemned empirics, their ignorance of authoritative texts, was shifting beneath their feet. In the sixteenth century some maverick medical practitioners like Paracelsus encouraged empiricism, arguing that medical treatment should start with observation rather than textual authority. Such an attack on accepted Galenic medicine stung university-trained physicians, and they responded, predictably, with ferocious condemnation. In 1573 the university physicians of Montpelier joined the master surgeons in a call to " exterminate all empirics from this city." Seven years later the physician André Du Breil of the University of Paris warned King Henri III that empirics "were ruining your republic," and Thomas Courval de Sonnet, a physician from Rouen, sought to "combat and vanquish such a pernicious and diabolical sect."[50] These physicians lumped all unlicensed or noncorporate practitioners, including Paracelsists, into the category "empiric." This could be a motley grab bag indeed. For Du Breil they included "vagabonds, atheists, exiles, priests, monks, shoemakers, carders, drapers, weavers, masons, madams and prostitutes."[51]

Such condemnations became all the more shrill because physicians and surgeons gradually replaced textual Galenism with empiricism themselves. In the eighteenth century military medical personnel were engaging in innovative forms of health service delivery based in clinical practice and empirical observation, an approach that spread into the civilian sector in hospitals. As a result, the epistemological foundations of medical authority were profoundly shaken. This advance of empiricism made it increasingly difficult for the licensed medical corps to continue to base its attack on empirics in terms of method because the "core" and "penumbra" of medical practitioners increasingly shared one. The only basis left for rejection of the practices of empirics was legal (encroachment on privileged monopolies) and social (empirics were morally inferior to licensed practitioners).

Female Medical Practitioners

The advancing corporatization of medical practice in the sixteenth century reduced the status of women practitioners. Women had been excluded from universities in France since the fourteenth century, and in 1484 a decree by Charles VIII barred them from legally practicing surgery. The king exempted widows of surgeons, a window that was closed in 1694 by Louis XIV, who now ordered that a widow could keep her deceased husband's shop open only if she employed a qualified, male, surgeon's assistant. Women continued to practice medicine, of course, but mostly in the penumbra of folk healers and unlicensed nursing activities. In sixteenth-century Lyon, for example, the male administrators of the Hôtel Dieu hired women to attend the sick in the outpatient unit, where women shared some of the tasks with men. These women were hired part-time and on an ad hoc basis as demand required, however, suggesting stopgap measures responding to a shortage of male personnel for the jobs.

Indeed, during the early modern centuries the only licensed medical practice left open to women was midwifery, and even here we see encroachment by male personnel, first as overseers and then as practitioners themselves. We need not look far in the early modern period to find men's negative views of midwives. These women were often condemned on the same grounds as empirics, for ignorance, but misogynistic opprobrium was added to the invective. In 1587, for example, Gervais de la Tousche wrote that midwives were "this idiot and incompetent race . . . who, to speak plainly and truthfully, we should rather call executioners and murderers of innocent blood, by their perverse incompetence." He located their faults in their lack of medical knowledge, their gender, and their low social status. He continued his tirade with this: "They are a heap of poor deprived little women, not only in mind and understanding but also in all manner of living."[52]

During the sixteenth century, midwives were usually supervised by the church rather than a medical faculty, revealing an emphasis on moral reputation as much as medical capacity and knowledge. However, in the same century we begin to see the intrusion of the state and its male representatives. In 1556 a royal edict required midwives to be enrolled on the local bailiff's register, an action that prompted the Parisian midwives to draw up statutes of incorporation. This is not a sign of autonomy or female empowerment, however, because these statutes reflect a licensing imposed on women. The statutes were officially recognized by the crown in 1560. The bylaws of these statutes required the prospective midwife to be examined by a jury composed of a male physician, two male master surgeons, and two experienced midwives. Similar developments occurred in other French cities; indeed, we frequently find that medical examinations were preceded by oaths to municipal authorities (all male, of course).

As we move into the seventeenth century a general trend of bringing midwives more under the control of male surgeons accelerates, again sanctioned by royal legislation. In many towns and cities midwives increasingly were examined and licensed by representatives of the local community of surgeons. The women had to be at least twenty years of age, and be apprenticed for a two-year period with a local midwife or in a local *hôtel dieu*, or hospital. In 1730 royal legislation commanded that most of these regulations be applied to every town that had a corporation of surgeons. Though unintended by men, these developments also contributed to a gradual professionalization of female midwifery. By the early seventeenth century more and more urban centers had their approved midwives, and increasingly the same women were serving in these positions year after year. This suggests a public recognition of a particular obstetrical expertise, and it began to take precedence over the traditional notion that any woman who had given birth could be a birthing expert.

Among the best known of female midwives of early modern France is Louise Bourgeois. Between 1601 and 1609 she served as the royal midwife to Queen Marie de Medici, wife of Henri IV, and by 1617 Bourgeois was the first French woman to write and publish obstetrical treatises. In one of them she suggested how female midwives might cope with the increasing demand for male interventions in deliveries. Despite Bourgeois' reservations, such intervention would increase during the seventeenth and eighteenth centuries.

Male midwives, or *accoucheurs*, had the advantage of cultural associations of medical knowledge with maleness, but they had several obstacles to overcome to gain acceptance. They were usually surgeons, and at first were called on only after days of unsuccessful labor. Because such attempted deliveries usually ended in the death of the child, the mother, or both, the *accoucheur* was frequently associated with death. Such negative perceptions were compounded by the sometimes necessary action of dismembering a dead child in the womb simply to extract it. Finally, surgeons had to confront the stigma of sexual impropriety, seeing and touching female body parts that modesty permitted only to husbands.

To convince patients/clients to hire them, during the seventeenth century *accoucheurs* employed social and cultural means to sell themselves and to diminish negative cultural assumptions about their character and practice. Judging from obstetric manuals written by male surgeons who also practiced as *accoucheurs*, these men drew on accepted theories of the day to present their character in a positive light. These theories held that a person's character was legible in his or her bodily appearance and facial features, proper bodily comportment, dress, and language. A tranquil face, for example, signified a disciplined character (a positive attribute), and in these obstetrical manuals authored by *accoucheurs* we often see on the first page a portrait of the author revealing just this quality, a form of "strategic display," in the words of the medical historian Lianne McTavish.[53]

Male midwives also had to overcome the traditional assumptions that women had bodily knowledge of birthing while males had only theoretical knowledge, and that it was inappropriate for males to have such intimate knowledge of a woman's body. As empirical method gradually entered medical practice in the seventeenth century, *accoucheurs* embraced it and again used image projection to display it and to legitimize their practice. A close look at the portrait of the *accoucheur* and author Cosme Viardel, for example, reveals how *accoucheurs* might resignify the hands, demasculinizing them by emphasizing delicacy, and in their general comportment portraying nonmasculine qualities such as modesty and tenderness (the caressing of a newborn's head, for example).

They thereby appropriated traditional conceptions of maternal knowledge (empirical and bodily) associated with female midwives, and blended them with traditional masculine attributes of theoretical knowledge. In McTavish's words, they displayed in their portraits and in their books "the learned anatomical touch embodying both practical and intellectual knowledge."[54]

Accoucheurs did not completely supplant female midwives, however, for in the eighteenth century we still find the male learned assault going on. In the 1750s and 1760s a concern for the importance of population growth and its fundamental connection to the preservation of the kingdom as a European power took hold. Many men consequently became concerned about death in childbirth and, not surprisingly, again pointed the guilty finger at the "crass

Figure 5.1. Cosme Viardel, author portrait, *Observations sur la pratique des accouchemens naturels*, 1671, engraving, National Library of Medicine, Bethesda, Md.

ignorance" of female midwives. After 1760 the royal government, provincial estates, and municipalities all tried to offer obstetrical training for existing and future midwives. Concerning Paris, Mercier informs his readers that "there is at present in Paris a public course in midwifery where practitioners can learn." In what is a typically breezy overstatement, he continues that "there is no lack of skill in the capital; where, indeed, it has become as easy and pleasant to bear a child as to conceive one."[55]

Mercier also pointed out that such skill did not extend to the provinces, a problem that the crown and Madame Angélique Du Coudray tried to rectify. In 1759, despite opposition from male surgeon-*accoucheurs*, Du Coudray received a royal license and annual pension of eight thousand livres with the charge to "travel to any province where she will be useful" in the training of midwives. Between 1760 and 1783 she traveled to most of the *généralités* of the kingdom (expressly invited by the intendants there), and gave around sixty courses to midwives in fifty different towns.[56] She taught as many as five thousand women. She also trained male surgeon-demonstrators to carry on the training after her departure, thus indirectly reaching perhaps ten thousand more. Du Coudray also wrote a manual on obstetrics that went through five editions.

Men of the Law

The late medieval period saw the emergence of a judicial system based on verifiable proofs (increasingly eyewitness testimony and physical evidence), inquisitorial and accusatorial procedure, and adversarial debate, and such a legal universe called for people with expertise capable of representing the parties involved. The shift from oral to written proceedings further complicated the legal process and heightened the demand for lawyers, who were the only ones who could disentangle the increasingly convoluted legal process. Behind these developments was the emergence of what historians call the "judicial monarchy," a state system that, for the maintenance of public order, relied on the administration and adjudication of law for regulation and enforcement rather than "police" activity (the recourse to licensed violence to maintain peaceful relations among subjects). As we will see, the apparatus of this judicial state expanded dramatically during the early modern years, a development that at least until the eighteenth century called for ever more men of the law. Since the sixteenth century the educational system had responded, training would-be barristers in painstaking analyses of legal texts that positioned them to assume reputations as acknowledged experts in the interpretation and understanding of the law. French jurisprudence was so complex by the eighteenth century (the baroque system was jammed with courts of all different stripes and jurisdictions—Paris alone contained thirty-five separate courts!) that manuals for aspiring barristers routinely noted that basic mastery took decades of applied study.

The monarchy, of course, nurtured and developed the system. A royal ordinance of 1345 confirmed the stipulation of a royal edict of 1274 that prescribed that only "legitimate" causes might be pleaded (no lawyer could represent a case he knew to be unjust), and added twenty-four rules the lawyer had to swear to uphold. It stipulated that no person may plead in court if he is not a lawyer, except in his own defense. The king's own prosecutors and his royal court, the Parlement, would determine if a lawyer were worthy of such a privilege, and retained the right to expel the unworthy from the bar. And finally, although a law degree did not guarantee admission to the bar, it was a necessary precondition.

Barristers

During the seventeenth century the world of French barristers (*avocats*) underwent significant changes. Lucien Karpik, a historian of the French legal profession, distinguishes between the "State Bar" and the "Classical Bar."[57] Lawyers in the State Bar, or "old bar," were equally involved in courtroom defense and the exercise of state power. Lawyers of the State Bar had access to high public office and so were instrumental in the emergence and functioning of the judicial monarchy that elevated the administration and adjudication of justice and gave form to legal procedure. Lawyers, especially the jurisconsults among them, were central to the formation of monarchical power defined in and through the law. These lawyers of the "old bar" were not an independent liberal profession or a corps, but rather a state-dominated group of practitioners. The Classical Bar, in contrast, emerged as lawyers lost access to public power, filled almost entirely after 1650 by bureaucratic venal officials with little input in determining government policy. This forced barristers to recast their internal order and their relations with the state. The result was an independent bar association marked by self-government and a common strategy. Barrister and magistrate went their separate ways.

Ever since the Renaissance barristers possessed, in David Bell's words, "most of the criteria generally associated with modern professions, such as a distinct vocational identity, an established body of theory taught in universities, and uniform standards for training and performance."[58] During the sixteenth century, with growth in the economy, population, and institutional apparatus of the state, the numbers of judges and lawyers expanded apace. The services of legally educated personnel were in sharply escalating demand. Many barristers entered the bench (the number of royal courts, as we have seen, increased dramatically), many purchasing the increasingly available venal offices that a cash-strapped monarchy was putting on the market at a dizzying pace. Indeed, the relationship between barrister and judge was far from competitive, being rather, in Bell's words, "practically symbiotic."[59] In 1579 King Henri III even ordered that all judicial magistrates serve time as barristers before entering office.

By 1600, however, tensions between bar and bench became apparent. And barristers who wrote about the breakdown of the traditional cordiality between bar and bench named the venality of office as the culprit. As the price of office spiraled upward, the openings for barristers to judgeships became more and more limited. Antoine Loisel, a renowned legal commentator, moaned in 1602 in his *Dialogue of the Barristers* that "the day is past when men were sought [for the bench] for their merit and value."[60] With venality and the appropriation of public function by venal magistrates, lawyers gradually lost both their public function and their social status. Some men in the new, wealthy royal magistracy ascended to nobility (of "the robe") as barristers sank into a diminished and less socially prestigious role, the provision of a service to a private clientele.

As venality more sharply excluded barristers from higher offices, they were driven to redefine their identity and redirect their actions. An independent Order of Barristers was established in the 1660s. It was not a corps, and thus was not regulated by the state, but it did establish standards of conduct and discipline its members. Occupational competence was stressed as well, resting on the new requirements for aspiring barristers to complete a two-year internship before they could apply and hopefully gain formal acceptance into the Order of Barristers. An overhaul in legal education in the latter years of the seventeenth century facilitated the barristers' increasing emphasis on competence and professional identity, as the curriculum at the University of Paris added Roman and French law to canon law in 1679. In the same year Louis XIV created the position of royal professor in French law at French universities.

Until 1750 the legal profession crafted a self-image of dignified barristers obedient to a professional code of conduct and assigned to themselves the place of high-minded commentary on the virtues of the judicial monarchy. After midcentury, however, as "new men" flooded into the bar, many barristers placed themselves in the vanguard of political reform by becoming deeply involved in public debates about governance. They did this by using the special privilege of publishing factums or "judicial memoirs" about particular cases that legally evaded censorship because they required no royal approval before publication.

Lawyers wrote hundreds of these in thousands of printed copies in the years leading to the Revolution, seizing on sensational cases and highlighting the hot-button political or social issues of the day. By railing against ministerial despotism of the crown or a decadent and predatory aristocracy, some barristers, as Bell points out, became self-proclaimed defenders of the public's rights and behaved before 1789 as if France were already a republic. They contributed enormously to the formation of public opinion and the politicization of society in the years leading up to the Revolution.

When revolution broke out, most barristers favored political reform and the suppression of privilege that had characterized the political and social order of the Old Regime, but they harbored a great fear of anarchy and so seldom supported the more radical directions the Revolution took. The Order of Barristers was abolished by the Constituent Assembly in 1790. Lawyers, men of moderation with a trust in law and legal process and a lingering loyalty to the past, tended to support the federalist move of the Revolution, and generally supported Napoleon when he came to power. The Order of Barristers was officially restored in 1811.

Notaries and Attorneys

The same forces that led to an increase in the numbers of barristers in early modern France affected notaries and attorneys (*procureurs*) as well. The expansion of the judicial monarchy and the increased involvement in the law of a growing French population triggered an exuberant growth in the demand for legal services. Notaries, as recorders of documents stipulating the conditions of loans and leases, marriages, wills, property transactions, and the like, became the gateways to the legal system that increasingly privileged written evidence. Although such practitioners certainly existed in the late Middle Ages in France, their business mushroomed in the sixteenth century as an increasingly commercialized economy intersected with an expansive judicial state. More producers, consumers, borrowers, and lenders required their services in drawing up enforceable contracts, while the crown relied on them as crucial and elemental cogs through which the state could extend its power by legally regulating the lives of its subjects. In the absence of a police force or an extensive bureaucracy, notaries were key mediators between the judicial state and the subject. In 1560 the crown reorganized the notariat, fixing the numbers of royal notaries and designating them as the official makers and repositories of public records. Historian Julie Hardwick found that in Nantes between 1560 and 1660, for example, the average notary recorded seventy-eight acts per year, although some drew up far more than that (Robert Poullain, for example, drew up 347 in one year).[61]

The explosive growth in the ranks of notaries and attorneys in the sixteenth century softened in the seventeenth, but their tasks servicing the judicial monarchy through record keeping and litigation continued to be vital. One change that is quite clear, however, is that a sharper hierarchical arrangement came more into focus within the world of the notary, attorney, and barrister. Barristers became further separated from attorneys beneath them in social and professional prestige (and wealth), while attorneys came to hold a rank superior to notaries (in the sixteenth century notaries had also often been attorneys; this was rarely the case in the seventeenth century). The office of notary and attorney were both venal, but the price of the latter became more expensive than the former, effectively making it prohibitive for one individual to own both. Between the 1560s and the 1620s in Nantes, for example, the cost of a notary office went up, reaching 725 livres, but the cost of an attorney office rose more sharply, to about 3,000 livres. By midcentury the notary office had climbed to 1,650 livres, more than that of a bailiff, which went for about 800, but much less than that of an attorney, which had climbed to 7,000. Notaries, in other words, were falling behind their former peers, resulting in a loss of status and wealth. Once again the three primary motors of change in early modern France—the expansion of the market, the growth of the judicial state, and the firmer grip of rank hierarchy—had a profound impact on the men of the law.

Officials

Did France's officialdom become a "bureaucracy" during the early modern centuries? The answer is no—and (a qualified) yes. The ambivalence hinges on whether the offices we speak of were venal or not. If we adopt the great German sociologist Max Weber's definition of bureaucracy as an administration, either public or private, by full-time salaried officials, who were professionals recruited for the tasks at hand, graded and organized hierarchically, with regular procedures and formalized record keeping, then no early modern European state had a bureaucracy. No state had at its disposal an entire body of professional officials before the end of the eighteenth century. Indeed, many officials were still considered the personal servants of the king and most were not directly paid by the state.

The number of public servants grew enormously in the early modern years. In 1515, according to Roland Mousnier, there were at least 4,081 officials in the kingdom, or one for every 115 square kilometers and every 4,700 inhabitants. By 1665 France had over 46,000 public servants in a population of 18 million, or one for every ten square kilometers and every 380 inhabitants. Ostensibly, this reflects a dramatic growth of a governmental infrastructure.

But was it a bureaucracy, according to Weber's definition? Were these offi-cials directly responsible, and responsive, to the dictates of the state? The need for money for waging war—the perennial pastime of kings—triggered venality of offices (begun under kings Louis XII and Francis I in the late fif-teenth and early sixteenth centuries) and spurred its expansion (strong through the seventeenth, although the demand for office softened in the eighteenth century). Initially venal offices were not inheritable, but that changed in 1604 with the Paulette, an official table of values of offices and the stipulation that if the holder paid an annual tax of one-sixtieth the value of the office then he could pass it down to an heir. This led to family dynas-ties within the world of officialdom and produced a privatization of public service. The investment was substantial. By 1665 the value of the nearly 46,000 offices represented a capital investment of 417,630,842 livres, which corresponded to the equivalent of four and a half years of royal expenditure.[62]

Alongside venal offices, kings created nonvenal ones, largely in response to the loss of royal control over venal ones. Here we can glimpse the outlines of modern bureaucracy. Commissioners (*commissaires*), masters of requests (*maîtres des requêtes*, advisers in the royal household and eventually junior members of the king's royal council), royal councilors (*conseillers d'Etat*), and, above all, intendants were officials who continued the medieval notion of personal service to the king, but were appointed to their office, served at the pleasure of the king, and could be dismissed by the king. Offices of this type multiplied in the seventeenth century, and, not surprisingly, created jurisdic-tional conflicts with venal offices.

The best known and most studied of these offices—the intendancies—were staffed by nonvenal appointees of the crown, usually selected from the ranks of the masters of requests. Resident commissioners in most provinces, these officials were titled "intendants of justice, police, and finances," sig-naling sweeping authority. They worked alongside local officials, but the king granted them power to impose their will. Given the revenue demands of the warfare state, the intendants' concerns were primarily fiscal, but the inten-dants nonetheless had extensive police and judicial powers. In the second half of the eighteenth century the duties of the intendant had expanded to encompass public welfare in general. Intendants were to be not only the guardian of law and order in the provinces, but now also an "active public improver."[63] Not surprisingly, they encountered opposition to their expand-ing claims to public authority, an opposition spearheaded especially after 1750 by jealous and threatened provincial *parlements* and estates.

Next to the intendancies, an example of an emerging bureaucracy is the Corps of Commis des Manufactures (called *inspecteurs* from the 1690s), created by Colbert in 1669 and recently studied in scrupulous detail by the historian Philippe Minard. These nonvenal posts were created to count and control textile manufacture, first woolens but soon silks and linen. Colbert initially targeted urban workshops for inspection, but promptly expanded the scope to rural industry. As the purview of the corps of inspectors expanded, so did its numbers, from fifteen in 1669, to twenty in the 1680s, to thirty-eight by 1704. Throughout its existence (the corps was suppressed in 1791), the corps' responsibilities were to verify the application of rules and norms of textile manufacture, and to gather information about markets, equipment, technology, location of raw materials, and the nature of the workforce. The objective of the inspectors was to provide the government with information deemed necessary for the administration of an informed and "rational" political economy. Inspectors were constantly writing reports, and in the eighteenth century these became more statistical. Their field also expanded beyond textiles to papermaking, tanning, and glass and faience manufacture. At their inception inspectors were steeped in the value system of Colbertism, which held that regulation was necessary for improvement, an assumption the rank-and-file officials of the corps never relinquished. Under the influence of the Enlightenment in the eighteenth century, they framed their work by the values of public utility and improvement, and saw their work as an important contributor to progress and the public welfare, but they never wavered from their commitment to the value of government regulation.

The eighteenth century witnessed a professionalization of the corps of inspectors (and other *fonctionnaires*, like royal engineers), especially after 1750 with the creation of state schools complete with examinations to certify the competence of their graduates. Matriculation was increasingly by merit as well, although the older system of recommendation and selection, clientelism, did not disappear. Good recommendations from powerful men were still needed to get into the school (not surprisingly, then, familial clans took root in the heart of the corps), but placements in jobs after graduation were increasingly based on merit. Furthermore, the institutionalization of an apprenticeship system of subinspectors guaranteed competence and contributed to the sense of unity in the corps.

Financiers

Tax farming, too, underwent changes marked by the growth of the state and increased centralization and bureaucratization. Recall that tax farmers would guarantee the crown an annual revenue in advance, then collect taxes that covered the advance plus an interest for themselves. Largely independent operatives before the mid-seventeenth century, after that several farms were brought together by the crown into one large one, formally organized by Colbert in 1681 as the *Compagnie des fermes générales*. This body collected indirect taxes and was effectively a company of private capitalists with a contract with the king. The *fermiers généraux* acted collectively, as a corps with legal privileges, with each member receiving funds corresponding to the percentage of capital he had invested in the company. In the absence of a national bank, the corps provided funds to the state; these funds were secured by the corps' own credit. Importantly, it thus underwrote the credit of the state. There were forty seats in the company in 1726, a number that expanded to eighty-seven before it was reduced to forty-eight in 1774.

Like the inspectors of manufactures, the men of the Ferme générale were highly competent and the most capable could expect promotion up the ranks. The corps was comprised of a hierarchy of committees, and the best and brightest moved up through them. At the top was the *Comité des caisses*, the central administrative council where all the important decisions were made. It dealt directly with the controller-general, the king's chief finance minister. After 1750 the Ferme générale had a central office in Paris and employed thirty thousand men throughout the provinces. Also like the inspectorate of manufactures, recruitment generally worked through families. Between 1726 and 1791, the 223 *fermiers généraux* came from 156 different families, and many of the financiers had brothers, cousins, nephews, and fathers in the ranks of treasurers, receivers, and so forth.

Under Louis XV in the eighteenth century the Ferme générale became one of most powerful institutions in France. Before the consolidation in the seventeenth century, the risks confronted by the financiers were high, and many financiers went bankrupt (of the 367 seventeenth-century financiers studied by the historian Françoise Bayard, 53 went broke).[64] With the formation of the Ferme générale, such risks receded. The crown's constant need for revenue, above all to equip the military, forced it into the arms of the financiers. Men like Samuel Bernard became fabulously rich. For over ten years from 1701 he furnished the king 1.3 million livres per month. In one advance of 1.5 million livres, he gained 407,000 livres in interest![65]

The golden age of the financiers was from 1730 to 1760, when they were heavily invested in military provisioning, of both the navy and the army. Like Jacques Coeur centuries before, they seamlessly blended their role as official personages of royal finances with that of private capitalists. After France's defeat in the Seven Years' War (1756–1763), however, periodic calls for fiscal reform could be heard. Kings Louis XV and XVI were still committed to great power competition with Great Britain, and royal expenditures therefore continued to soar. And the crown remained completely dependent on the Ferme générale.

In the late 1770s Controller-General Jacques Necker wanted to eliminate the ferme altogether and replace it with a state-administered system of public finance that would include the direct collection of taxes. During his tenure as controller-general Necker was able to reduce the number of treasurers and receivers, but he was unable to deny that financiers were the masters of state credit. Without them the state commanded no confidence in the credit markets. Reform of the fiscal system would come only with the Revolution, when the Ferme générale was abolished (and twenty-eight *fermiers généraux* and many treasurers and receivers were guillotined).

Notes

1. Laurence Brockliss and Colin Jones, *The Medical World of Early Modern France* (Oxford: Oxford University Press, 1997), 8, 18–19.

2. Matthew Ramsey, *Professional and Popular Medicine in France, 1770–1830: The Social World of Medical Practice* (Cambridge: Cambridge University Press, 1988), 244.

3. Ramsey, *Professional and Popular Medicine*, 190.

4. Quoted in Susan Broomhall, *Women's Medical Work in Early Modern France* (Manchester: Manchester University Press, 2004), 51.

5. Alison Klairmont Lingo, "Empirics and Charlatans in Early Modern France: The Genesis of the Classification of the 'Other' in Medical Practice," *Journal of Social History* 19, no. 4 (1986): 586.

6. Quoted in Ramsey, *Professional and Popular Medicine*, 132.

7. Quoted in Broomhall, *Women's Medical Work*, 100.

8. Louis-Sébastien Mercier, *Panorama of Paris*, ed. Jeremy Popkin, trans. Helen Simpson (University Park: Pennsylvania State University Press, 1999), 104.

9. Philippe Minard, *La Fortune du Colbertisme: Etat et industrie dans la France des Lumières* (Paris: Fayard, 1998), 75.

10. Zoe Schneider, "The King's Bench," unpublished manuscript, 31. Now available as *The King's Bench: Bailiwick Magistrates and Local Governance in Normandy, 1670–1740* (Rochester, NY: University of Rochester Press, 2008).

11. Schneider, "King's Bench," 166.

12. Schneider, "King's Bench," 92.

13. Quoted in Guy Chaussinand-Nogaret, *Gens de finance au XVIIIe siècle* (Paris: Editions complexe, 1993), 19 (my translation).

14. Fernand Braudel, *The Wheels of Commerce*, trans. Siân Reynolds (New York: Harper and Row, 1986), 540.

15. Toby Gelfand, "A 'Monarchical Profession' in the Old Regime: Surgeons, Ordinary Practitioners, and Medical Professionalization in Eighteenth-Century

France," in *Professions and the French State, 1700–1900*, ed. Gerald L. Geison (Philadelphia: University of Pennsylvania Press, 1984), 149.

16. Svante Beckman, "Professionalization: Borderline Authority and Autonomy in Work," in *Professions in Theory and History: Rethinking the Study of the Professions*, ed. Michael Burrage and Rolf Torstendahl (London: Sage, 1990), 115–38.

17. Lingo, "Empirics and Charlatans," 591.

18. Brockliss and Jones, *Medical World*, 230.

19. Quoted in Christine Adams, *A Taste for Comfort and Status: A Bourgeois Family in Eighteenth-Century France* (University Park: Pennsylvania State University Press, 2000), 186.

20. Quoted in Pamela H. Smith, *The Body of the Artisan: Art and Experience in the Scientific Revolution* (Chicago: University of Chicago Press, 2004), 156.

21. Mercier, *Panorama*, 58.

22. Alison Klairmont Lingo, "Women Healers and the Medical Marketplace of Sixteenth-Century Lyon," *Dynamis* 19 (1999): 91.

23. Broomhall, *Women's Medical Work*, 102, 105.

24. Gelfand, "'Monarchical Profession,'" 149.

25. Quoted in Lucien Karpik, *French Lawyers: A Study in Collective Action, 1274–1994*, trans. Nora Scott (Oxford: Clarendon Press, 1999), 39.

26. Robert Nye, *Masculinity and Male Codes of Honor in Modern France* (New York: Oxford University Press, 1993), 42.

27. Lenard Berlanstein, *The Barristers of Toulouse in the Eighteenth Century (1740–1793)* (Baltimore: Johns Hopkins University Press, 1975), 28.

28. David Bell, *Lawyers and Citizens: The Making of a Political Elite in Old Regime France* (New York: Oxford University Press, 1994), 36.

29. Bell, *Lawyers and Citizens*, 14, 6.

30. Quoted in Adams, *Taste for Comfort*, 130.

31. Claude de Ferrière, *Dictionnaire de droit et de pratique*, 2 vols., 2nd ed. (Paris, 1740).

32. Claire Dolan, *Le Notaire, la famille et la ville* (Toulouse: Presses Universitaires du Mirail, 1998), 168.

33. Dominique Julia, "L'Education des négociants français au 18e siècle," in *Cultures et formations négociantes dans l'Europe moderne*, ed. Granco Angioline and Daniel Roche (Paris: Editions de l'EHESS, 1995), 234.

34. Minard, *Fortune du Colbertisme*, 115.

35. Quoted in Minard, *Fortune du Colbertisme*, 78

36. Robert Forster, *Merchants, Landlords, Magistrates: The Depont Family in Eighteenth-Century France* (Baltimore: Johns Hopkins University Press, 1980), 42.

37. Forster, *Merchants*, 125.

38. Schneider, "King's Bench," 155.

39. Kathleen Daly, "Private Vice, Public Service? Civil Service and *Chose Public* in Fifteenth-Century France," in *Concepts and Patterns of Service in the Later Middle*

Ages, ed. Anne Curry and Elizabeth Matthew (Woodbridge, UK: Boydell Press, 2000), 102.

40. Quoted in Daly, "Private Vice," 101.

41. Quoted in Daly, "Private Vice," 111.

42. Mercier, *Panorama*, 172–73.

43. Mercier, *Panorama*, 216.

44. Françoise Bayard, *Le Monde des financiers au XVIIe siècle* (Paris: Flammarion, 1988), 335.

45. Bayard, *Monde*, 311.

46. Braudel, *Wheels of Commerce*, 541.

47. Ramsey, *Professional and Popular Medicine*, 58.

48. Brockliss and Jones, *Medical World*, 620.

49. Quoted in Broomhall, *Women's Medical Work*, 47.

50. Quoted in Lingo, "Empirics and Charlatans," 583.

51. Quoted in Lingo, "Empirics and Charlatans," 584.

52. Quoted in Broomhall, *Women's Medical Work*, 33.

53. Lianne McTavish, "On Display: Portraits of Seventeenth-Century Men Midwives," *Social History of Medicine* 14, no. 3 (2001): 392.

54. McTavish, "On Display," 408.

55. Mercier, *Panorama*, 105.

56. Jacques Gélis, "Sages-femmes et accoucheurs: L'Obstetrique populaire aux XVIIe et XVIIIe siècles," *Annales: Economies, Sociétés, Civilisations* 32, no. 5 (1977): 941.

57. Karpik, *French Lawyers*.

58. Bell, *Lawyers and Citizens*, 41.

59. Bell, *Lawyers and Citizens*, 43.

60. Quoted in Bell, *Lawyers and Citizens*, 46.

61. Julie Hardwick, *The Practice of Patriarchy: Gender and the Politics of Household Authority in Early Modern France* (University Park: Pennsylvania State University Press, 1998).

62. Jean-Marie Constant, "Absolutisme et Modernité," in *Histoire des élites en France du XVIe au XXe siécle*, ed. Guy Chaussinand-Nogaret et al. (Paris: Editions Tallandier, 1991), 170.

63. Forster, *Merchants*, 129.

64. Bayard, *Monde*.

65. Chaussinand-Nogaret, *Gens des finances*, 22.

~

Conclusion

Market, State, Hierarchy

This book on work and culture in early modern France has engaged the "critical issue" of the relationship between material life—specifically, work activities (of both men and women)—and the culture in which these activities were embedded. This culture helped shape the nature of work, invested it with meaning, and fashioned the identities of the people across the social spectrum. The focus has been early modern France, and we began our exploration of the history of work in the countryside, in the world of the peasant and rural artisan. Our attention then shifted to the towns and cities, the urban world of common laborers (lumped by the French into a general category of the *menu peuple*, or "lesser folk"), domestic servants, craftsmen and craftswomen, and merchants. We concluded with an examination of the emergent professions of law, medicine, finance, and bureaucratic governance. Each chapter was divided into three parts, the first two treating constants and continuities in which the nature of various kinds of work activities and the cultural aspects of them were explored, while the third examined and explained the multifarious changes in the world of work.

These changes were so profound and sweeping that France—and its work world—would be forever transformed and ushered into the modern age. The world of work was especially affected by three salient, interconnected, and at times conflicted developments that I have emphasized throughout this book: the extension and integration of the market economy, the growth of the state's functions and governing apparatus, and the intensification of social hierarchy.

Throughout Europe in the early modern centuries we cannot miss the growing interconnections among widening markets, and France was no exception. Indeed, France was Europe's largest market. More and more people unmistakably oriented their lives toward the market, stimulating an ebullient—if discontinuous—demand. The primary site of such demand, I have emphasized throughout this book, was the city. Urban populations experienced sustained growth across the early modern years, even as the overall population went through phases of growth and contraction. Market disturbances and bottlenecks there certainly were, but in the long run the extension and integration of a market system fueled economic growth, however incremental it may have been. By no means, however, did this development equally benefit all French men and women. Indeed, as a redistributor of resources and wealth, market growth resulted in pronounced inequality, as some reaped enormous profits from it while the vast majority did not. The market, then, can be seen as an important motor not just for economic growth, but also for the polarization of wealth and the intensification of social hierarchy that we have observed in each chapter in this book.

A distinct and intensifying social hierarchy held sway in the rural world as the market reached ever deeper into peasants' lives. At the top of the social pyramid was the *laboureur*, or farmer, distinguished by the ownership of land that was an important marker of social status. At the other end of the social scale were the men and women hired as farm laborers, owners of very little, if any, land, and so considered inferior to the *laboureur* and ranked below him in the social hierarchy. Ranged in between were varieties of tenant farmers and sharecroppers, large and small. A finely graded legal and economic hierarchy structured social relations in the countryside. This was a society of inequality, and one that was accepted by everyone from the king to the lowest peasant as natural and sacred.

The connection to the land immersed the peasant in an economic relationship to the market—of land, commodity, and labor—but it also entailed a political relationship to the *seigneur* (landlord) and the state, the latter of increasing importance as the governing apparatus of the state grew and extended its reach. The seigneurie and the state were both mechanisms for surplus extraction from the land in the form of dues, fees, sharecropping, rental arrangements, and taxation, a squeeze on the peasantry's resources that mounted inexorably during the centuries of this study.

A central argument of this book emphasizes the importance of the growth of cities and the trade networks that increasingly connected them in creating markets that were a primary motor of economic growth. Attuning production to these conditions, which we now recognize many, perhaps even most, peasants did, testifies to an innovative peasant mentality eager for profit, and reveals changes in the rural world that were marked by incremental and specialized adaptations to geographic, climatic, and above all market conditions. These adaptations, which often included peasant involvement in rural manufacture, had an aggregate effect and resulted in growth, discontinuous, sporadic, and regional though it may have been.

The *menu peuple*, or "lesser folk" as they were described by their social superiors, were affected no less by market forces, intensification of social hierarchy, and expansion of the state. Men, women, and children of this social group comprised probably at least half of the urban population but also included vast numbers of rural folk, many of whom alternated work in fields and unskilled labor in towns, flowing back and forth as demand required. Most of these people—with the exception of domestic servants—survived by an economy of makeshifts. They worked at whatever tasks they could find to piece together a subsistence living for the family. The laboring poor of France were a highly disparate group, and a shifting one where people often specialized in not specializing in anything.

Among these folk, despite the fluidity and seeming lack of structure, a stratified hierarchy tended to emerge, mirroring the rest of society. Port workers and loaders, for example, openly simulated corporate status and clearly organized themselves into disciplined bands, defending their "turf" against interlopers as any official guild might do. After all, work of whatever kind was seen by everyone as a means to place one in society and to identify one with a group. Participation in social life was conditioned by submission to certain bonds of the group—family, corporation, neighborhood, friends, what have you. For respectable folk the fundamental community ordering society and bestowing status was the corporation, a community bound by an oath of solidarity. These people looked on the day-laboring poor as dangerous precisely because they seemed *not* to have ties to communities, above all corporate ones, and so were *gens sans aveu* (literally, people without oath), masterless men and women. Even servants, despite their physical closeness to their masters and mistresses, were likewise outside the corporate regime, and so had no legal basis for social recognition.

Jan De Vries called our attention to an "industrious revolution" among the working folk of Europe where more and more workers (husbands, wives, and children, rural and urban) were working harder and longer at their jobs, exchanging leisure time for work. The result was the generation of a growing surplus, modest though it might have been. This surplus not only further stimulated the extension and growth of the market system, it also returned cash to these workers, who in turn entered the market as consumers. It seems likely that this phenomenon was related to the consumer revolution of the late seventeenth and eighteenth centuries that many historians have observed.

Artisans were caught up in the same forces of market growth, intensification of hierarchy, and expansion of the state. Decentralization of production, galloping specialization, widespread subcontracting—both within the guild structure and outside it—had profound results. First, they splintered the division of labor, not only among trades, but within them as well. Second, the labor force tended to separate into a peripheral majority of mobile semi-skilled wageworkers who floated in and out of the workplace as demand dictated, and a core, sedentary minority who learned the mysteries of the trade from their masters (that is, they were skilled). Yet despite all the economic fluidity, hierarchy held sway, and before the eighteenth century, even intensified. Masters ranked above journeymen, who counted apprentices and unskilled wageworkers beneath them.

I have cautioned here and elsewhere that we must guard against viewing the operation of the craft economy only through the lens of the guild. Still, guilds obviously were important to early modern artisans, and so we must ask why. After all, they existed legally for half a millennium! The answer is status. Status was paramount to an artisan's identity, and thus a keen sense of honor was felt by craftsmen of all stripes. Guilds served an important function in establishing and proclaiming status, and fundamentally served as institutions for ordering the world and making sense of it. Indeed, I would go so far as to say that guilds were likely *more* important to artisans for their social value than economic; guild membership was a recognized, legally sanctioned and recognizable badge of status and respectability, affirming publicly and legally the artisan's place in the social firmament.

Let me be clear, for I have been misunderstood on this point before. I am not trying to argue that the guild system or even government regulation in general was economically irrelevant. (Indeed, recent research suggests that state involvement appears to have been effective in *stimulating* economic growth in some sectors, specifically through the industries it directly sponsored). Regulation did have a stultifying effect on economic growth in some places and at some times, but the more research that is done into the *overall* operation of the early modern urban craft economy over the long term, the more we realize how much was happening *beyond the purview and reach* of the guilds and of government regulation. Recent research strongly suggests that the regulatory reach of guilds was short and incomplete, the magnitude of violation of the normative guild bylaws enormous. Ebullient urban demand (not to mention rural manufacturing) no doubt contributed mightily to this development.

Merchants, not surprisingly, were the linchpins of the early modern market economy. We find their footprints everywhere—in long-distance, regional, and local commerce, in public finance (especially as the costs of governance skyrocketed), in land acquisition and management, in rural manufacturing, in credit transactions, indeed, anywhere a profit could be spied and realized. The merchant, large or small, lived in a world of risk and chance, and all merchants shared a calculating profit-oriented mentality that encouraged the development and employment of pragmatic business techniques that minimized risk and maximized predictability.

Hierarchy among traders emerged and intensified, too. Everywhere in the work world of early modern France we have seen an increase in the division of labor during the early modern years, and the mercantile world is no exception. Likewise, this development exacerbated inequalities among merchants. A "trade hierarchy" became increasingly pronounced, with financiers perched at the top of the pyramid, followed closely by a new class of extremely wealthy merchants engaged in long-distance trade. At the bottom were poor peddlers and street vendors, many of them women, who hawked a meager stock in the countryside or in the countless urban marketplaces. In between were artisan shopkeepers, small wholesale merchants who bought goods and produce in the nearby countryside and sold them in the city, and mercers, retailers who, according to a French proverb, "sell everything, make nothing."

Early modern French people tended to think of work in physical terms, and framed their conceptions of status according to who worked with their hands (a sign of social inferiority) and who did not. The situation became more complicated than this simple dichotomy suggests, for increasingly we find men (and some women) involved in nonphysical activity describing their actions as "work." This was true of medical practitioners, men of the law, and government officials. As we have seen, the conceptualization of intellectual work was closely related to the historical process of professionalization, and "professional" work identity throughout the early modern period is inextricably bound up with personal honor, social esteem, and hierarchy.

The intensification of hierarchy was only one force that told the history of the professions. The growth of the market and the state were others. The numbers of the men and women of the medical world increased steadily as the demand for medical services grew. Indeed, the commercialization of health delivery accelerated dramatically in the eighteenth century. Licensed physicians, corporate surgeons, and apothecaries (who comprised a tripartite hierarchical division within the official medical community) were insufficient in number to meet the demand, so around this core there grew a "penumbra" of unincorporated empirics, hawking their services and cures in markets large and small, wherever a buyer could be found. What distinguished the core from the penumbra was, primarily, the law: the crown legally granted this core the corporate privileges that bestowed a legal identity and social status. This penumbra, however, was impossible for either corporations or the state to control.

Hierarchy, market, and state went a long way in defining the history of legal practitioners, too. The numbers of barristers, attorneys, and notaries grew exuberantly over the early modern years. As in most emergent professions, an increasing self-awareness of the specificity of their work marked these men. Identification with their work deepened as they increasingly defended their collective privileges. The early modern centuries also witnessed the emergence and growth of a state system that historians call the "judicial monarchy," whose fundamental tasks and justification were the maintenance of public order and the legal preservation and transfer of property. The expansion of the judicial monarchy and the increased involvement of a growing French population in the law triggered an exuberant growth in the demand for legal services.

The growth of the judicial state, of course, entailed the mushrooming of officialdom—royal, seigneurial, and municipal, much of it venal. As with the medical world, it is useful here to distinguish between a center and a periphery, the former closer to the center of power (the king) than the latter (those who worked in the provinces, and though they might be royal officials, their interests and tasks would be firmly tied to the locale). A hierarchy radiating from the center to the periphery designated the relative status of these officials. The numbers of men working in all these categories swelled over the early modern years. Much of this growth was fueled by the war-driven fiscal needs of kings, and so within this officialdom a venal, expansive, and complex financial administration can also be seen.

Much of the history of work has been, *per force*, written in gendered terms—male—because women all too often do not appear in the records historians must use to write their accounts of the past. This does not mean, of course, that women did not work, but it does make it especially difficult to determine where and how they fit in the history of work. We know, for example, that large numbers of them participated in and were integral to the functioning of the growing market economy—as petty traders, seamstresses, prostitutes, medical empirics, midwives—and that vast numbers of them staffed households up and down the social scale as domestic servants. Part of the reason that they are shielded from our eyes is the advancing corporatization of work, which defined work in masculine terms. Thus, for instance, women were increasingly pushed out of the craft guilds (the seamstresses are a shining exception), and midwives found their place in obstetrics taken over by men. Given these developments, it is very difficult to sketch a history of women's work that can account for female work identity, but within these limitations we can safely speculate that the same forces that structured the world of work for men—market, state, hierarchy—exerted their forces on women as well.

What's in a Word? Labor and Work

In modern French dictionaries the words "work" and "labor" are translated by the same word, *travail*, with another word, *oeuvre*, denoting a product of such directed effort. The verb form is invariably *travailler*, the archaic *oeuvrer* having fallen out of usage. If one looks more closely at the dictionary entries for these terms, however, one sees subtle differences determined by the kind of effort involved, either physical or mental. These differences have historical reasons, for the meanings of labor and work underwent important transformations during the early modern period. It was during these centuries that, as we have seen, intellectual activity was more generally included in the meaning of work. Moreover, the connotation of manual labor subtly began to shift from solely pejorative to one that mixed negative with positive aspects. How and why these transformations in meaning occurred had much to do with the processes we have examined in this book that altered the nature of work and the lives of the men and women experiencing it in the early modern centuries: the intensification of hierarchy, the expansion and integration of the market economy, and the growth of the state. It seems appropriate, therefore, to conclude this book with an examination of the meanings of the words that have described the activity we call "work."

Let's begin with the word "labor." During the early modern era the meaning of labor began with a pejorative definition. It will never lose this meaning, but, at least in the minds of some theorists, it will be awkwardly joined by a more positive one rooted in a respect for productivity. Here, in part, we are on our way to the modern "work ethic" usefully defined recently as this:

> Attitudes towards labour found in modern industrial society. The phrase ["modern work ethic"] refers to a mentality which regards work in a positive light and which perceives it as beneficial, rewarding and improving. The

normal expectation is that work will occupy a high proportion of our time, and that excessive idleness is morally wrong. Following from these assumptions, work is conducted within a framework of rules and norms. Workers are expected to commit themselves to their tasks diligently and effectively, and to accept discipline and supervision. In return, employees can expect to be fairly rewarded by receiving a just wage and other benefits. Leisure is precisely defined as an alternative to work, but is not mere idleness. It should be organized and even be purposeful and constructive.[1]

Attitudes toward labor were not always thus. For much of the period from the late Middle Ages until the eighteenth century, labor (tellingly, *travail* in French, from whence the English, "travail"), so all the dictionaries and many commentators tell us, is closely associated with necessity, pain, suffering, and fatigue. Until the mid-fifteenth century *travail* meant torment, suffering, and physical fatigue provoked by a painful and difficult activity. Fatigue and torment in the definition take primacy over the act of production. We also find the words *labour* (noun) and *labourer* (verb) carrying the same connotations where the productive aspect of the activity described is clearly of secondary importance, the emphasis instead being placed on the pain, suffering, and fatigue that come with the activity. When we find these words used in the twelfth century their synonym is *besogne*, or *besoin*, that is, need or necessity. Labor was purely physical and even slavish because it was necessitated by bodily needs. Moreover, it lacked value because it was ephemeral and left nothing lasting behind—the result of its effort being consumed almost immediately. And consider the etymology of *travail*: it comes from the Latin *tripalium*, which was an implement of torture in the High Middle Ages! Pain indeed.

This negative, painful meaning of *travail* and *labour* is further reinforced in this Christian society because of its association with the Fall of mankind. Adam and Eve, and their descendants, were fated to painful labor to survive and reproduce. And because the sin of Adam and Eve was disobedience, their penance was labor as a form of servitude. Significantly, as the postulates of sin and servitude were joined they justified the principles of hierarchy and discipline. This was a very old idea dating at least to Saint Augustine in the fifth century CE, but it had a powerful hold on European minds for a very long time. So, the postulates of pain, suffering, sin, servitude, necessity, and inferiority gathered around the words *travail* and *labour* in the High and late Middle Ages, a meaning that was bequeathed to the early modern era. The medieval meaning of labor, in short, was cast in a moral register, not a productive one.

Beginning in the fifteenth century we will find significant nuances in the meaning of *travail*. It does not shed its pejorative connotation, nor does it lose its association with suffering, pain, and fatigue,[2] but now it can be found more explicitly describing "the ensemble of activities exercised by man, generally productive or creative, and directed towards an immediate objective . . . an effort that man must sustain in order to make something."[3] *Labour* has parted company with *travail* by now as well, making specific reference to agricultural activity, of cultivating the land. By the seventeenth century *travailler* has supplanted *oeuvrer*, which falls out of common usage, *travail* now carrying the explicit meaning of "executing a work" (*exécuter un ouvrage*).

Despite the emerging inclusion of creative production in the meaning of labor in the early modern years, such activity was still explicitly associated with the men and women who worked with their hands—peasants, urban day laborers, artisans—and it was no accident that these folk occupied the lower rungs on the hierarchical ladder, often dismissed as *grossier* (crude) or *vil* (vile) by their social superiors (who, significantly, made a point of the fact that they did *not* work with their hands). Such assumptions rested on the notion that hierarchy descends from the spiritual to the bodily, that the will is the obedient servant of reason transmitting commands to the body. This was a theory of the individual as well as of society, and so activities associated with bodily actions (like manual labor) were considered vile.[4] As hierarchy intensified in the sixteenth and seventeenth centuries, it brought in its train the meaning of work as a badge of a certain inferior social rank.

The Problem of Poverty

The increasingly pressing problem of poverty in the early modern years was an important catalyst for the evolving meaning of work that brought productive activity more to the forefront. Here's why. The increase in the numbers of the poor and indigent who tramped the kingdom's roads and swarmed into its cities and towns in the sixteenth century, a development well documented by many historians, pushed many commentators to ponder the causes of and formulate solutions to such a pressing social problem. Along the way the meaning of labor was further defined. These transient indigent folk were feared by society's elites and also condemned by them as immoral because they were cut free from the authority structures of society—above all the family, village, or master. Visibly doing no work, beggars contrasted sharply with those who did. Unemployment and pauperization, whatever their demographic or economic causes, were seen as willful idleness, and thus the sin of disobedience that must be corrected by discipline—and toil.

Indeed, some commentators spied productive value in putting the poor to work. In 1615 Antoine de Montchrestien, for example, observed that the kingdom of France's idle poor were a vast, untapped reservoir of a workforce. In the second half of the century mercantilists like King Louis XIV's chief finance minister and mastermind of the king's economic policies, Jean-Baptiste Colbert, looked on the new workhouses springing up across the land as potential contributors of labor for new manufactories as much as institutions for moral correction (their original design). In good mercantilist fashion, Colbert focused on increasing the wealth of the kingdom by internal measures, and concluded that productivity would be increased and wealth created if as many individuals as possible were at work as much of the time as possible. For Colbert, labor is the creator of wealth, but hierarchy and social discipline are still prevalent in his mind, for he assumed that work is the creator of order and that every man and woman put to work is a victory over disorder.

Colbert was not alone in these views that mixed the moral value of labor with the productive. Pauperization had become a severe social problem by then, and various solutions were advanced for it. Confinement was one. Jean Guérin, a late-seventeenth-century advocate for the incarceration of the poor, dismissed paupers and beggars as "the refuse and dregs of the world, and if one may put it thus, the excrement. But now [incarcerated in workhouses] they are no longer as before useless burdens upon the face of the earth, nor gangrenous members that had to be cut off; rather, they have become *by their labor* necessary parts in the growth of towns."[5]

A similar sentiment informed the king's creation of the General Hospital system in Paris in 1656. Paupers (both men and women) were to be confined in the Bicêtre and Salpetrière, more prisons than hospitals, to be employed in manufacturing and other works, its founder convinced that idleness was both a sin and a drag on productivity. Work was penance, and productive. As with Colbert's assumptions, we see here a combination of a moral valorization of labor and an appreciation of its productive capacity.

This melding of the moral and the productive that came together in thinking about poverty and work can be seen elsewhere. During the seventeenth century devout men and women thought that a combination of prayer and labor would solve the problem of pauperization, and they advocated and even established primary schools to accomplish this. "Little schools" popped up in cities throughout the realm and the curriculum was heavily religious. Such a basic education would, these godly reformers hoped, instill moral values, but in step with the views of the time, it also was expected to encourage productive labor. According to the priest Charles Demia, the author of a

1666 tract encouraging primary instruction, the uneducated were likely to become "idlers, libertines, blasphemers . . . drunks, and thieves, the most depraved and fractious people in the kingdom." The school, in contrast, would assure order in the city and would put "children to work in most of the arts and professions."[6] By the end of the century almost all of the students in the little schools came from the world of manual labor.

The problem of poverty continued into the eighteenth century, but we can perceive a shift in attitudes toward poverty as the language of "utility" entered the discourse about it. More and more we find the primacy of work as penance for the sin of idleness fall away, nudged to the background by a more secular view that work should be valued because it was productive and therefore useful to the economy and the state. By the 1750s Jean Le Rond d'Alembert, coeditor of the *Encyclopédie*, spoke for a generation of philosophes when he asserted that the strength of the realm depended on an increase in productivity, and this in turn required that the habit of idleness be broken. The rational incentive to work must be complemented by sanctions against idleness, a state of being now shorn of its religious connotation of sin.

Montesquieu shared these views by crisply pronouncing that "a man is not poor because he has nothing, but because he is not working."[7] Guillaume François Le Trosne joined the enlightened chorus, asserting that "it is assuredly not work which is lacking, but a willingness to work. . . . Any able-bodied man . . . has only to choose one of any kind of employment. Whoever has difficulty finding one, has only to offer himself for board, or even ask less than the ordinary rate; he is sure not to fail."[8] Véron de Forbonnais concurred that idleness was voluntary and must not be tolerated, asserting that "in a well-ordered society, men who are poor and without industry must not find themselves clothed, fed and healthy: the others will soon imagine that there is greater happiness in doing nothing."[9]

The eighteenth-century French state was fully in step with these ideas, as the establishment of Dépôts de mendicité shows. Created by royal command in 1764 and 1767 and placed under the authority of the most important royal officials in the provinces, the intendants, these institutions were to impel the idle either to seek work or to be drawn into them. Enlightened administrators would then subject the idle to a rigorous work discipline and thereby transform them into a useful productive citizenry.

Directors of public institutions like the Bureau des Ecoles Charitables (Office of Charitable Schools) in Grenoble shared the same assumptions. These men wanted to produce not good Catholics, but productive workers. As Kathryn Norberg succinctly puts it, "Labor was the key, and the Grenoblois had a near mystical faith in its powers" to order and perfect society.[10] Indeed, enlightened elites everywhere sang the praises of the education of the work-force as the only means, according to Imbert de Saint Paul in 1778, "to instill in the people a taste for industry." Dupont de Nemours added that proper education would "inspire in the people a love of work."[11]

During the eighteenth century, then, the meaning of labor finds its productive quality brought more into primacy, and its pejorative connotation, though not shed entirely, clearly falling into the background. The concept and value of labor (*travail*) holds a central place in the monumental *Encyclopédie* and in the mind of its chief architect, Denis Diderot. Here labor is defined as "the daily occupation to which man is consigned by his needs, and to which he owes at the same time his health, his subsistence, his serenity, his reason, and his virtue."[12] As was typical of Enlightenment thinkers, labor is shorn of its Christian trappings and its moral force gives way to its productive power, by which nature is transformed and humankind improves its condition. Labor, in other words, becomes the wellspring of progress. Abbé Malvaux summed it up in 1777: "The philosopher's stone, so long sought after, has been found—it is work."[13]

Work, Thought, and Leisure

Such was the history of the concept of "labor" in the early modern centuries. But what about "work" (*oeuvre*)? Or more specifically, what changes do we see in that other kind of labor that lay alongside physical exertion (by this I mean thought or mental activity)? How did contemplation and study come to be viewed as work? Let's begin with the words *oeuvre* (noun) and *oeuvrer* (verb). The etymology of these words links their meaning with simply acting or doing, and here the connotations are not necessarily pejorative. The roots of this notion of work lie deep in the Christian Middle Ages and, indeed, reach back to antiquity.

Among Greek philosophers like Plato and Aristotle, leisured contemplation (in Latin, *otium*) was considered an activity (it was decidedly *not* idleness), and an activity that was considered superior to manual labor or even to commerce (the Latin *negotium*, or the negation of otium, from which the French *négoce*, or commerce, derives). This positive notion of "work" was adapted to Christianity during late antiquity and the early Middle Ages as the worship of God and the contemplation of salvation became the most valued activity. True, manual labor was an important component of monastic life, but monks engaged in it to subdue the temptations of the flesh, to provide subsistence for the community, and to provide possibilities for charity (such labor was decidedly *not* intended to alter the material world for human benefit). By the thirteenth century *oeuvre* connotes both an activity (*oeuvrer*) and something lasting (*une oeuvre*, or its derivative, *un ouvrage*), a production of "a work," a material embodiment that lasts, that is memorial.

Medieval theologians theorized little about the meaning or significance of work, but university professors did.[14] Perhaps moved to define their own activities as worthy, they sharply separated the liberal arts from the mechanical arts, the fundamental distinction between them being the intellectual component. In fact, the liberal arts (such as philosophy and theology) were deemed superior to the mechanical precisely *because* they were intellectual pursuits. According to these theorists, hierarchy divided the mechanical arts as well. They were ranked within themselves by the degree of intellectual activity required in the fashioning of an object. Therefore, for example, goldsmithing was a superior activity to weaving because the former was deemed to demand a greater amount of thought than the latter.

These distinctions were embraced widely by secular theorists in the early modern centuries and given clearest voice by Charles Loyseau in his hugely influential *Treatise of Orders and Plain Dignities* (1610).[15] Manual labor came to be the key factor defining the frontier between respect and contempt, and intellectuals hastened to place themselves on the right side of the line. So did the new aristocracy emerging at the time. As historian Jacques Le Goff puts it, "Across from the *manouvriers* and *brassiers*, who worked with hands and arms, was the patrician world, the new aristocracy, consisting of all those who did no manual labor."[16] This model would grip the minds of European men for centuries, loosening its hold only in the eighteenth century.

Behind this schematic picture, however, there were occurring in society subtle yet profound changes that elaborated the meaning of work. As labor gradually gathered positive, productive connotations alongside its moral ones, it crowded on the definition of *oeuvre*, driving the verb form (*oeuvrer*) into disuse and calling on the word *travail* to signify a range of meanings defined by context. Thus in the first modern dictionaries of the seventeenth century—Richelet, Furetière, the Académie française—we find multiple definitions listed under the same word.

In the Middle Ages, as we have seen, theologians and university professors were defining their cerebral activities as an art, but sociologically speaking, this definition and its application to specific social strata was not consistently extended beyond but a few occupations (like professor or theologian). In the early modern period it was. Now we find "work" and intellectual activity more tightly associated and broadened into new sectors of society. In 1636 we find work defined as "a product executed, manual, artistic or intellectual, considered as a result of manual operations relevant to a technique or as the sum of erudite research."[17] Late in the century Furetière includes in his definition of *oeuvres* this: "compositions of the intellect, writings of an author." Work as cerebral (often called an art) continues to be more highly valued than "mindless" manual labor. There is an explicit correlation between social rank and the kind of work activity performed. In other words, the meaning of work is increasingly *sociologically* defined.

In their feeling their way toward an understanding of the meaning of work, contemporaries thought and wrote a great deal about what it was *not*. Today we contrast work with leisure, or free time, but those concepts are historical products of a work regime that is closely tied to disciplined notions of time. When one is not "on the job" and "under the clock," one has free time or leisure time. In the early modern period such concepts as leisure or free time were only just beginning to come into being. This is partly because work (and labor) were largely task oriented rather than time disciplined. And even when manual workers were hired "by the day," they drifted in and out of the workplace with a frequency that would drive a modern employer to distraction. Certainly, contemporaries had words to describe nonwork activities, and significantly, the educated elite (men) busied themselves with considerable thinking and writing on the subject.

As we have seen, idleness was roundly denounced. Sloth was one of the seven deadly sins, and in the twelfth century we find the word *paresse* describing such laziness in terms of indolence, torpor, lassitude, and the repugnance for work or effort. During the Middle Ages and through the early modern years we find a parade of terms with similar, pejorative meaning: *oisif*, *oisiveté* (inactive, negligent, useless, superfluous); *fainéant* (one who does nothing, refuses to work), *désoeuvré* (inactive).[18]

Now, in contrast, consider the meaning of the words *passe-temps* (pastimes), *divertissement* (diversion), *récréation* (recreation), and *loisir* (leisure), which also described nonworking activity, but positively and associated with society's elite. No negative connotations here. By the seventeenth century the meanings and application of these terms for idleness reveal a hierarchical mediation of the meaning of nonwork activity. *Oisif*, *oisiveté* (or any of the other pejorative terms for idleness) stand in stark contrast to *loisir* and its synonyms. Nonworking laborers or journeyman artisans were branded *oisif* (willfully idle, and thus indisciplined and sinful). Nonworking activity among the elite, however, carried no such opprobrium.

Consider the etymology of *loisir*. In the twelfth century, *loisible*, the root of *loisir*, meant "to be free to do what one wants." By the sixteenth century *loisir* had come into usage, and meant "to be able to dispose of one's time freely," and described activities away from one's habitual occupation.[19] Furetière notes in the late seventeenth century that "the devotion of all of one's time in applying oneself to study" is an *honnête loisir* (an honest or respectable leisure).[20] According to the dictionary of the Académie française in 1740, *loisirs* now meant "distractions in which one can deliver oneself during moments of freedom," and carried synonyms of amusement, diversion, pastime, pleasure, and, tellingly, *recréation*. This last term carried the positive sense of needed refreshment and recreation, or a restoring of the faculties needed for effective work. The emphasis throughout is on freedom, a state not permitted to everyone in society, and stands in contrast not only to *oisiveté* (indisciplined idleness) but also to *travail* as a slavish activity of necessity, the antithesis of liberty. Once again, the meanings of words are mediated by hierarchy.

The value of work and even its meaning, as this brief etymological review illustrates, is determined by who is doing it. We thus find lawyers, doctors, and the new officeholding class of government administrators referring to their activities as *travail*, without the slightest sense of social derogation. Here we can see definitions of and distinctions between work and manual labor as a form of ideological masking, self-serving justifications for social hierarchy. This ideological commitment to hierarchy, however, was fashioned in a context of market expansion and intermittent yet unmistakable economic growth. Indeed, the ideological intensification of hierarchy (and patriarchy) and the corresponding emphasis on the importance of status in the seventeenth century is, I have suggested in this book, in part a response to unsettling market forces and the social changes that accompanied them.

The intensification of hierarchy and extension and integration of the market economy, however, were but two of several changes that transformed the work worlds of early modern French men and women from the top to the bottom of the social hierarchy, in city and countryside, among peasants, the lesser folk (from day laborers to servants), artisans, merchants, medical practitioners, lawyers, notaries, financiers, and government officials. The other salient and interconnected developments that I have emphasized throughout this book are the growth of the state's governing apparatus and urbanization. As France's social structure became increasingly hierarchical, more and more of its elites lived in cities and possessed most of the kingdom's wealth, making the city the primary motor powering a growing market economy. The city was also the dominant if not exclusive seat of government, and so was fundamentally important to the growth of the state—in both numbers of officials and in the power the state exerted over ordinary French men and women, thus fundamentally influencing their worlds of work.

Work and labor are basic to the creation of the human environment, and in this book I have explored the varied ways in which French men and women worked, and how and why these activities changed over the early modern years. I have emphasized, however, that work is more than just an economic activity, as important as that is, but also a cultural one. In short, work activities—making things and performing services that are of value to oneself and to others—are how men and women make contact with material reality, *and* how they see themselves and are seen by others in the ever-shifting constellation of social relations.

Notes

1. Christopher Dyer, "Work Ethics in the Fourteenth Century," in *The Problem of Labour in Fourteenth-Century England*, ed. James Bothwell, P. J. P. Goldberg, and W. M. Ormrod (York: York Medieval Press, 2000), 21.

2. See Edmond Huguet, *Dictionnaire de la langue Française du seizième siècle* (Paris: Didier, 1967), s.v. "travail."

3. *Le Grand Larousse de la langue française* (Paris: Larousse, 1971–1978), s.v. "travail."

4. See Mikhail Bakhtin, *Rabelais and His World*, trans. Irene Iswolsky (Cambridge, Mass.: MIT Press, 1968).

5. Quoted in Thomas McStay Adams, *Bureaucrats and Beggars: French Social Policy in the Age of Enlightenment* (New York: Oxford University Press, 1990), 30 (my italics).

6. Kathryn Norberg, *Rich and Poor in Grenoble, 1600–1815* (Berkeley: University of California Press, 1985).

7. Adams, *Bureaucrats and Beggars*, 33.

8. Adams, *Bureaucrats and Beggars*, 41.

9. Adams, *Bureaucrats and Beggars*, 35.

10. Norberg, *Rich and Poor*, 166.

11. Quoted in Philippe Minard, *La Fortune du Colbertisme: Etat et industrie dans la France des Lumières* (Paris: Fayard, 1998), 246.

12. Denis Diderot and Jean Le Rond d'Alembert, eds., *Encyclopédie, ou Dictionnaire raisonné des sciences, des arts et des métiers*, 28 vols. (Paris: 1751–1766).

13. Adams, *Bureaucrats and Beggars*, 240.

14. See George Ovitt Jr., *The Restoration of Perfection: Labor and Technology in Medieval Culture* (New Brunswick, N.J.: Rutgers University Press, 1987).

15. Charles Loyseau, *Treatise of Orders and Plain Dignities*, ed. and trans. Howell Lloyd (Cambridge: Cambridge University Press, 1994).

16. Jacques Le Goff, *Time, Work and Culture in the Middle Ages*, trans. Arthur Goldhammer (Chicago: University of Chicago Press, 1980), 70.

17. *Le Grand Larousse*, s.v. "travail."

18. See Huguet and Antoine Furetière, *Le Dictionnaire universel* (Paris: SNL-Le Robert, 1978; orig. ed. 1690), s.vv. "oisif," "oisiveté," "paresse," "fainéant."

19. *Le Grand Larousse*, s.vv. "loisible," "loisir."

20. Furetiére, s.v. "loisir."

Bibliography

Adams, Christine. *A Taste for Comfort and Status: A Bourgeois Family in Eighteenth-Century France.* University Park: Pennsylvania State University Press, 2000.

Adams, Thomas McStay. *Bureaucrats and Beggars: French Social Policy in the Age of Enlightenment.* New York: Oxford University Press, 1990.

Applebaum, Herbert. *The Concept of Work: Ancient, Medieval and Modern.* Albany: State University of New York Press, 1992.

Arcangeli, Alessandro. *Recreation in the Renaissance: Attitudes towards Leisure and Pastimes in European Culture, 1350–1700.* London: Palgrave, 2004.

Aston, T. H., and C. H. E. Philpin, eds. *The Brenner Debate: Agrarian Class Structure and Economic Development in Pre-Industrial Europe.* Cambridge: Cambridge University Press, 1987.

Bakhtin, Mikhail. *Rabelais and His World.* Translated by Irene Iswolsky. Cambridge, Mass.: MIT Press, 1968.

Bayard, Françoise. *Le Monde des financiers au XVIIe siècle.* Paris: Flammarion, 1988.

Beckman, Svante. "Professionalization: Borderline Authority and Autonomy in Work." In *Professions in Theory and History: Rethinking the Study of the Professions,* edited by Michael Burrage and Rolf Torstendahl, 115–38. London: Sage, 1990.

Bell, David. *Lawyers and Citizens: The Making of a Political Elite in Old Regime France.* New York: Oxford University Press, 1994.

Benabou, Erica-Maria. *La Prostitution et la police des moeurs au XVIIIe siècle.* Paris: Perrin, 1987.

Berlanstein, Lenard. *The Barristers of Toulouse in the Eighteenth Century (1740–1793).* Baltimore: Johns Hopkins University Press, 1975.

———, ed. *Rethinking Labor History.* Urbana: University of Illinois Press, 1993.

Bloch, Marc. *Les Caractères originaux de l'historie rurale française.* Cambridge, Mass.: Harvard University Press, 1931.

Bouwsma, William J. "Lawyers in early Modern Culture." *American Historical Review* 78, no. 2 (1973).

Braudel, Fernand. *The Wheels of Commerce*. Translated by Siân Reynolds. London: Harper Collins, 1986.

Breen, Michael P. *Law, City, and King: Legal Culture, Municipal Politics, and State Formation in Early Modern Dijon*. Rochester, N.Y.: University of Rochester Press, 2007.

Brockliss, Laurence, and Colin Jones. *The Medical World of Early Modern France*. Oxford: Oxford University Press, 1997.

Broomhall, Susan. *Women and the Book Trade in Sixteenth-Century France*. Aldershot, UK: Ashgate, 2002.

——. *Women's Medical Work in Early Modern France*. Manchester, UK: Manchester University Press, 2004.

Brunelle, Gayle K. *The New World Merchants of Rouen, 1559–1630*. Kirksville, Mo.: Sixteenth Century Journal Publishers, 1991.

Burke, Peter. "The Invention of Leisure in Early Modern Europe." *Past and Present* 146 (1995): 136–50.

Burstin, Haim. "Unskilled Labor in Paris at the End of the Eighteenth Century." In *The Workplace Before the Factory: Artisans and Proletarians, 1500–1800*, edited by Thomas M. Safley and Leonard N. Rosenband, 63–72. Ithaca, N.Y.: Cornell University Press, 1993.

Butel, Paul. *Les Négociants Bordelais*. Paris: Aubier, 1974.

Cacérès, Benigno. *Loisirs et travail du moyen âge à nos jours*. Paris: Seuil, 1973.

Chartier, Roger, Guy Chaussinand-Nogaret, Hugues Neveux, and Emmanuel Le Roy Ladurie. *Histoire de la France urbaine: La Ville classique*. Paris: Seuil, 1981.

Chaussinand-Nogaret, Guy. *Gens de finance au XVIIIe siècle*. Paris: Editions complexe, 1993.

Chaussinand-Nogaret, Guy, et al., eds. *Histoire des élites en France du XVIe au XXe siècle*. Paris: Editions Tallandier, 1991.

Coornaert, Emile. *Les Corporations en France avant 1789*. Paris: Les éditions ouvrières, 1968.

Cross, Gary. *A Social History of Leisure since 1600*. State College, Penn.: Venture Publishing, 1990.

Crowston, Clare Haru. *Fabricating Women: The Seamstresses of Old Regime France (1675–1791)*. Durham, N.C.: Duke University Press, 2001.

Daly, Kathleen. "Private Vice, Public Service? Civil Service and Chose Public in Fifteenth-Century France." In *Concepts and Patterns of Service in the Later Middle Ages*, edited by Anne Curry and Elizabeth Matthew, 99–118. Woodbridge, UK: Boydell Press, 2000.

Davis, Natalie Z. *Society and Culture in Early Modern France*. Stanford, Calif.: Stanford University Press, 1975.

——. "A Trade Union in Sixteenth-Century France." *Economic Historical Review*, 2nd ser., 19 (1966): 49–68.

——. "Women in the Crafts in Sixteenth-Century Lyon." In *Women and Work in Preindustrial Europe*, edited by Barbara Hanawalt, 167–97. Bloomington: Indiana University Press, 1986.

De Vries, Jan. *The Economy of Europe in an Age of Crisis, 1600–1750*. Cambridge: Cambridge University Press, 1976.

———. *European Urbanization, 1500–1800.* Cambridge, Mass.: Harvard University Press, 1984.

———. "The Industrial Revolution and the Industrious Revolution." *Journal of Economic History* 54, no. 2 (1994): 249–70.

Dewald, Jonathan. *Pont-St-Pierre, 1398–1789: Lordship, Community, and Capitalism in Early Modern France.* Berkeley: University of California Press, 1987.

Dewald, Jonathan, and Liana Vardi. "The Peasantries of France, 1400–1800." In *The Peasantries of Europe from the Fourteenth to the Eighteenth Centuries*, edited by Tom Scott. London: Longman, 1998.

Diderot, Denis, and Jean Le Rond d'Alembert, eds. *Encyclopédie, ou dictionnaire raisonné des sciences, des arts, et des métiers.* 28 vols. Paris, 1751–1766.

Dolan, Claire. *Le Notaire, la famille et la ville.* Toulouse: Presses Universitaires du Mirail, 1998.

Doyle, William. "Myths of Order and Ordering Myths." In *Social Orders and Social Classes in Europe since 1500: Studies in Social Classification*, edited by M. L. Bush, 218–29. London: Longman, 1992.

Dubin, Robert. *The World of Work.* New York: Prentice Hall, 1963.

Dyer, Christopher. "Work Ethics in the Fourteenth Century." In *The Problem of Labour in Fourteenth-Century England*, edited by James Bothwell, P. J. P. Goldberg, and W. M. Ormrod. York: York Medieval Press, 2000.

Epstein, S. R. "Crafts Guilds, Apprenticeship, and Technological Change in Preindustrial Europe." *Journal of Economic History* 58 (1998): 684–713.

Fairchilds, Cissie. *Domestic Enemies: Servants and Their Masters in Old Regime France.* Baltimore: Johns Hopkins University Press, 1984.

Farge, Arlette. *La Vie fragile: Vouloirs, pouvoirs et solidarités à Paris au XVIIIe siècle.* Paris: Hachette, 1986.

———. *Fragile Lives: Violence, Power and Solidarity in Eighteenth-Century Paris.* Translated by Carol Shelton. Cambridge, Mass.: Harvard University Press, 1993.

Farr, James R. *Artisans in Europe, 1300–1914.* Cambridge: Cambridge University Press, 2000.

———. *Authority and Sexuality in Early Modern Burgundy, 1550–1730.* New York: Oxford University Press, 1995.

———. "Consumers, Commerce, and the Craftsmen of Dijon: The Changing Social and Economic Structure of a Provincial Capital, 1450–1750." In *Cities and Social Change in Early Modern France*, edited by Philip Benedict, 134–73. London: Unwin Hyman, 1989.

———. "The Disappearance of the Traditional Artisan." In *A Companion to Nineteenth-Century Europe, 1789–1914*, edited by Stefan Berger, 98–108. Oxford: Blackwell, 2006.

———. *Hands of Honor: Artisans and Their World in Dijon, 1550–1650.* Ithaca, N.Y.: Cornell University Press, 1988.

———. "On the Shop Floor: Guilds, Artisans, and the European Market Economy, 1350–1750," *Journal of Early Modern History* 1, no. 1 (1997): 24–54.

Fitzsimmons, Michael. *The Parisian Order of Barristers and the French Revolution.* Cambridge, Mass.: Harvard University Press, 1987.

Forster, Robert. *Merchants, Landlords, Magistrates: The Depont Family in Eighteenth-Century France.* Baltimore: Johns Hopkins University Press, 1980.

Fossier, Robert. *La Travail au moyen âge*. Paris: Hachette, 2000.

Franklin, Alfred. *Dictionnaire historique des arts, métiers et professions*. New York: Burt Franklin, 1968; orig. ed. 1906.

Furetière, Antoine. *Le Dictionnaire universel*. Paris: SNL-Le Robert, 1978; orig. ed. 1690.

Garden, Maurice. *Lyon et les lyonnais au XVIIIe siècle*. Paris: Flammarion, 1975.

Gascon, Richard. *Grand commerce et vie urbaine au XVIe siècle: Lyon et ses marchands (environs de 1520–environs de 1580)*. 2 vols. Paris: SEVPEN, 1971.

Gelfand, Toby. "Deux cultures, une profession: Les chirurgiens français au XVIIIe siècle." *Revue d'histoire moderne et contemporaine* 27 (1980): 468–84.

———. "A 'Monarchical Profession' in the Old Regime: Surgeons, Ordinary Practitioners, and Medical Professionalization in Eighteenth-Century France." In *Professions and the French State, 1700–1900*, edited by Gerald L. Geison, 149–80. Philadelphia: University of Pennsylvania Press, 1984.

———. *Professionalizing Modern Medicine: Paris Surgeons and Medical Science and Institutions in the Eighteenth Century*. Westport, Conn.: Greenwood, 1980.

Gélis, Jacques. "Sages-femmes et accoucheurs: L'Obstetrique populaire aux XVIIe et XVIIIe siècles." *Annales: Economies, Sociétés, Civilisations* 32, no. 5 (1977): 927–57.

Geremek, Bronislaw. *Inutiles au monde: Truands et misérables, 1300–1600*. Paris: Gallimard, 1980.

———. *Le Salariat dans l'artisanat parisien aux XIIIe–XVe siècles*. Paris: SEVPEN, 1962.

Goubert, Pierre. *The Ancien Regime*. Translated by Steve Cox. New York: Harper and Row, 1973; orig. ed. 1969.

———. *Familles marchandes sous l'Ancien Regime: Les Danses et les Mottes de Beauvais*. Paris: SEVPEN, 1959.

———. *The French Peasantry in the Seventeenth Century*. Translated by Ian Patterson. Cambridge: Cambridge University Press, 1986.

Grenier, Jean-Yves. *L'économie d'Ancien Régime: Un monde de l'échange et de l'incertitude*. Paris: Albin Michel, 1996.

Gresset, Maurice. *Gens de justice à Besançon de la conquête par Louis XIV à la revolution française*. 2 vols. Paris, 1978.

Gutton, Jean-Pierre. *La Société et les pauvres en Europe, 16e–18e siècles*. Paris: PUF, 1974.

Hafter, Daryl M. "Women in the Underground Business of Eighteenth-Century Lyon." *Enterprise and Society* 2 (March 2001): 11–40.

Hardwick, Julie. *The Practice of Patriarchy: Gender and the Politics of Household Authority in Early Modern France*. University Park: Pennsylvania State University Press, 1998.

Hartman, Mary S. *The Household and the Making of History*. Cambridge: Cambridge University Press, 2004.

Hoffman, Philip T. *Growth in a Traditional Society: The French Countryside, 1450–1815*. Princeton, N.J.: Princeton University Press, 1996.

Hufton, Olwen. *The Poor of Eighteenth-Century France, 1750–1789*. Oxford: Oxford University Press, 1974.

Huguet, Edmond. *Dictionnaire de la langue Française du seizième siècle*. Paris: Didier, 1967.

Hunt, Lynn, and George Sheridan. "Corporatism, Association, and the Language of Labor in France, 1750–1830." *Journal of Modern History* 58 (1986): 813–44.

Jeannin, Pierre. *Merchants of the Sixteenth Century.* Translated by Paul Fittingoff. New York: Harper and Row, 1972.

Johnson, Martin Phillip. "From Guild to Academy: Absolutist Culture and Social Differentiation among Artisans and Artists in Seventeenth-Century Paris." *Halcyon* 17 (1995): 175–91.

Jones, P. M. *The Peasantry in the French Revolution.* Cambridge: Cambridge University Press, 1988.

Joyce, Patrick, ed. *The Historical Meanings of Work.* Cambridge: Cambridge University Press, 1987.

Julia, Dominique. "L'Education des négociants français au 18e siècle." In *Cultures et formations négociantes dans l'Europe moderne,* edited by Granco Angioline and Daniel Roche. Paris: Editions de l'EHESS, 1995.

Jütte, Robert. *Poverty and Deviance in Early Modern Europe.* Cambridge: Cambridge University Press, 1994.

Kagan, Richard. "Law Students and Legal Careers in Eighteenth-Century France." *Past and Present* 68 (1975).

Kaplan, Steven L. "Social Classification and Representation in the Corporate World of Eighteenth-Century France: Turgot's Carnival." In *Work in France: Representations, Meaning, Organization, and Practice,* edited by Steven L. Kaplan and Cynthia Koepp, 176–228. Ithaca, N.Y.: Cornell University Press, 1986.

———. *Provisioning Paris: Merchants and Millers in the Grain and Flour Trade during the Eighteenth Century.* Ithaca, N.Y.: Cornell University Press, 1984.

Kaplow, Jeffrey. *The Names of Kings: The Parisian Laboring Poor in the Eighteenth Century.* New York: Basic Books, 1972.

Karpik, Lucien. *French Lawyers: A Study in Collective Action, 1274–1994.* Translated by Nora Scott. Oxford: Clarendon Press, 1999.

Koepp, Cynthia. "The Alphabetical Order: Work in Diderot's *Encyclopédie.*" In *Work in France: Representations, Meaning, Organization, and Practice,* edited by Steven L. Kaplan and Cynthia Koepp, 229–57. Ithaca, N.Y.: Cornell University Press, 1986.

Larson, Magali Sarfatti. *The Rise of Professionalism: A Sociological Analysis.* Berkeley: University of California Press, 1977.

Lave, Jean, and Etienne Wenger. *Situated Learning: Legitimate Peripheral Participation.* Cambridge: Cambridge University Press, 1991.

LeBrun, François. *Se soigner autrefois: Médecins, saints et sorciers aux 17e et 18e siècle.* Paris: Seuil, 1995; orig. ed., 1983.

Le Goff, Jacques. *Marchands et banquiers du moyen âge.* Paris: PUF, 1969.

———. *Time, Work and Culture in the Middle Ages.* Translated by Arthur Goldhammer. Chicago: University of Chicago Press, 1980.

Le Roy Ladurie, Emmanuel. *The French Peasantry, 1460–1660.* Translated by Alan Sheridan. Berkeley: University of California Press, 1987; orig. ed. 1977.

———. *The Peasants of Languedoc*. Translated by John Day. Urbana: University of Illinois Press, 1974; orig. ed. 1966.

Lingo, Alison Klairmont. "Empirics and Charlatans in Early Modern France: The Genesis of the Classification of the 'Other' in Medical Practice." *Journal of Social History* 19, no. 4 (1986).

———. "Women Healers and the Medical Marketplace of Sixteenth-Century Lyon." *Dynamis* 19 (1999): 79–94.

Loyseau, Charles. *A Treatise of Orders and Plain Dignities*. Edited and translated by Howell A. Lloyd. Cambridge: Cambridge University Press, 1994.

McTavish, Lianne. "On Display: Portraits of Seventeenth-Century Men Midwives." *Social History of Medicine* 14, no. 3 (2001): 389–415.

Ménétra, Jacques-Louis. *Journal of My Life*. Edited by Daniel Roche and translated by Arthur Goldhammer. New York: Columbia University Press, 1986.

Mercier, Louis-Sébastien. *Panorama of Paris [Selections from Le Tableau de Paris]*. Edited and translated by Jeremy Popkin. University Park: Pennsylvania State University Press, 1999.

Minard, Philippe. *La Fortune du Colbertisme: Etat et industrie dans la France des Lumières*. Paris: Fayard, 1998.

Mousnier, Roland. *The Institutions of France under the Absolute Monarchy, 1598–1789: Society and the State*. Translated by Brian Pearce. Chicago: University of Chicago Press, 1979.

Musgrave, Elizabeth. "Women in the Male World of Work: The Building Industries in Eighteenth-Century Brittany." *French Historical Studies* 20, no. 1 (1993): 30–52.

Neveux, Hugues, Jean Jacquart, and Emmanuel Le Roy Ladurie. *Histoire de la France rurale: L'Age classique*. Paris: Seuil, 1975.

Norberg, Kathryn. *Rich and Poor in Grenoble*. Berkeley: University of California Press, 1984.

Nye, Robert. *Masculinity and Male Codes of Honor in Modern France*. New York: Oxford University Press, 1993.

Ovitt, George, Jr. *The Restoration of Perfection: Labor and Technology in Medieval Culture*. New Brunswick, N.J.: Rutgers University Press, 1987.

Pahl, R. E., ed. *On Work: Historical, Comparative and Theoretical Approaches*. Oxford: Blackwell, 1988.

Panckoucke, Charles Josèph, ed. *Encyclopédie méthodique*. 206 vols. Paris: Panckoucke, 1782–1832.

Perkins, Wendy. "Midwives versus Doctors: The Case of Louise Bourgeois." *Seventeenth Century* 3, no. 2 (1988): 135–57.

Poisson, Jean-Paul. *Notaires et société: Travaux d'histoire et de sociologie notariales*. Paris: Economica, 1985.

Poitrineau, Abel. *Ils travaillaient la France: Métiers et mentalités du XVIe au XIXe siècle*. Paris: Armand Colin, 2003; orig. ed., 1992.

Prak, Maarten, Catharina Lis, Jan Lucassen, and Hugo Soly, eds. *Craft Guilds in the Early Modern Low Countries: Work, Power, and Representation*. Aldershot, UK: Ashgate, 2006.

Ramsey, Matthew. *Professional and Popular Medicine in France, 1770–1830: The Social World of Medical Practice*. Cambridge: Cambridge University Press, 1988.

Reyerson, Kathryn. *Jacques Coeur: Entrepreneur and King's Bursar*. New York: Pearson Longman, 2005.

Rifkin, Jeremy. *The End of Work: The Decline of the Global Labor Force and the Dawn of the Post-Market Era*. New York: Putnam, 1994.

Robertson, Kellie. *The Laborer's Two Bodies: Labor and the 'Work' of the Text in Medieval Britain, 1350–1500*. New York: Palgrave Macmillan, 2006.

Robertson, Kellie, and Michael Uebel, eds. *The Middle Ages at Work: Practicing Labor in Late Medieval England*. New York: Palgrave, 2004.

Roche, Daniel. *France in the Enlightenment*. Translated by Arthur Goldhammer. Cambridge, Mass.: Harvard University Press, 1998.

———. *Le Peuple de Paris*. Paris: Aubier, 1981. English translation *The People of Paris: An Essay in Popular Culture in the Eighteenth Century*. New York: Berg, 1987.

———. "Talent, Reason, and Sacrifice: The Physician during the Enlightenment." In *Medicine and Society in France*, edited by Robert Forster and Orest Ranum. Baltimore: Johns Hopkins University Press, 1980.

Rosenband, Leonard N. "Hiring and Firing at the Montgolfier Paper Mill." In *The Workplace Before the Factory*, edited by Thomas M. Safley and Leonard Rosenband, 225–40. Ithaca, N.Y.: Cornell University Press, 1993.

———. *Papermaking in Eighteenth-Century France: Management, Labor, and Revolution at the Montgolfier Mill, 1761–1805*. Baltimore: Johns Hopkins University Press, 2000.

Roupnel, Gaston. *La Ville et la campagne au XVIIe siècle: Etude sur les populations dijonnaises*. Paris: SEVPEN, 1955.

Schneider, Zoe. "The King's Bench." Unpublished manuscript, now available as *The King's Bench: Bailiwick Magistrates and Local Governance in Normandy, 1670–1740*. Rochester, N.Y.: University of Rochester Press, 2008.

Sewell, William H., Jr. "Visions of Labor: Illustrations of the Mechanical Arts before, in, and after Diderot's *Encyclopédie*." In *Work in France: Representations, Meaning, Organization, and Practice*, edited by Steven L. Kaplan and Cynthia Koepp, 258–86. Ithaca, N.Y.: Cornell University Press, 1986.

———. *Work and Revolution in France*. Cambridge: Cambridge University Press, 1980.

Sheridan, Bridgette. "At Birth: The Modern State, Modern Medicine, and the Royal Midwife Louise Bourgeois in Seventeenth-Century France." *Dynamis* 19 (1999): 145–66.

Simpson, Richard L., and Ida Harper Simpson, eds. *Research in the Sociology of Work*. Vol. 5, The Meaning of Work. Greenwich, Conn.: JAI Press, 1995.

Smith, Pamela H. *The Body of the Artisan: Art and Experience in the Scientific Revolution*. Chicago: University of Chicago Press, 2004.

Simonton, Deborah. *A History of European Women's Work, 1700 to the Present*. London: Routledge, 1998.

Soll, Jacob. "Healing the Body Politic: French Royal Doctors, History, and the Birth of a Nation, 1560–1634." *Renaissance Quarterly* 55, no. 4 (2002): 1259–86.

Sonenscher, Michael. *The Hatters of Eighteenth-Century France.* Berkeley: University of California Press, 1987.

———. *Work and Wages: Natural Law, Politics, and the Eighteenth-Century French Trades.* Cambridge: Cambridge University Press, 1989.

Speier, Hans. "Honor and Social Structure." In *The Truth in Hell and Other Essays on Politics and Culture, 1935–1987,* edited by Hans Speier. Oxford: Oxford University Press, 1989.

Vardi, Liana. *The Land and the Loom: Peasants and Profit in Northern France, 1680–1800.* Durham, N.C.: Duke University Press, 1993.

Woronoff, Denis. *Histoire de l'industrie en France.* Paris: Seuil, 1998.

Index

Note: Page numbers in *italic* type indicate illustrations.

weaving, 24–25. *See also* textile industry
Weber, Max, 9, 125–26, 183
Wenger, Etienne, 100
West India Company, 136
widows: in commerce, 112; medical
  practice by, 162, 175; and
  prostitution, 62; in retail, 58; in
  trades, 87–88
wine, 35, 40, 130, 139
witchcraft, 150–51
women: in domestic service, 75–77; and
  femininity, 99; identity of, 162;
  medical practice by, 151–52, 162,
  175–77, 179; and prostitution,
  60–63, 66–67, 73–75; in trades, 82,
  87–91, 98–99; types of work
  performed by, 58; work of *menu
  peuple*, 58–63, 66–67. *See also*
  gender; widows
wool production, 24, 30
work: of artisans, 79–92; children and,
  22; corporatism and, 9–10; defining,
  1–3; gender and, 7–9, 21–22, 57–64,
  92, 99, 196–97; and hierarchy, 4–7,

27, 65, 203–5; and identity, 92, 98,
  162, 165–66; intellectual, 5–6, 8,
  125, 147–48, 166, 195, 197, 202–5;
  labor vs., 197–99, 202; manual, 5–6,
  93, 125, 140, 148, 161, 197, 199,
  202–5; meaning of, 2–3, 7, 9, 10, 14,
  15, 25, 65, 197–206; of *menu
  peuple*, 47–64; of merchants, 111–22;
  of peasants, 21–25; poverty and,
  48, 199–202; and productivity,
  197, 200–202; religion and, 198,
  202–3; social order and, 9–10;
  sociocultural meanings of, 2–3;
  unskilled, 50–51, 53, 72–73. *See also*
  work ethic
workers. *See menu peuple* (lesser folk);
  wageworkers
work ethic, 65, 125–26, 160, 165,
  167–68, 197–98
workhouses, 200
working conditions: of artisans, 85–86;
  of domestic servants, 59, 64

Young, Arthur, 93

~

About the Author

James R. Farr is the author of several books on French and European history, most recently *A Tale of Two Murders: Passion and Power in Seventeenth-Century France* (2005) and *Artisans in Europe, 1300–1914* (2000). He also is the author of *Hands of Honor: Artisans and Their World in Dijon, 1550–1650* (1988) and *Authority and Sexuality in Early Modern Burgundy, 1550–1730* (1995). He served as coeditor of *French Historical Studies* from 1991 to 2000, and has been the recipient of a Guggenheim Fellowship (1998–1999), a Shelby Cullom Davis Center Fellowship (1994–1995), and an American Council of Learned Studies Fellowship (1994–1995). He received his PhD from Northwestern University and is professor of history at Purdue University in West Lafayette, Indiana.